Andy,
Thank you for your patience, positive attitude and smiling face. You enrich our lives every day.
We love you!

Mom and Dad

How to Start a Home Based Travel Agency

Tom and Joanie Ogg

**How To Start a
Home Based
Travel Agency**

Published by:
Tom Ogg and Associates
P. O. Box 2398
Valley Center, California 92082
1-619-751-1007
FAX 1-619-751-1309

Printed in the United States of America

ISBN# 1-888290-00-5
10 9 8 7 6 5 4 3 2 1

TABLE OF CONTENTS

Chapter 9
YOUR HOME COMPUTER

Chapter 10
SELECTING YOUR KEY
TRAVEL SUPPLIERS

Chapter 11
YOUR AUTOMATED TRAVEL
RESERVATION SYSTEM

Chapter 12
SETTING UP YOUR SUPPLIER FILES

Chapter 19
TRAVEL MARKETING TECHNIQUES FOR THE NINETIES

Chapter 20
COLD CALLS, CANVASSING, AND TELEMARKETING

Chapter 21
ORGANIZING YOUR MARKETING FILES

Chapter 22
DEVELOPING YOUR PROFESSIONAL KNOWLEDGE AND SKILLS

Chapter 27
TRADE GROUPS AND ASSOCIATIONS

Chapter 28
TRADE MAGAZINES, PUBLICATIONS AND REFERENCE MATERIALS

Chapter 29
A CHECKLIST FOR GETTING STARTED

Chapter 30
WHERE DO I GO FROM HERE?

Chapter 31
COMMON TERMS AND PHRASES

Chapter 32
WHERE CAN I GET A PROFESSIONAL TRAVEL EDUCATION?

PREFACE

I cannot believe that it is already 1997. I am paddling back out to the lineup at Rincon Point wondering if I will ever complete this book. Joanie and I have committed ourselves to the task and everything is done but the forward. How am I going to introduce this book? The surf has good size but the swell is crossed up with section after section and there has been a constant WSW wind....not at all the quality surf we normally get on our annual Santa Barbara/New Years trip.

I was enjoying thoughts about trips I have taken all over the world chasing perfect surf when the wind quit, the ocean glassed off and a slight off shore breeze developed. The surf got immensely better. The off shore wind was holding the lips up creating wide open tubes. In a matter of minutes the surf went from lousy to epic with very few guys in the water...nature has so many wondrous ways.

Then it happened. I was paddling from the Second Point to the Indicator when a ten foot set poured through. I pushed over the first three or four waves trying to scramble outside. The wind was now howling offshore. The spray from the set waves showered me as I scratched further out. I was right on a peak outside the second point when I turned, stroked hard and started to drop into the largest set wave. The offshore gust was furious! It was all I could do to get my 7'6" Brewer to drop. I practically free fell down the face and hit the bottom of the wave with so much force my knees almost collapsed. I managed an off balance bottom turn and ended up extremely high on the wall now behind peak. My adrenaline was pumping. It was like my surfboard was hanging on the face of the wave held their by the shrieking off shore wind. I started to drop........

The lip of the wave threw out like an avalanche. A huge volume of water hissed over my head and smashed into the flat area to my left......I was frozen in a cavern large enough for ten guys. The moment was awesome, the noise deafening. The emerald liquid ceiling backlit from the afternoon sun....everything in slow motion.....the fear, the excitement....truly one of life's most exhilarating experiences.

It made me think of all the wonderful times Joanie, Andy and I have had on our adventures all over the world. The first time Andy rode Threes and Pops in Hawaii.....and Andy's first tube ride. It reminded me of Honolua Bay and of course, the North Shore. I remember the outrageous tubes around Rio in Brazil, and Kirra in Australia....Uluwatu on Bali...Mexico and Baja. Surfing is so much fun and I am so lucky Andy loves it as well. I can't wait to show Andy all of the breaks in the

How To Start a Home Based Travel Agency

world.

I think of the fun our family has had visiting various places and on cruise ships. I just can't believe some families still haven't traveled with their children. What could be more important? I remember taking Joanie's Mom, Elizabeth on a Caribbean cruise on the Crown Princess. We wouldn't trade that trip for a million dollars. Shortly after our cruise Elizabeth became ill and it was to be our last trip together.

I remember Andy's first steps at the Tower of London in England when he was just eleven months old, his first swim in the ocean outside of La Paz, his first snorkle trip at Mayreau in the Grenadines, his first green water wave inside first break in Waikiki when he was just four. I remember dancing with Joanie at Foxy's in Lahaina when I first met her....asleep in the back of a taxi with Andy in her arms going to the hotel in Europe....skiing Utah....shopping in San Juan....winning thousands at Bingo on two consecutive cruises...first on the Star Princess and then the next week on Celebrity's Zenith.

People dream about having an adventure one day. About going places they haven't been. About doing things they have always wanted to do. About taking risks, exploiting the moment.....About traveling. About really living their lives.........

Ooooowwwww! The shouts brought me back to reality. I could see guys paddling over the green wall in front of me shouting and hooting as I screamed out of the cavernous tube I was in. It seemed like an eternity since I was covered up but it was really only a split second. I will remember that barrel forever. After all, isn't that what life is all about? Those moments that create the memories we savor more than anything? About the experiences that happen so quickly yet impact our lives so much? About exploring new ideas, and places, and feelings?

Oh well, I had better get back to work....Lets see, where can I begin on the forward to this book?

Chapter 1
THE TRAVEL INDUSTRY, OPPORTUNITY OF THE 1990s

Imagine selling tours and cruises to interesting, successful and happy people from all walks of life, attending trade shows and conventions located in exotic destinations around the world, cruising the world's finest ships, savoring the world's choice hotels and resorts, enjoying the freedom of working from your own home with maximum time to enjoy your family, and receiving outstanding tax benefits to boot! This is the reality of owning your own home based travel business. Once, this scenario could have only been a dream for travel agents but today it is a lifestyle for thousands who work from their home selling all types of travel services and products.

Some of the reasons for the evolution of travel agents out of store fronts and into home offices is well documented by the progressive advancement in telecommunications and personal computer technology. Many businesses have seen dramatic change in their structure of distribution as a direct effect of the impact of technology. Most information based enterprises have seen the transition from mainframe computer to desktop microcomputers and portable automation. Personal computers have revolutionized small business by permitting even the smallest entrepreneur software applications as efficient as Fortune 500 companies at cost effective prices. Ten years ago when John Naisbitt predicted the explosion of cottage industry, the entrepreneurial era, and the maturation of the information society in his book *"MEGATRENDS"*[1], it is doubtful even he could see the overwhelming transformation that was about to take place.

Probably the best example of the evolution is the change in structure Merrill Lynch, the conservative investment brokerage, has undergone to remain competitive. Until recently, Merrill Lynch would only consider large, metropolitan areas to open their 460 offices. Each office would house 20 to over 100 brokers that would solicit investments from regional areas. During the same period Edward D. Jones focused solely on small town markets and successfully opened one broker operations in over 2,600 cities with names like Thief River Falls, Minn (pop, 8,010). These one man offices developed local rapport with their markets and with the advent of personal computers, facsimile machines, and modems are ever as efficient as their big city competition. So effective has Jones become that Merrill Lynch has now decided they had better change their marketing plans to include small office markets. "What makes small markets so appealing? Powerful computers, fax machines and satellite communications now make it possible to set up a full service office without a lot of fixed costs. As recently as the 1960s some brokerages used Morse code to order a trade. Offices needed a cashier, two wire operators and a bookkeeper to perform functions now done in a minute by a single broker." says Merrill Lynch spokesman Bill Clark.[2]

THE TRAVEL INDUSTRY, BENEFICIARY OF TECHNOLOGY

If you think that telecommunications and personal computers have changed the investment industry you won't believe the impact technology has had on the travel industry. Only twenty years ago travel agents hand wrote airline tickets using manual tariffs to resource fares and schedules. They depended on personal experience and stacks of brochures for information about every nook and cranny around the world. Being a travel agent consisted of painstaking details in every transaction.

Today, even a casual computer user can access more information in a single minute that would take a travel agent several hours only a few years ago.....and the databases are increasing in size and availability every day. Virtual reality and Multi Media have already changed the travel industry forever and their applications are still in their infancy. The merging of television, personal computer, and telecommunications will even further change the way travel is marketed.

No longer does a travel agent need to be just one agent of many in a large automated storefront agency location. By taking advantage of technology and personal computers a whole new breed of home based travel agent has evolved and is becoming a dominant factor in travel marketing.

THE TRAVEL INDUSTRY, THE UNITED STATE'S #1 GROWTH INDUSTRY

Even though travel and tourism is the United State's second largest contributor to the GNP (6%+) with annual sales in excess of three hundred billion dollars, USA Today continues to tout the travel industry as the nation's number one growth industry into the twenty first century. In a world economy the United States has dramatic appeal as a destination for every country in the world. Travel and tourism is just about the only segment of our economy that enjoys a positive trade balance and further development of our sector will offset trade deficits in manufacturing and other areas. Taxes derived from travel and tourism represent huge amounts of revenue for the federal, state and local governments who all favor expansionist viewpoints. This favorable political climate coupled with our incredible natural resources guarantees substantial growth for the industry for the foreseeable future.

When you consider that fewer than 5% of the total population own passports you can grasp the opportunity for growth. Imagine if only 6% of the population of the U.S. owned cars? Would you think there is opportunity for increased automobile sales? How about personal computers? There was a time when very few folks had either. Investment by companies with an agenda to create markets inundated the public with products and developed vast industries by simply creating demand through advertising, sales and distribution. Think of a passport as a license to travel. 94% of our total population, hundreds of millions of Americans, do not even own a license to travel and can afford to travel if convinced through advertising, sales and distribution.

Less than 6% of the American population has ever taken a cruise yet the repeat ratio of those that have is extremely high. The cruise lines are investing billions of dollars in new ships and the total inventory of the cruise lines has doubled, doubled again, and then doubled again over the last eight years. This investment continues into the twenty first century and virtually guarantees incredible opportunity for travel agents that can market the cruise lines products. All sectors of the travel industry have experienced awesome growth and beg for marketers to fill their ships, hotels, resorts, airplanes, car rentals, and so on.

THE TRAVEL INDUSTRY, THE ENTREPRENEUR'S DREAM

In his book *"MORE WEALTH WITHOUT RISK"*, Charles J. Givens advises people to consider starting their own travel agency to earn extra money, enjoy excellent tax benefits at home and while travelling, and to defray the cost of travel itself. He cites many examples of his own exploits in the travel industry and really hits the nail on the head with this statement.

"During the seventies, I personally took hundreds of people to Hawaii, Mexico, England, Ireland, France and South America. As an outside agent putting trips together, I knew I would enjoy myself. My share of the commissions amounted to about $5,000.00 per week, plus free airfare and hotels. Not a bad way to travel. You can get the same bargains by becoming a successful outside agent."[3]

If you have considered entering the travel industry there has never been a better time to start. Personal computers, telecommunications, the entrepreneurial era, the dramatic changes in the dynamics of travel marketing, and airline deregulation have created a small business opportunity for everyone desiring the rewards of operating their own small business from their home.

THE TRAVEL INDUSTRY, YOUR VEHICLE TO SUCCESS

It is always easy to talk about starting your own business or to dream about visiting far off places. To make your dreams reality requires action. Action on your part to improve your life and environment, to take control of your own fortune and to realize your ambitions.

"HOW TO START A HOME BASED TRAVEL AGENCY" is written for action to help you start your business today. It is laid out in an action oriented format so you can start with chapter one and work your way through the development of your own travel business step by step. There really is no reason to wait, unless you are not ready to make the commitment to your hopes and dreams.

You will find, as many before you have, that operating your own home based travel agency is one of the most satisfying and fulfilling businesses there is. Your commitment to yourself, your family and your desires will yield huge returns.

---

[1] *"MEGATRENDS"* John Naisbitt, Warner Books, 1984 Chp.1,2,6.

[2] *USA Today,* February 6th, 1994 "Merrill Lynch turns Bullish on rural USA, STREET TALK.

[3] *"MORE WEALTH WITHOUT RISK"* Charles J. Givens, 1991, Simon & Schuster, pp263

Chapter 2
A BRIEF HISTORY OF TRAVEL RETAILING

In order to recognize the trends affecting retail travel agencies today and to identify the major turning points in the development of our industry, following is a brief history of the evolution of retail travel agencies.

IN THE BEGINNING

Travel agencies were businesses possessing some area of special expertise. If a client wanted to tour Europe they would likely seek out an expert travel agent who would charge the client to organize an itinerary around the specific requests of the client. The travel agent would communicate with the various hotels, transfer companies, railroads, airlines and so forth to make the arrangements on the clients behalf. Rarely did these F.I.T. (Free Independent Travel) agents work for commissions but rather tacked on a service charge for their efforts and costs incurred on behalf of their clients. Many of these early travel agents have grown into major companies by virtue of their excellent reputations and opportunities for expansion during periods of the evolution. Generally, these early travel agencies were not focused on airline ticketing but specialized in planning leisure travel.

During the 1950s and early 1960s some of the first tour packaging began to occur. This had an extraordinary impact on the agent's ability to earn money since the cost of operating the reservation was dramatically reduced. Instead of having to communicate with each and every component of a given itinerary the agent could simply sell the "tour product" and leave the details to the tour operator. The tour operator paid the travel agent a commission for consummating the sale. These organized tours and charters were the forerunner of today's travel marketing. Some of the early tour programs were priced with a 10% tax and service charge that was added by the travel agent. This was actually the travel agent's commission and the tour operators were sure to include this service charge provision on their brochures.

During this period the travel agents relied heavily on "agency desks" at the airlines for reservations information. The client would visit the travel agent who would then work from a manual tariff published by the Air Traffic Conference and possibly an Official Airline Guide (OAG). To confirm a flight reservation for a client the travel agent would call the specific airline and complete the reservation with the agency desk reservationist. The travel agent would then hand write an airline ticket for the reservation and claim a commission as part of the process. This service was valuable to consumers as there were no toll free telephone lines to call the carriers and they would have to wait in long lines at the airport while the carrier's ticket desk personnel hand wrote the ticket. The airlines loved the help from the travel agent because at this time all airline employees were unionized and very expensive. The small commission paid the travel agent was far less expensive than the carrier's own unionized employees.

THEN CAME COMPUTERS

It was only 1975 or so when the very first travel agency received a Carrier Reservation System (CRS). This single event ushered us into the current environment that is creating dramatic change in the retail distribution of travel products.

When the first computerized reservations system (CRS) was installed in that first travel agency, just imagine the impact. First, the airline was relieved of having to pay a union employee to man the "agency desk" to process reservations. This was a major benefit in itself. Next, the airline did not have the cost of providing an automated work station for the employee they no longer employed, another major savings. Best of all, the travel agent that replaced the employee was willing to pay, and pay big, for the privilege of having automation available in their agency. The rush was on.

Initially, a travel agent had to qualify to be considered for a CRS. If they did not have enough revenue to qualify they simply could not obtain automation at any price. During the following four or five years over 16,000 retail travel agencies were automated. Automated travel agents could offer their clients instant ticketing by computer with boarding passes and a computerized itinerary and invoice. When you consider that no airline offered toll free reservations at the beginning of this period, the boom was on! Travel agents advertised "Airport Prices in Town", "Never a Service Charge for Airline Tickets" or, "Guaranteed Lowest Airfares" to develop the mass conversion of clients who traditionally booked direct with the airlines, into the agencies new customers.

Travel school graduates would find jobs immediately upon finishing their automation training much to the chagrin of more established and professional travel counselors. These "instant agents" paved the way for rapid expansion of the retail travel agency population that exploded in the seventies. It seems anyone who completed the airlines one week automation training class could do the work of a professional agent without enduring the years of experience once necessary to become competent as a travel professional.

The recession of the early eighties, deregulation, and the advent of satellite telecommunications and wide availability of inexpensive toll free telephone numbers brought a rapid close to the rate of expansion of retail travel agencies. Virtually every client willing to switch from booking directly with an airline had been converted, every commercial account locked up, and every frequent flyer and repeat leisure traveller spoken for. The inflation experienced during the late seventies and early eighties had led to the spectacular productivity squeeze being put on retail travel agencies today.

PERSONAL COMPUTERS, THE END OF AN ERA

More recently, the evolution of personal computers and telecommunications has had a most dramatic impact on retail travel agencies. In the beginning, only the airlines were automated with substantial databases, then during the mid to late seventies, travel agents became automated as well through the use of the exclusive data lines connecting them to the CRS. Today consumers enjoy access to the same CRS databases once reserved exclusively for the airlines and travel agents. By using the various on-line services that offer a wide choice of dial up access into the databases, consumers can make their own reservations from home and once again purchase their airline tickets direct form the airline of their choice.

While the retail travel industry was once airline ticket driven from the mid seventies until most recently, it is very apparent that the future of travel agency retailing is dependent on revenues generated in areas other than airline tickets.

THE COMMISSION CAPS AND ELECTRONIC TICKETING

In early February 1995 the major U.S. trunk carriers led by Delta Airlines capped their domestic airline commissions to travel agencies at $25.00 for one way tickets and $50.00 for round trip airline tickets. The caps were put into place by the airlines supposedly to control their distribution costs and enhance opportunity for operating profits. Industry insiders believe that the caps were set in place to reduce travel agency profitability and to force the travel community to charge service fees for issuing low yield airline tickets. Short haul regional carriers who enjoyed pre-cap distribution through travel agents bore the brunt of the new environment. Their commissions were not sufficient for retailers to continue distributing their tickets without imposing a transaction fee to offset the losses from commission income lost by the commission caps.

At the same time airlines have reduced their dependency on physical airline tickets by instituting "electronic ticketing", or E-Tickets. Ticketless travel has some obvious advantages over using the established traffic documents. By eliminating the physical ticket itself airlines are more able to handle the passenger directly with a minimum of expense. At press time American Airlines, United Airlines and surely most trunk carriers are pursuing paperless transactions as their primary method of documenting a reservation. The airlines are exploring the use of "smart cards" so consumers can purchase their airline tickets on-line and execute the transaction with an airline credit card. These airline credit cards will be encoded with their frequent flyer information and other pertinent data to secure the airlines and client alike in this new electronic environment.

PERSONAL COMPUTERS, THE BEGINNING OF AN ERA

So if airlines are more interested in selling their tickets directly to consumers rather than through travel agents, where, if any, is there opportunity? Mr. Jeffrey Katz, President of American Airline's SABRE Travel Information Network, the largest vendor of CRS to the industry sums it up this way. "As travel automation becomes more and more widespread and sophisticated, the role of the leisure travel agent is far less likely to be diminished than that of the business travel agent." According to Katz, "The leisure travel decision is complex, and the purchase value can be high; for example, when a client is buying a cruise or tour. These decisions are less likely to be made without some form of personal consultation or expert assistance."[1]

There you have it. Personal computers are paving the way for travel agents to forego the traditional store front travel agency in favor of a home based business focused on niche markets. By utilizing the effectiveness of modern personal computers, a one man operation can out market, out perform, and out earn their store front counterparts.

---

[1] _TRAVEL TECHNOLOGY,_ Oct.4th, 1993, pp 26

Chapter 3
HOME BASED TRAVEL AGENCIES OF THE NINETIES

The transition of retailing travel from store front locations to home based locations during the late eighties and nineties is occurring for many diverse reasons. While the transition is fueled in part by advances in personal computers, telecommunications, and an entrepreneurial spirit that blossomed during the eighties, much of the transition is motivated by the changing financial climate of which retail store front agencies are faced.

ERODING STORE FRONT PROFITS

The Deregulation Act that took full effect in 1981 created a more competitive environment in the airline industry. Initially deregulation was followed by a flurry of new opportunity for travel agents who benefitted from the increased competition of the airlines. As deregulation wore on, the continuing airfare wars drove the productivity level of domestic airline ticketing below the cost of providing the transaction for most agencies. Vertical integration by the airlines into commercial accounts, ethnic groups, frequent flyers programs, and wholesale tour programs created a more demanding scenario for retailers. Following is an overview of some of the more important trends that have occurred.

INFLATION VS. PRODUCTIVITY

One of the primary reasons retailers have chosen the move from store front to a more cost effective home base is the consequence of the increasing cost of operating a retail location. This caused diminishing remuneration from the productivity of the blended revenue of a retail store fronts. The inflation of the late seventies and eighties drove up all of the costs of operating a retail store front including, rent, utilities, postage, labor, automation, supplies, equipment and communications. Virtually every cost incurred by retailers increased dramatically. While most other industries enjoyed dramatic increases in the prices of their products to offset the effects of inflation on their operating overhead, retail travel agencies have actually experienced a decrease in the overall revenue.

One measure of retail travel agency viability is the average Yield Per Transaction (YPT). The YPT is indicative of an agency's ability to earn money. As an agency's YPT increases so does its profits given the same cost structure. Retail travel agencies' YPT has been on a constant downward spiral since the onset of deregulation and is currently in the low twenty dollar range for most agencies.

During the same period the Cost Per Transaction (CPT) has increased dramatically. The effects of inflation have propagated havoc on the average cost per transaction. So much so, that the average cost per transaction in most urban areas of the United States is in the mid twenty dollar range. It is not uncommon to find agencies in the Southern California area with YPTs of $19 and CPTs of $26. There is little wonder retail store fronts are having a difficult time.

The third factor that influences a retail agency's ability to create profit is the Average Transactions Per Employee Week (ATPEW). During the eighties many agencies tried to correct the diminishing YPT and increasing CPT by streamlining their operations and increasing their employee's productivity. Large commercial agencies are the best examples of this effort. The expansion of chains of agencies with centralized reporting, accounting and management was another variation of the effort. Generally, though, about 80% of the appointed retail store front locations in the United States lack the volume of business and staffing to meaningfully influence their ATPEW. Most smaller agencies have had flat growth in their average transactions per employee week since 1975.

If the simple measure of productivity for travel agents is ATPEW x (YPT-CPT) we can easily understand the problems that travel agencies face. As profits become slimmer travel agents can only remain profitable by increasing their YPT, reducing their CPT or increasing their ATPEW. Given most agencies have little ability to impact the majority of their YPT and little control over their ATPEW, the only opportunity is to decrease their CPT by increasing their volume to better amortize the fixed operating costs. This effort has driven up the break even point for most retail store front travel agencies to around $1.2 to $1.5 in annual gross revenues. Unfortunately the vast majority of retail travel agencies are primarily small businesses with revenues of $600,000.00 to $1,000,000.00.

THE CULPRIT, DOMESTIC AIRLINE TICKETS

Deregulation has taken its toll on airlines, sure, but look at the impact it has had on retailers. In 1977, approximately 70% of all retail agency revenue was created from airline tickets. The arrival of computerized Reservations Systems (CRS) and the automation of thousands of travel agents drove billions of dollars worth of domestic airline ticketing into retail travel agents at a time when airfares were high and operating costs were low. There was an explosion of retailers that enjoyed immediate profits. Then average YPTs were $24 to $28 and average CPTs $12 to $14, therefore agencies couldn't miss.

Today, average YPTs on domestic airline tickets vary between $16 and $22 depending on the market the agency is in. Agencies in markets served by some of the low cost regional carriers are even less. Imagine selling tickets on Southwest Airlines, as an example, for $39.00 including a companion ticket. You must make the reservation by calling Southwest after waiting on hold for ten or fifteen minutes, issue two separate tickets, issue an itinerary/invoice and deal with the client. All for a whopping $3.50 commission. Of course your direct costs were substantially above the commission not to mention the impact of allocating the agencies fixed operating costs on top of the variable costs. You can see what a loser it is. Or worse yet, imagine issuing a ticket for $439.00, then the next fare war comes along and you have to reissue it for $339.00 refunding a good part of the original commission and doing the work a second time for free. Then, lo and behold, the fares drop once more creating a third reissue and another commission refund. This scenario is not at all uncommon in today's competitive airline environment. You can see the dramatic impact this series of events has on both YPT and CPT. Most travel agents incur a large amount of their fixed overhead to sustain their ability to issue airline tickets to the public. More and more agents now feel that it is less and less viable to continue the service for the general public.

Larger commercial accounts are now dominated by large agencies specializing in business travel who have found the ability to operate in today's YPT climate by selecting accounts with higher than normal commissions per ticket and offering "revenue sharing" programs. Basically these programs allow the client to earn rebates, or share in the revenue, of the commissions the travel agency earns from their ticketing. Generally revenue sharing programs start at around $26 YPT and cap at $30 YPT with the vast majority of the balance of the commission paid to the account The existence of revenue sharing programs has practically ensured that low levels of yield for domestic airline tickets are guaranteed. This drain on travel agencies' productivity has rendered most store front locations unviable.

Another chief reason many travel agents are abandoning their store fronts is the drastic increase in the cost of employees. Workman's Compensation Insurance, the employer's contribution to payroll taxes, unemployment plans and other employee related contributions are exploding. The threat of mandatory health insurance and other government mandated policies only further damage the employee environment. As employees demand more and more salary to keep pace with inflation and the cost of payroll tax contribution and government mandated employee benefits spiral, employees become a luxury only the most effective agencies can afford without major increases in productivity.

THE LAST STRAW, COMMISSION CAPS

In February of 1995 when the United States trunk carriers capped their commissions on domestic airline tickets at $25.00 on one way tickets and $50.00 for round trip domestic airline tickets it virtually knocked most agencies for a loop. Because they were blending the yields from low yielding airline tickets with the outstanding yields from first class, business, and coach tickets to arrive at an acceptable blended yield agencies went from modest profitability to losing substantial amounts of money overnight. All at once it became obvious that they would either have to start charging fees for issuing domestic airline tickets, which consumers were not ready for, or they would have to forsake their airline ticketing business for other more profitable ventures.

Concurrent with the commission caps was the airline's effort to develop consumer automation through the various bulletin board services. The ticketless environment created by the carriers is proving to be their most successful vehicle for reducing their distribution costs. The information age has bought an unprecedented level of consumer sophistication.

It is obvious that the face of travel retailing will continue to change as domestic airline commissions stay depressed and agents are faced with a new economic challange. Travel agents must both embrace technology and reduce operating costs. The information age will bring these changes.

AUTOMATION, THE HIGHWAY TO CHANGE FOR THE HOME BASED TRAVEL AGENT

In November of 1992 the United States Department of Transportation ruled that the existing Computerized Reservations Systems (CRS) of the various vendors could not restrain other carriers and suppliers that marketed their products through the CRS from competing with them. This revolutionary decision has paved the way for the demise of the small store front travel agency dealing in general airfares. We know that YPTs and CPTs are creating difficulty for smaller agencies but imagine the impact of diversity of automation. Suppliers can now offer direct access to their databases to whomever they like. .

Access to the industry databases will be via PC modem rather than a dedicated data line as current store fronts use. Access will be in the shape of all of the on-line services such as CompuServe, AOL etc. The largest opportunity for growth in electronic distribution is the Internet and possible Intranet solutions as well.

Currently, when an offline carrier sells flight segments through one of the existing CRS they pay a revenue segment fee to the host CRS for the transaction. The segment fee can be a large portion of the total transaction. The cost, as an example, to sell a $99.00 fare through the CRS is as follows:

TYPICAL COST OF CRS DISTRIBUTION

Basic Airfare	**$99.00**
Transportation tax (10%)	9.00
Base Airfare	$90.00
Travel Agent Commission (10%)	9.00
Revenue Segment Fees (4 segments @ $3.00)	12.00
Total marketing cost	21.00
Net Fare to Carrier	**$69.00**

You can see the relative expense in the CRS system of distribution. A company called Lanyon Industries in England has created a PC gateway board and software for the travel industry that will allow any PC user equipped with Lanyon to access any travel supplier equipped with Lanyon. It remains to be seen how this development will manifest itself but one thing is crystal clear....retail store fronts dependent on CRS for airline ticketing revenue are in jeopardy.

ENTREPRENEURIAL ERA

The recession of the early nineties has created an entrepreneurial era. Numerous middle management, aerospace, military and other professionals have found themselves without the prospect of employment. While they have acquired substantial assets they are seeking entrepreneurial opportunity in lieu of corporate positions. Agents disenchanted with dwindling resources and opportunity in

Agents disenchanted with dwindling resources and opportunity in traditional storefront agencies are opting for their own operation from which to serve their clients. Many full time employees or business owners are looking at the travel industry for part time income and a diversion away from the toils of day to day efforts in their primary business. Whatever the reason, more and more folks are entertaining their own business and the challenge of directing their own destiny.

Many new entrepreneurs are opting for the independence and effectiveness of working from home. Information based businesses have been the beneficiaries of the vast capabilities of personal computers. Travel is one of these businesses that can be operated anywhere there is an electrical outlet, telephone line and VCR. The demand for in home leisure travel sales has created a whole new environment displacing store front agencies. Entrepreneurs working from home go into clients homes with dial up reservations automation, travel videos and brochures. They are able to set the travel agency up on the client's own kitchen table offering the ultimate in convenience to the consumer.

EVOLUTION OF THE TRUE INDEPENDENT CONTRACTOR

For years retail travel agencies have been using sales forces that were identified as "commissioned outside sales people". Travel agencies that use this type of sales organization to develop clients normally pay them a straight commission without making payroll tax deposits on behalf of the sales person. During the financial crunch of the nineties the E.D.D. quickly found that these agencies had not classified these outside sales people correctly. They went after agencies with large commission payments by auditing the outside sales force to verify their independent contractor status. Needless to say, travel agencies had not met the test for independent contractor status and the agency was then hit for back payroll tax deposits, a penalty for misclassification of employees, penalties for not filing and interest. The E.D.D. then notified the I.R.S. who followed the E.D.D. into the agency with more penalties and fines. So severe were the repercussions that agencies were going out of business weekly because of federal tax liens that were filed against the business.

The pressure to either start treating outside sales people like employees, with all of the benefits attached to such a designation, or perfect the true independent contractor status of the outside sales person that the industry gave way to the latter. Following are just some of the criteria the I.R.S. looks at when determining the classification.

CONTROL

If an agency exercises any control whatsoever over an individual it usually would indicate that the person is an employee. Having the employee answer phones for the agency, mandatory hours in the office, sales quotas, mandatory seminar attendance, etc. are all signs of control by the agency. An independent contractor is free to work when and where they like at their own discretion.

FORMAL WRITTEN CONTRACT

Every independent contractor has a formal contract with their suppliers, especially their primary ticketing agency. The lack of a contract indicates that the outside sales person is an employee....period. The contract must indicate the terms of the agreement between the independent contractor and the principle (agency). It must also include the declaration that the outside sales person is in fact an independent contractor and must not include anything that would violate any of the ingredients necessary for the perfection of the independent contractor status before the I.R.S..

EXCLUSIVITY

The true independent contractor is free to do business with whom ever they would like and the principle cannot restrict the I.C.s activity in any way. Agencies that require their outside sales force to put all of their business through their agency only and do not make payroll tax deposits for the outside sales person as if they are an employee should take a careful look at this practice.

TOOLS OF THE TRADE

Independent contractors supply their own tools of the trade. If the agency is supplying reference material, dial up automation, itinerary/invoices, desk space, time on the agencies CRS, or any other "tool of the trade" this may violate the I.C. status of an otherwise perfected outside sales person. Many agencies have begun charging monthly service fees to cover such costs as they are passed to the independent contractor.

TRAINING

An agency may not train their outside sales force with their inside agents. By commingling both employees and independent contractors into one training session the I.R.S. might disqualify the

I.C. status for the sales force. Ideally; Independent contractors should pay for any training the agency provides and it should be isolated to include only I.C.s.

SEPARATE LEGAL ENTITY

The independent contractor should be a clear and separate legal entity from the agency. The best separation is for the I.C. to operate under a separate fictitious business name. If the I.C. is to operate under the agencies name the formal contract should be entered into by the I.C. as a separate business rather than an individual. Recognition of commissions paid the I.C. should always be made on an I.R.S. form 1099. Recognition of outside sales people that are treated as employees should always be reported on I.R.S. form W-2.

WHAT IS SO DIFFERENT ABOUT AN INDEPENDENT CONTRACTOR?

Today's true independent contractor is a travel professional that generally operates from a home base and serves an established clientele of leisure travellers. They are generally members of CLIA and belong to a cruise consortium for overrides, they deal directly with tour companies by using "pseudo ARC numbers" that the operators themselves provide. They buy international airline tickets directly from consolidators, and they may work with one or more retail travel agencies or independent contractor networks to obtain their domestic airline tickets.

These new breed of travel marketers are not interested in selling domestic airline tickets but have specialized in one aspect of the travel industry or another. They have formidable marketing plans, more so than their store front counterparts and they tend to exist in more sophisticated areas of the travel industry. Most important is their profitability. By focusing on areas where yields are substantially higher than domestic airline tickets they have found a way to once again earn a good living in the travel industry.

CONCLUSION

It is very clear that the nature of travel distribution is changing. Increasing costs of operation have not been offset by concurrent increases in commissions. Domestic airline commissions no longer warrant the investment into retail store fronts from a cash flow perspective. The opportunity cost of operating a retail store front is not offset by potential profit. As more and more small agencies become unprofitable, agency owners are moving their higher yielding clientele into a home based agency and foregoing the traditional "walk-in" ticketing business. The move to perfect a true independent contractor status for agency sales people has led to a new breed of agent.

Home Based Travel Agencies of the Nineties

Chapter 4
DEVELOPING A BUSINESS CONCEPT

Like any business venture, starting a home based travel business is bound to be more successful if you have an established business concept and destination in mind. Without defining a profile of your intended business you run the risk of becoming lost in the myriad of opportunity that exists in the travel industry. So many times folks get involved to make money and end up spending most of their time running around delivering $29 airline tickets thinking that someday the folks will buy a cruise or something profitable from them. Of course, if and when they eventually do call, you are still to busy running around delivering airline tickets to properly service them. Worse yet, you have spent all of your resources, time, and effort delivering tickets and not preparing for the eventual call for information about a high yielding product or service.

Focus is the only way to ensure you stay on course in your business. By maintaining your focus during the planning, start-up, and early stages of your business you will almost always guarantee your success. In this chapter we will look at traditional yields for the various products you might sell and various areas of focus you might consider to maximize profitability. We will look at developing some basic business objectives.

COMMISSIONS AND OVERRIDES

Virtually all travel products and services are commissioned to travel agents. Airline tickets, tours, cruises, hotels and resorts, rail travel, and so on all have a travel agent's commission built right into the pricing. A client does not pay more to purchase through a travel agent but simply pays the same price as if they had booked direct with the supplier. The supplier actually pays the travel agent for selling the particular service or product.

Overrides are extra commissions a travel agent can earn by giving a particular supplier enough revenue to qualify. Overrides are commonly paid after the fact the first year and then are deducted at time of final payment in subsequent years. Many agency consortiums have been formed for the express purpose of offering overrides to the member agencies. Overrides are extremely important as they tend to have a dramatic impact on the profitability of an agency. Following is an example of the importance they play.

NET PROFIT FROM SALES

C & O SALE	COMMISSIONS	8% COST	PROFIT
10% $1,000	$100	$80	$20
12% $1,000	$120	$80	$40
15% $1,000	$150	$80	$70
20% $1,000	$200	$80	$120

As discussed in Chapter Three CPT and YPT are crucial factors. Note that the CPT remains constant but that as the YPT increases the impact on the net profit from the transaction is dramatic. Just an increase from 10% to 12% yields a 100% increase in profitability. You can see how important overrides can be. Following are the levels of commission and overrides you might expect to find in the industry.

DOMESTIC AIRLINES

Most domestic carriers offer a flat 10% commission (actually 9% when you deduct the 10% transportation tax) to travel agents. In some instances carriers will offer up to 15% for sales of "disproportionate market share". This means that the agency must put their clients on the carrier at a rate substantially higher than the other travel agencies within their specific market area. This is a mixed bag. On one hand you make an additional 5% commission but on the other you risk losing clients by continually favoring one carrier over another. However, overrides on domestic carriers may be the only way to turn a non profitable business into a profitable one providing the current yields on domestic tickets.

American Airlines, United Airlines, Delta, TWA, Northwest, USAir, and Continental Airlines have all capped the commission they pay on domestic airline tickets at $25.00 for one way and $50.00 for a round trip regardless of the value of the airline ticket over $250.00 for one way and $500.00 for round trip. On tickets of less value than the cap the carriers pay 10% on the base fare.

Given that your business concept will probably not include selling a lot of domestic airline tickets it is safe to assume that you may contract with another travel agency to perform this service on your behalf. Generally, the commission split would dilute your yield but would also free you up to pursue more profitable ventures to focus on. Most agents are willing to give up 30% to 50% of the commission for this trade off. In some instances where you demand instant response you may be willing to give up all of the commission just so your client's domestic airline needs are handled properly and they still rely on you for the rest of the leisure travel needs.

INTERNATIONAL TICKETS

Selling International airline tickets can be a whole other story. Huge commissions can be realized by shopping various tour operators and consolidators. Chapter 13 will delve into this in much more depth. Commissions anywhere from 8% to 36% and more can be realized on international airline tickets.

TOUR COMPANIES

Tour companies will pay a minimum of 10% commission with override programs up to 18% and sometimes more. Depending on the destination, commissions and overrides of 12% are readily obtainable through your own productivity. Even more commissions are available from a good number of travel agency consortiums. Many times commissions in excess of 10% on domestic airline tickets are available directly from the tour operators so they may meet their contractual numbers with the airline.

CRUISE LINES

Here is the opportunity of the century in the travel industry. Be sure to read *"HOW TO START A CRUISE ONLY TRAVEL AGENCY"* to fully understand the nature of the opportunity. Cruise lines pay 10% on all cruises to CLIA and ARC agents. Overrides up to an additional 5% are generally available from the cruise lines for productivity and other substantial overrides are available from a good number of cruise consortiums that can increase the total commission to 28% and above. When you consider the large sales price of cruises and the ease of sale plus the high percentage of commission, cruises are an excellent way to make lots of money in the travel industry.

HOTELS AND RESORTS

Most hotels and resorts pay 10%. Some will pay more in off seasons. A good number of smaller hotels do not pay commission at all so be sure to check before you book your clients.

CAR RENTAL COMPANIES

Commissions vary widely from car rental companies. Large companies like Hertz, Avis and National on pay a pittance to travel agents. Some companies like Alamo are very generous. I bet you wonder why Alamo has done so well lately? Commissions anywhere from $2.00 per reservation (regardless of value) to 20% are available. Again, there is not much money in renting cars which goes hand in hand with domestic airline tickets.

AMTRAK

Amtrak pays 10% commission on all sales.

TRAVEL INSURANCE

Insurance pays anything from 10% up to 35% and more. Sometimes independent insurance policies are better than the tour operator's or cruise line's and will pay substantially more commission.

CHARTERS

Most airline charters pay at least 5% with the normal being 10%. If you are contracting a substantial number of seats the commission becomes more negotiable.

SIGHTSEEING TOURS, LIMOUSINE SERVICES, GREETING SERVICES, AND OTHER MISCELLA-NEOUS TRAVEL PRODUCTS

10% to 20% generally, sometimes more for good productivity.

GROUP TRAVEL

Generally group travel is priced from the ground up and most group rates are quoted net of commission. For a group to be successful there is customarily a 25% to 35% commission built into the final selling price. This is to allow for the extraordinary costs associated with the formation and marketing of the group movement and the supplier's net rates are commonly discounted this much to allow for this markup.

TRAVEL AGENCY FEES

Since the commission caps of early 1995 many travel agencies have implemented fees for certain services. Usually travel agents charge a $10 to $25 fee for issuing airline tickets in amounts lowere than $300. Ticket reissues, cancellations, deliveries are other fee areas.

15 AREAS OF OPPORTUNITY TO MAKE LOTS OF

MONEY IN THE TRAVEL BUSINESS

Sure the low yields on domestic airline tickets have taken their toll on orthodox retailers but there are still many areas in the travel industry that are very lucrative. By forsaking the store front environment, a travel marketer is free to focus on specific areas where yields are far more attractive. Following are 15 areas of specialization that make sense in today's environment.

GROUP TRAVEL

By specializing in organizing, marketing, and operating group travel you can generate excellent profitability. Groups may become repetitive each year and in a few years you can build an extremely nice business.

CRUISE TRAVEL

Becoming a cruise specialist has excellent rewards. The cruise lines have put numerous ships into service over the last five years and have created great demand for cruising. They have vehemently supported the agency distribution system and encouraged agents to sell cruises by offering overrides and other marketing incentives to stimulate agents. Outstanding profitability can occur for cruise only agents operating from their homes. Be sure to read *"HOW TO START A CRUISE ONLY TRAVEL AGENCY"*.

INTERNATIONAL AIRLINE TICKETS

Specializing in selling international transportation can be very attractive especially if you operate in regions not dominated by consolidators. Commissions from 15% to over 35% can be obtained.

SPECIAL INTEREST TRAVEL

Do you have a special interest shared by many folks throughout your community, city, state, or country? If so, you may be able to polarize folks with similar interest into groups or individuals for travel around the special interest.

SMALL COMMERCIAL ACCOUNTS

Sure domestic airline ticket yields are low but if you can find smaller commercial accounts that have not been approached by the revenue sharing mega agencies, you may be able to capture their business by simply offering personal service. If the account is willing to pay for extra services you may be able to do extremely well handling their special requests. Most larger agencies are unable to because of their volume.

ADVENTURE AND SPORTS TRAVEL

Do you ski, surf, run, hike, bike, fish, golf, play tennis, mountain climb, windsurf, hunt or participate in any other sport? Adventure travel for photo safaris, white water rafting, exploring and so on are all opportunities to make money from a home based travel business.

SENIOR TRAVEL

Everyone knows that seniors have the money, time, and inclination to travel. When you consider that the baby boomers are now coming of senior age you can really see the opportunity. Seniors can travel off season and love to go in groups which make this sector very profitable.

MEETING PLANNING

If you happen to live in a place where corporations, associations, or other organizations come to meet you may have the opportunity to get into the business of planning the meetings and associated meals and events surrounding them.

ETHNIC TRAVEL

Many cultures prefer to purchase goods and services from their own ethnic groups rather than going into the community at large. If you are in a position to polarize distribution within your ethnicity you stand to make an excellent income. Especially if you can deal in destinations not already saturated with independent distributors.

SEMINARS

If you have a specific area of expertise you may be able to combine seminars with travel to greatly enhance your profitability from the seminars. Financial seminars, professional seminars, "How To" seminars are all great examples of opportunities to enter the cruise seminar or resort seminar business.

REGIONAL OR DESTINATION SPECIALIZATION

If you specialize in a particular region of the world or a specific destination clients will seek you out for the information. If you specialize in areas with a high concentration of visitors like Hawaii, Mexico, England, Hong Kong you will be successful. More exotic areas also can lead to success if you can reach your potential market either through other travel agents or some cost effective media.

GEOGRAPHIC ADVANTAGE

If you have a geographic advantage over any competing travel agencies you can do very well. Many communities are without retail agencies located within them and rely on an agency in an adjoining town. This is a classic example of an opportunity to start a home based travel agency.

DEMOGRAPHIC ADVANTAGE

If you specialize in products of high demographic appeal and are located in an area of high demographics this would represent a great opportunity. Rich and Famous Travel is a great name for this type of operation.

ECOTOURISM

Many home based travel businesses have been successful designing and operating tours to ecologically sensitive areas of the Earth and give a financial motivation for countries to preserve their rain forests, ocean environment and culture.

HANDICAPPED TRAVEL

Arranging travel for folks with handicaps can be very rewarding both personally and monetarily. There is a large demand for travel agents who can communicate with and service their needs.

SAMPLE INCOME STATEMENTS OF HOME BASED AGENCIES

By thoroughly understanding your business concept and primary focus it becomes an easy task to determine a path to follow. By maintaining your focus you can easily avoid being side tracked by incidental sales that will erode your time and energy for the task at hand. Specializing in areas of higher than normal YPTs you can establish a highly profitable travel venture.

Following are income statements from successful home based travel entrepreneurs for your review. Note the range of gross sales and net income they produce.

AGENCY A

GROSS INCOME

Commissions from sales	37,222.17
Interest Income	216.77
TOTAL INCOME	**$37,438.94**

EXPENSES

Advertising	860.00
Automobile	6,765.00
Depreciation (Equipment)	564.00
Entertainment	516.70
Insurance	812.00
Licenses	173.00
Office Supplies	295.00
Postage	2,756.33
Printing	3,770.00
Professional Fees	600.00
Subscriptions and Dues	385.00
Telephone	4,778.16
TOTAL EXPENSES	**22,275.19**
OPERATING PROFIT	**$15,163.75**

This is a classic example of a home based business making money where a store front could not. This is a home based business in a rural area of Oregon with no agencies within almost 40 miles. Much of the expenses were actually a benefit to the owner. Automobile, entertainment, and telephone expenses were incurred in business but were private expenses before the agency was started.

This agent would have to double her existing business before she could afford to relocate into a store front and get her ARC appointments.

AGENCY B

REVENUE

Cruise Sales	$397,944.90
Tour Sales	67,300.55
Airline Commissions	13,734.16
Misc. Commissions	2,660,28
TOTAL REVENUE	**$481,639.89**

COST OF SALES

Cruise Sales	$344,349.68	
Tour Sales	58,887.98	
TOTAL COST OF SALES	**403,237.66**	
GROSS PROFIT		**$78,402.23**

EXPENSES

Advertising	$3,774.00	
Automobile Lease	4,245.00	
Bad Checks	270.00	
Contributions	130.00	
Dues and Subscriptions	716.00	
Insurance	1,354.00	
Interest and Bank Chgs	213.55	
Office Supplies	788.14	
Postage and Fedex	1,573.89	
Printing	2,843.93	
Sabre Expense	947.16	
Seminars and Meetings	1,744.00	
Telephone Expense	4,777.14	
Travel (Educational)	6,829.16	
Utilities	1,755.33	
TOTAL EXPENSES		**31,961.30**
NET PROFIT		**$46,440.93**

Here is another excellent example of a home based agency that is very attractive from a net profit standpoint yet would not be viable in an ARC accredited store front location. This happens to be a former store front agency owner that closed her business, gave up her ARC appointments and let her employees go. She high graded her clientele and took only the best for her own and now operates part time from a home base. Note the heavy cruise business that yields over 13% average. Note also that even by sharing her airline ticket commissions with another agency she still is very profitable. She uses Corporate Sabre and queues the reservation to an ARC location for quality control and ticketing on 50/50 split.

AGENCY C

GROSS SALES	$910,756.71

COST OF GOODS SOLD

ARC Expense, Credit Card	266,813.51
ARC Expense, Cash	428,205.42
Business Expense, Hotel	11,280.24
Business Expense, Tour	57,636.59
Business Expense, Cruise	27,597.70
Other Commissions	13,742.50
Seminars and Conventions	2,030.17
Client Transport	10,803.50
Apollo	7,093.25
TOTAL COST OF GOODS SOLD	**$825,202.88**

GROSS PROFIT	85,553.83

EXPENSES

Commissions	$ 29,189.02
Office Expense	2,625.56
Insurance	2,477.38
Rent	8,400.00
Banking Charges	293.75
Postage	281.50
Advertising	3,707.95
Utilities	2,562.94
Automobile Expense	1,478.19
Subscriptions and Dues	1,877.15
Accounting Fees	1,075.00
Legal Fees	1,045.00
Interest Expense	653.29
TOTAL EXPENSES	**55,666.73**

TOTAL PROFIT	**$ 29,887.10**

Here is a great example of an independent contractor that is "renting" a desk from an agency that specializes in working with independent contractors. The agent is paying $700.00 per month rent and receives 100% of the commission from her sales. The agency keeps all of the air overrides and provides automation and office space. The agent pays her pro-rata portion of the utilities and office maintenance. The agent also has three other outside sales/independent contractors that place their business with her on a 70/30 commission split. While this agency is starting to show signs of viability as a store front location, the agent wants to stay in the current relationship because of the comfort.

AGENCY D

TOTAL COMMISSIONS $ 4,882.04

EXPENSES

Automobile Expense	$2,577.00
Education and Seminars	385.00
Office Expense	618.85
Postage and Delivery	188.00
Subscriptions and Dues	645.00
Telephone	833.17
Travel	1,905.37

TOTAL EXPENSES   7,152.39

NET PROFIT (LOSS)   ($2,270.35)

As you might imagine, this agency has just started in business but managed to generate sales in sufficient volume to obtain an IATAN ID card. Her losses are deceiving when you consider that she took an NACTA fam/cruise/seminar aboard Carnival's Holiday, visited Hawaii on a Familiarization tour, and also took a west coast Mexican Riviera cruise as well. Her automobile expenses were justified but were actually mileage she was driving before she started her home based agency so now represent a legitimate deduction.

While this agent is serious about her business she doesn't envision going full time and is very satisfied with the results of her business so far.

AGENCY E

REVENUES

Cruise Sales	$388,276.98	
Cost of Cruise Sales	338,237.78	
Cruise Commissions		$ 50,039.20
Tour Sales	177,446.42	
Cost of Tour Sales	158,814.55	
Tour Commissions		18,631.87
Air Commissions		8,233.72
Miscellaneous Commissions		2,566.29
Interest Income		328.66
TOTAL REVENUE		**$79,799.74**

EXPENSES

Advertising	$3,672.99
Automobile	1,667.24
Commissions	3,774.62
Depreciation (Equipment)	1,422.00
Equipment Rental	948.00
Insurance	1,378.01
Postage and Delivery	2,773.78
Printing (Brochures)	612.00
Printing (General)	1,445.07
Subscriptions and Dues	1,267.88
Supplies	1,744.23
Telephone Expense	3,278.36
Worldspan Automation	1,140.00
TOTAL EXPENSES	**25,124.18**
NET OPERATING PROFIT	**$54,675.56**

This is a wonderful example of a home based entrepreneur making the most of a good thing. This same operation in a store front would not even come close to breaking even. By focusing on cruises and tours with minimal domestic air sales this agent has produced excellent profitability for a one man operation. The agent is extremely happy with his results and does not envision growing much more. "I would like to increase my cruise sales, however" is his only comment regarding his operation.

Chapter 5
DEVELOPING A BUSINESS PLAN

Even the smallest of home based travel entrepreneurs should invest the time and effort to develop a business plan so you can get under way in the right direction. Many books have been written on how to piece business plans together so this chapter will just look at some of the criteria that might be included. Your plan doesn't have to be a formal document, in fact it doesn't even need to be written down. As long as you are aware of your own expectations from your business effort and have thought out the level of income, benefits, mid and long term goals and investment, that is all that is necessary.

Once you have developed a business plan starting and maintaining your business will be a snap. Many folks get into trouble in the travel industry for the lack of a proper business plan. They end up spending way to much money and time in pursuit of revenues not consistent with their objectives. Following are key ideas to consider in your business plan.

DEFINE YOUR EXPECTATIONS

When considering your home based travel business what are your expectations? What sort of income do you expect the business will generate in its first month? Its first six months? Its first year, second year and so on? Is your motivation for getting into the travel industry to travel? If so, where do you want to go? When? So many people get into the industry and get too busy to take the trips when they do become available. What is your eventual goal? Do you intend to start out part time and build the business into something that will support your full time effort? Maybe you just want to operate part time for a second income.

You can see the wide variety of choices you can make and all of them are potentially correct depending on your expectations. By understanding your expectations from your business you can easily decide whether your business plan is viable or not long before you spend your first dime.

STATE YOUR SPECIFIC OBJECTIVES

Once you understand your expectations from your business you should be able to state them as specific objectives. "I intend to generate $10,000.00 income the first year by focusing on selling cruises only via direct mail and advertising" is a stated objective. "I intend to take at least three cruises per year on different lines to increase my knowledge of the cruise industry" is another objective. "I intend to start out as a small home based business, build it gradually, and commit to it full time in five years" is yet another objective.

Objectives are very important when we set priorities. If an opportunity does not have continuity with your stated objectives you must carefully evaluate the "opportunity costs" of the decision to pursue the new opportunity. If the opportunity is within your stated objectives then it is certainly worth pursuing.

PROJECT YOUR INCOME

Once you know what your business is going to be you can start to project the income you desire. Lets say you are going to focus on cruises and you are going to sell to the middle of the market. It is a safe bet that your average yield per transaction will be a minimum of $600.00. If you need to make $20,000.00 your first year you will need to sell 34 cruises to meet your income needs. By projecting your income you can now start to get an idea of the nature of the business you are contemplating. At this point specific direction is a must. There is simply no way you can guess what your income might be if you merely open your doors and hope someone buys their travel from you.

Your income projections don't need to be to the penny but should be as accurate as possible. If you have expectations of developing your business into a full time effort you should prepare income projections for at least three to five years with five years being better.

PROJECT YOUR EXPENSES

Go through the same effort with your expenses. Try to figure out what sort of capital expense you will need to invest in your business for start up costs, equipment, training, and so forth. Try to budget your monthly operating overhead and establish a break even baseline for your intended operation. Your variable marketing expenses will be reflected in your marketing plan, but at this time you can easily compare your anticipated income with your anticipated expenses to see if your proposed business is viable.

FUNDING YOUR BUSINESS

Assuming the numbers add up and your expectations can be met by starting your venture it is now time to fund the effort. You should set aside the necessary funds to grow your business according to your business plan. Many folks do not isolate their funding from other monies and either end up dipping into the funds or continually putting more money into a venture that is clearly not working. By identifying the funds from the very start you can instantly tell if your plan is working or needs modification.

BUSINESS PLAN REVIEW

While this is a very simplistic look at the development of a business plan yours need not be any more sophisticated. The best way to monitor a business is to schedule review periods often and block time from your schedule to do the review. Every thirty days for a new business is not to frequent to make sure you are on course. If your revenue is failing to materialize or your expenses are skyrocketing you may want to completely redo your plan. On the other hand if business is rolling in and expenses are lower than anticipated this might call for a total revision of your plan. Your business plan is your safeguard from incurring losses from an undeveloped business.

WRITING A FORMAL BUSINESS PLAN

If you wish to write a more formal business plan for control purposes or probably to obtain investment funds or a loan you should complete a more detailed plan that would include all aspects of your proposed business or expansion. There are several great software applications available that make this task quite simple. BizPlan Builder is one such program. With BizPlan Builder you can start from scratch and by using the word processing templates and spreadsheet templates you can complete a formidable plan by just following the bouncing ball. I have included a sample of the beginning of a business plan for a business known as Mobile Cruise Source of San Diego. Note that just the executive summary and vision and mission statement are shown. The complete business plan would include detailed information on the following:

Company Overview
Product or Service Strategy
Thorough Market Analysis
Complete Marketing Plan
Complete Financial Plan including all Financial Statements

While a great business plan will not make a lousy idea better it can help you crystalize your thoughts and cement your direction for a good idea. A formal business plan can entice investment much more effectively than any other means.

MOBILE CRUISE SOURCE OF SAN DIEGO, Inc.

January 1996

Business Plan Copy Number 1

John Doe
Chief Executive Officer
1234 Main Street
San Diego, California 92021
619-123-4567
FAX 619-234-5678

Table of Contents

Executive Summary

Vision / Mission

In 1995 the San Diego area franchise of Mobile Cruise Source was negotiated and contracted for a ten year period to allow the establishment of San Diego's first cruise only travel agency that brings the travel agency to the client's home.

Overall, our company can be characterized as a inovative high-profile retail cruise only travel agent selling cruises at competitive rates with the distinct advantage of offering our clients the luxury of in-home presentations.

> Mobile Cruise Source is a highly recognized national franchiser supported by a notional advertising budget in excess of one million dollars. The San Diego franchise is expected to be one of the largest in the system

Background

> For many years people have had to visit retail travel agency locations during their hours of operation (usually between 9AM to 5PM Monday through Friday) to obtain and book various cruise vacations.

The state of the art condition of the industry today is such that;.

> The cruise segment of the travel industry is in a fantastic growth period and while Cruise Only specialists have evolved within the traditional travel industry, clients are still forced to visit the agency location to purchase cruises. Clients, however, have responded overwhelmingly to the in-home service offered by Mobile Cruise Source in all markets.

San Diego represents an excellent opportunity for the establishment of Mobile Cruise Source as it is one of the largest cruise markets in the United States. We have just started a novel and proprietary service that both our suppliers, the cruise lines, and our clients agree is long over due.

The legal form of Mobile Cruise Source of San Diego is a Subchapter S-Corporation located at 1234 Main Street, San Diego, California 92021. We elected to operate as a S-Corporation to allow maximum tax pass through to our federal tax returns.

Objectives

It is the objective of Mobile Cruise Source of San Diego to establish itself as the primary seller of cruises by utilizing in-home presentations and 24 hour, 7 day a week availability.

It is the objective of Mobile Cruise Source of San Diego to recruit and develop Affiliates in the following markets within the first twelve months of operation; North County Inland, North County Coastal, East County, South County, San Diego Proper, and La Jolla.

Revenue projected for fiscal year 1996 without external funding is expected to be $2,500,000.00. Annual growth is projected to be 50% per year through 1998. We feel that within 3 years Mobile Cruise Source of San Diego will be in a suitable position for further expansion. Our objective, at this time, is to propel the company into a prominent market position.

Capital Requirements

According to the opportunities and requirements for Mobile Cruise Source of San Diego described in this business plan, and based on what we feel are sound business assumptions, our initial capital requirements are for $75,000.00 by January 1st, 1996.

To accomplish this goal we have developed a comprehensive plan to intensify and accelerate our marketing and sales activities, product development, services expansion, distribution and customer service. To implement our plans we require a investment totaling $40,000.00 for the following purposes:

> Acquire two vans equipped per Mobile Cruise Source franchise standards; Maximize sales with an extensive campaign to promote our products / services; Recruit targeted Affiliates, train and add vans from Affiliate investment.

Management Team

Our management team consists of 3 men and women whose backgrounds consist of 56 years of travel marketing with various travel organizations, and 17 years of corporate development with leaders in the cruise industry.

In-House Management

[1], President, John Doe, MCC, 22 years working in the cruise industry
[2], Vice President of Marketing, Paul Doe, MCC, 11 years as mar-

keting manager for cruise line
[3], Vice President of Operations, Jane Doe, MCC, 23 years experience with cruise lines and tour operators in operations.

Outside Management Support

[4], Accountant / CPA, Walter Doe, CPA, 34 years experience
[5], Corporate Attorney, Frank Doe, 22 years experience
[6], Travel Industry Consultant, Tom Ogg, 27 years experience

Additionally, our outside management advisors provide tremendous support for management decisions and creativity.

Marketing Strategy

Cruises enjoy the highest level of satisfaction and repeat purchase of any of the leisure travel products. The cruise industry has increased capacity at a rate of over 30% per year since 1988 and ships currently on order promise future expansion will meet or exceed that of the past.

Mobile Cruise Source of San Diego currently offers cruises on all CLIA and other cruise lines worldwide. Mobile Cruise Source is part of a national network of agencies that specialize in selling cruises only and participates in commissions and overrides that make it competitive to any seller of cruises in the San Diego market.

Market Analysis

San Diego County enjoys one of the largest cruise markets within the United States. Retirees and long time residents alike are drawn to exceptional travel value that cruises represent.

Market Definition

The cruise market is growing rapidly. The market for cruises amounted to $5 billion in 1995 representing a 700% growth over $775 million in 1985. According to industry reports, the overall market for the cruise industry worldwide is projected to be $20 billion by the end of 2005.

The area of biggest growth in the cruise market is in the area of cruise specialist. Currently, the market distribution is shared by 4,500 participants, with Cruise Holidays considered the market leader.

Customer Profile

Mobile Cruise Source of San Diego's target market includes vacationers with incomes of $40,000.00 and above. The typical customer of our products is someone who is in the business or professional fields, and who currently purchases leisure travel.

Competition

Companies that compete in this market are Cruise Holidays, Cruise One and AAA World Travel. All companies charge competitive prices but operate from retail store front locations

Key factors of cruise line over capacity and declining domestic airline ticketing yields have resulted in the present competitive position in the industry. Compared to competitive services our service will offer an unprecedented level of consumer convenience to clients who demand such conveniences in other types of products and services they purchase..

The ability to offer in-home cruise sales is a capability unique to Mobile Cruise Source of San Diego's services.

> Clients of Mobile Cruise Source of San Diego enjoy the convenience of having the agent visit them at home when convenient for the client, not the agent. Agents are available evenings and weekends for consultation with clients and are equipped with video, portable computers that access massive databases, brochures, and everything necessary to consummate the transaction. While clients enjoy the convenience of in-home sales and presentations, Mobile Cruise Source of San Diego offers the guaranteed lowest available price on cruises in the travel industry.

Currently no travel agency in San Diego county offers this service even though the majority of clients prefer to purchase cruises in this fashion. Our strategy for dominating the competition is client convenience and competitive pricing which is our unique selling proposition.

Risk

The top business risks that Mobile Cruise Source of San Diego faces as it begins to enter the San Diego market are the general economy failure in San Diego, a continued glut of space and price deterioration in the cruise industry and government regulation.

Marketing Plan

Responses from customers indicate that our service is enjoying an excellent reputation and we fully intend to continue this trend. Inquiries from prospective customers suggest that there is considerable demand for it. Relationships with leading cruise lines and clients substantiate the fitness of Mobile Cruise Source of San Diego for considerable growth and accomplishment in our industry.

Mobile Cruise Source of San Diego's marketing strategy is to aggressively enhance, promote and support the fact that our radio dispatched Mobile Cruise Source of San Diego's "Mobile Travel Agency Vans" are the most convenient and cost effective way to purchase cruises in San Diego.

Sales Strategy

Because of Mobile Cruise Source of San Diego's special market characteristics, our sales strategy includes a broad based advertising and promotional campaign.

Mobile Cruise Source of San Diego will advertise cruise specials weekly in the major travel sections of the San Diego Tribune and other local newspapers with travel sections. The Mobile Cruise Source of San Diego's vans will all feature display advertising on the exterior. A bi-monthly newsletter will be sent existing clients and potential clients. A one hour radio show on KCEO entitled "Cruising, the best way to vacation" will be sponsored by Mobile Cruise Source of San Diego.

By focusing on the demographic market as described above through focus advertising and direct mail Mobile Cruise Source can effectively gain dominant market share over its store front counterparts.

Public Relations

During 1996, Mobile Cruise Source of San Diego will focus on the following publicity strategies:

Mobile Cruise Source of San Diego will participate in every public gathering possible (Cobey's swap meet, farmer's markets, street fairs, community fairs and shows, etc.) to gain recognition of Mobile Cruise Source of San Diego's vans. We will release press releases on cruise issues via Fax blast to every conceivable party of interest. Mobile Cruise Source of San Diego will attend every cruise or other industry seminar and prominently display the vans.

We will track, wherever possible, the incremental revenue generated from our advertising, promotion and publicity efforts. We anticipate at least $800,000.00 of sales will be generated directly from our promotions, and possibly an additional $350,000.00 of indirect increase in sales through our various channels.

Conclusion

Mobile Cruise Source of San Diego enjoys an excellent track-record of excellent service for our customers. Their expressions of satisfaction and encouragement are numerous, and we intend to continue our advances and growth in the San Diego marketplace with more unique and effective service.

Mobile Cruise Source is a nationally recognized name in the United States and enjoys the respect of both the cruise industry and their combined clientele. The San Diego franchise will continue to offer exceptional cruise values to our clients at a level of convenience and personable service never obtainable before from traditional travel agencies.

Chapter 6
STARTING YOUR HOME BASED TRAVEL BUSINESS

Assuming you now have your business plan in place and have funded your business it is time to begin. The first things you want to accomplish is the formation and licensing of your home based travel agency and then the setting up of your office to do business. Following are some ideas you may be able to use. Remember though, that only an attorney is capable of giving you legal advice and an accountant competent accounting advice. Your best move is to consult with each of these professionals before making any decisions and letting them help you set up your business.

ESTABLISH YOUR BUSINESS NAME

You should file a Fictitious Business Name Statement with your local county recorder's office to establish a D.B.A. and rights to use a particular business name. The county recorder's office will have a list of names already being used in your area so you must first check to be sure your name is available for use. If you intend to incorporate you should contact the Secretary of State. in your state to check and reserve a corporate name availability and to file your articles of incorporation to perfect your business name.

The name you choose for your business should suggest the actual nature of your business as closely as possible. Avoid generic names like Ajax Travel, ABC Travel, and so on. If you can sum up your entire business concept in a few words this would be a good business name. Exotic Caribbean Cruises, or West African Safaris, Tours and Cultural Exchange, or International Dive Travel, or Tom's Discount Pacific Cruises, or Kaamaina Hawaii Travel are all good names that suggest the actual nature of the business.

ORGANIZING YOUR BUSINESS

Most home travel agencies are operated as sole proprietorships which are extremely easy to establish. Partnerships are also easy to establish but are much better done in a legal document prepared by an attorney. Partnerships once formed are binding on both partners and are sometimes very difficult to dissolve. Some home based travel agencies operate as corporations which allow a certain protection for their owners. Generally, clients cannot sue the shareholders of a corporation for the acts of the corporation. If you have considerable assets that might be exposed if you operated as a sole proprietor you should consult your attorney about the possibility of starting a corporation. A Subchapter S corporation allows for the legal protection of a corporation but allows the corporate losses to pass through the corporation directly to the shareholders. Subchapter S corporations are excellent vehicles for small home operated travel agencies that want the best of both worlds.

OBTAINING THE PROPER LICENSES

Most people are surprised to find that there is absolutely no licensing of travel agents either by the federal or state governments. Unlike real estate, insurance, securities and other agency businesses, there has never been a travel agent license required. You must check your local city hall or county authorities to see if you need a local business license to operate from your home base but these are usually inexpensive and easy to obtain.

Some states now require travel agents, travel promoters, and others advertising travel to register with the state attorney's office. These registration requirements vary from state to state and normally impose some sort of registration fee, trust account, possibly a bond, and so on. You can check with your state Attorney General's office about possible registration requirements or you might call your local ASTA representative to see if they are aware of any requirements. If you have a local ASTA, ARTA, NACOA, or NACTA representative they could also help as well. You can also visit your local library and look in the layman's version of the Business and Professional code under "Travel" to find all current laws in effect that govern travel agents in your state.

Some states that require registration are California, Oregon, New York, Florida, Massachusetts, Illinois and others.

OPENING YOUR BUSINESS BANK ACCOUNT

Once you have recorded your Fictitious Business Name Statement with the county recorder you may use that to open you business checking account before you actually comply with the publication of the Fictitious Name Statement as required by your state. Most home based businesses use self imposed trust accounts for their client's funds. By including the phrase "Client Security Trust Account" or some sort of similar statement on your checks you offer a level of security to your clients funds and mental security as well. You can open a second operating account under your business name to ensure funds are not commingled. When ordering checks be sure to select the most professional available. The more professional your checks look the more viable your clients and suppliers will perceive you and your business. Can you imagine receiving a check from the IRS that had a ski scene lightly printed over a pinkish base and that was handwritten? So many times the check in payment for services and reservations is the only visual exposure a client or supplier will have with your agency.

YOUR STATIONERY AND BUSINESS CARDS

This is your real first opportunity to establish your businesses identity. Your stationary and business cards are possibly the only exposure clients may have to your business and you should be sure that they reflect your business as closely as possible. So many times the image you present when your client asks "will you send me something" will either make or break your sale. Imagine trying to sell a $10,000.00 cruise if your response to a request for information arrived on typewritten letterhead, or worse, plain paper. How would you feel about sending a check to a business that couldn't afford professional stationary?

You should have your letterhead, envelopes, and business cards specially designed by a professional in the field. Avoid saving money by using desktop publishing programs that allow you 300 Dpi renditions of clip art and type. Once you have your stationary and business cards developed you can use the artwork forever and you have the advantage of being proud every time you send any correspondence to your client. It is well worth the extra money you invest at this point. Even the smallest part time travel business should go to this effort and expense. By handing a potential client a well designed business card you tell them you are serious about your business even if it is only part time from your home.

If you can afford to have a professional logo created around your specific business so much the better. A unique and attractive logo that reflects the nature of your business is just more confirmation of your professionalism and commitment. A good logo can actually create demand for your products if used with advertising specialties.

If your are short on start up funds you can purchase process color laser stationary sets from Paper Direct (1-800-4-PAPERS), Quill (1-800-789-5813), or Image Street by Moore (1-800-IMAGE-ST). These companies specialize in printing quality stationary papers and business cards you simply run through your laser printer in small quantities for professional stationary at affordable prices. Order each of their catalogs for use in special promotions and other printed materials you may use in your business.

ESTABLISHING AN OFFICE FOR YOUR HOME BASED TRAVEL AGENCY

OK, now that you have formed your travel business you need to establish your home office from which to operate. This could be a spare bedroom or den, an attic, converted garage, or it could just be a corner of your bedroom or kitchen table. Wherever you set your home office up needs to be as professional as possible. You will need desk space, files for brochures, client files and correspondence, shelves for reference material, a place for your computer and printer, fax machine and most important, telephone.

The level of commitment to your business will in part determine the extent you will want to develop your home office. If you are starting your business anticipating just an occasional sale maybe a corner somewhere in your house or apartment will work just fine. If you are going full time right out of the gate then close attention should be paid to your home office. Following are just some of the issues and items you should plan for.

EXCLUSIVITY OF SPACE

No matter what the scale of your business is you should reserve the space you are committing to your business exclusively. By segregating your business space from your residential space you can easily determine control interferences caused when your work materials have been misplaced or moved to make room for other activities. Imagine getting a call for a round trip ticket across the country and having to put your client on hold while you look for your OAG which is nowhere to be found. By making your home office a separate and exclusive place in your home you will always to be able to find everything when you need it and preserve your professionalism even on occasional telephone calls.

TELEPHONE AND ELECTRICITY

Most home offices may need more electrical outlets and telephone jacks than are currently in the area to function. You should anticipate your needs before you furnish the office. If needed, install additional electrical outlets on separate breakers as you will find you will need the electricity for a wide variety of things as your business grows. Most homes and apartments are wired with one pair, or two different telephone lines that will accommodate a local residence line, a local business line and a personal 800# on top of the local business line. This gives the home travel entrepreneur the opportunity to offer their clients toll free service and still have a free line to either dial into a reservation data base or send a fax while they are on their business phone line. The telephone company will work with you to install additional pairs of lines into your home office and are quite reasonable to work with.

There are a good number of telephones made for home offices. AT&T has a wide variety including those with multiple lines, voice mail, automatic dialing and many other features. There are several manufacturers that offer two line home office phones quite reasonably.

OFFICE FURNITURE

When establishing your home office special attention should be paid to your surroundings and working environment. Nothing is more counter productive than to engage in business from a desk that wobbles, or worse, is cluttered with so much stuff you can't find a thing. You should invest in a home office desk that will allow you ample space to operate effectively. Even if your intent is to only operate part time, a roomy functional desk will greatly enhance your productivity.

If you only have a small area you are going to dedicate to your business consider having a cabinet maker design an efficient piece of furniture to serve all of your needs. Many companies have gone into the business of making computer furniture for home offices that allows you ample storage for all of your office machines and files in small amounts of space. It is well worth the investment to improve your working conditions as best you can.

FILING AND STORAGE

The work of a travel agent involves much research into vast amounts of information. Destination and product files will require a minimum of four 4 drawer legal file cabinets or two 4 drawer lateral file cabinets. If you have space for more you will certainly find a use for it. While these file cabinets do not need to be in the same area as your desk they do need to be accessible. You will also need space for the reference library you will use in your daily business. Generally, a four shelve bookcase will suffice.

Chapter 7
SETTING UP YOUR BOOKS

Without question, the single most important document that will reflect the nature and health of your business is your income, or profit and loss, statement. Hopefully, you will generate income statements each month for the first years of your business.

By familiarizing yourself with the nature of the revenue and expense accounts of your business from the onset you will be in great control should your business take a change of course sometime during its building stages. Once you have established your business you may want to delegate the chore of keeping records and doing profit and loss statements to a bookkeeping service or accountant. The best way to start your business is on a cash basis rather than an accrual basis especially if you are starting on a small scale. You should always seek the advice of a competent professional when undertaking the development of an accounting system and starting a business.

Following is a list of accounts found on the income statements of home based retail travel agencies and small wholesale tour companies with brief descriptions to help understand the nature and source of the account. You or your accountant can choose from these lists to develop your chart of accounts for your system.

WHAT ARE THE MAIN REVENUE ACCOUNTS AND WHERE IS THEIR ORIGIN?

REVENUE CHART OF ACCOUNTS

Air sales, Domestic
Air Sales, International
Tour Sales
Cruise Sales
Other Sales
funds)
Hotel Commissions
Car Commissions
Other Commissions

Fees and Tuition
Advertising Income
Interest Income
Cost of Domestic Air Sales
Cost of Intl Air Sales(Re-
Cost of Tour Sales
Cost of Cruise Sales
Cost of Other Sales
(Refund Credits)

AIR SALES AND COST OF AIR SALES

Air sales are the single largest source of income for most agencies and are always reported as a separate item. Some agencies segregate domestic from international air sales, as well as, cash from credit card sales. This is helpful in determining the type of business an agency is doing. If you will be receiving only commission from your host agency you could call the accounts Air Commissions - Domestic and Air Commissions - International.

TOUR AND CRUISE SALES AND COST OF TOUR AND CRUISE SALES

Most tour and cruise sales are prepaid with your agency check in the net amount and can be verified by voucher check copies, stubs, hard copy client files, and entries in a sales or cash disbursements journal. Other tour and cruise sales may be prepaid by a M.C.O. through your host agency and the commission paid to you after the fact. These could be logged in an account such as Tour Commissions.

OTHER TRAVEL AGENCY SALES AND COST OF SALES

All other prepaid sales should be identified and reported with significant income categories reported separately on the income statement. Items such as group sales, incentive sales, tour product sales, convention sales, etc. should all be individually identified if their contribution is meaningful.

REFUNDS

Monies received from suppliers for refund to clients should be reported to reduce the cost of sales as well. Many agencies interpret this transaction improperly and post the amount of refund received from the supplier to a sales account thereby inflating overall revenue, not only by the original sale, but by the refunded amount as well. Be careful to understand how you have accounted for refunds and cancellations.

CAR, HOTEL, OVERRIDES AND OTHER COMMISSIONS

All should be reported as they are received in their net amount and not as a gross sale and cost of sale. Agencies reporting these commissions as sales and cost of sales are inflating their overall sales volume, and do not have proper supporting documentation to warrant these entries. Commissions paid in arrears will be verified by an appropriate journal entry and cash deposit.

FEES AND TUITION

Many agencies earn fees by providing consultation, seminars, or services and these fees should be identified as separate items on the income statement. If you are going to operate a travel school you should segregate tuition as well. If you derive considerable income from service fees you should segregate the various types of fees you are collecting so the effectiveness of your fee structure to offset low yield transactions can be measured

ADVERTISING INCOME

If you get involved in soliciting advertising contributions for brochures you are developing or advertisements you are placing and receiving cooperative advertising funds for this would be the place to account for it.

INTEREST INCOME

Interest earned from commercial checking accounts, money market funds, or other holding accounts of the agency should be reported as "other income" or "interest income".

REFUND CREDITS

Monies received from suppliers for refund to canceled client files should be shown as a contra account to the appropriate cost of sales account and reduce the account by the amount received.

WHAT ARE COMMON EXPENSE AREAS FOR HOME BASED TRAVEL AGENCIES?

EXPENSES CHART OF ACCOUNTS

Advertising (general)	Interest
Advertising (yellow pages)	Licenses
Advertising Specialties	Maintenance
Amortization	Payroll Taxes

Automation Equipment Rental
Bank Charges
Brochure Expense
Commissions
Depreciation
Donations
Dues Subscriptions
Telephone Equipment
Telephone and Telex
Temporary Help
Travel Expense
Utilities
Uncollectible Accounts

Postage and Delivery
Printing
Professional Fees
Promotion
Rent
Salaries
Entertainment
Equipment Rental
Familiarization Tours
Franchise Fees
Gifts
Insurance
Education

ADVERTISING (GENERAL)

Newspaper advertisements, radio, television, newsletters, magazines, trade publications and point of purchase displays would be general advertising. Most agencies don't use advertising to their benefit.

ADVERTISING (YELLOW PAGES)

Some home based agencies use this heavily, others do not. Most yellow page advertising is expensive with questionable results for the dollar spent.

ADVERTISING SPECIALTIES

Printed pens, calendars, matches, flight bags, clocks, bag tags, travel items, rulers and pocket flight guides are all used by home based agencies to promote business. If you have gone to the expense of developing a unique logotype, advertising specialties may amount to a large account.

AUTOMATED AIRLINE RESERVATION SYSTEMS

If you are going to use dial up automation in your business this would be the place to log the monthly user charges you will be paying.

AUTOMOBILE

Keep track of every dime you spend on business travel and post it here. The IRS requires you to maintain a mileage log for every business and personal mile

BROCHURE EXPENSE

Normally you would incur brochure expense only if you are producing groups or some sort of other travel where a substantial brochure would be needed.

COMMISSIONS

As an independent contractor you are free to hire other commissioned sales people to transact business on your behalf. Commissions you pay your commissioned sales people would appear hear.

DUES

Dues for the membership in various associations and organizations can mount up and by segregating them on your income statement you can keep a handle on them.

EDUCATION

The cost of your basic travel education may be recaptured as a deductible business expense as is all of the cost associated with your education such as transportation, books, parking, etc. The costs of attending most seminars, trade shows, and conventions can be written off as business expenses as well.

EQUIPMENT RENTAL

It is unlikely that a home based travel agency would be renting equipment but if a copier, telephone system, or computer is rented this is the correct account to post it to.

FAMILIARIZATION TOURS

An area of legitimate business expense that may result in substantial benefits to the home based travel entrepreneur.

FRANCHISE FEES, CONSORTIUM FEES, AND ROYALTIES

If you join an independent contractor network or agency consortium to obtain overrides this is the proper way to identify payments. If you join a cruise or other franchise and pay royalties again this is the proper place for the expenditure.

INSURANCE

Liability insurance, Errors and Omissions insurance, automobile insurance for a business automobile, health insurance (in some cases) can be written off.

PAYROLL TAXES

If you intend to hire an employee you need to make payroll tax deposits on their earnings. Failure to do so is a BIG problem.

POSTAGE AND DELIVERY

Stamps, Federal Express, Express Mail, Courier deliveries and UPS all go in this account.

PRINTING

Put all of your printing cost into this account with the exception of your business cards which should go into the advertising account.

PROFESSIONAL FEES

This is the account where your attorney, consultant, accountant, and other professional fees should be shown.

RENT

Lucky you! You may be able to write off part of your mortgage payment as monthly rent. Be sure to have your accountant set this up for you.

SALARIES

Again, this would be important only if you choose to employ people to help you handle your business.

SUBSCRIPTIONS

The O.A.G., Official Hotel Guide, Hotel and Travel Index, CLIA Cruise Manual, etc. are among mandatory publications required by successful home based travel agencies. Trade magazines, travel publications, and other printed media you use in your business should be recorded in this account

SUPPLIES

All of the supplies you purchase for your business can be written off and should be kept separate in this account.

TELEPHONE EQUIPMENT

If you have purchased separate telephone equipment for your business you can write it off in this account. If you are going to use your existing telephone equipment consult with your accountant to see if you can recapture some or all of the cost.

TELEPHONE AND TELEX

Your business usage of your telephone, telex, fax and other costs are posted here.

TRAVEL

Again, lucky you! You may be able to write off all of your travel expenses and a good portion of your meal and entertainment expenses while travelling.

UTILITIES

You may be able to deduct a good portion of your utility bill for your home based office. Talk with your accountant.

UNCOLLECTIBLE ACCOUNTS

If you have the unfortunate experience of having someone pass you a bad check, you can write off the loss in this account.

WHAT SOFTWARE IS AVAILABLE TO MAKE THE ACCOUNTING TASK EASIER?

There are a number of small business accounting programs available at affordable rates and you should talk with your accountant for recommendations. However, a couple of options seem to have gained the favor of many independent travel agents. Following are two of the more popular choices.

QuickBooks by Intuit

QuickBooks is a program available from Intuit that seems very compatible with home based travel businesses. It allows you to track your business easily without an accounting background and also makes the chore of generating statements quite easy. QuickBooks is a good choice if your are just starting out as the program allows you to develop more complexity as your business grows.

OATS by TRAMS

Another program that has been very successful for independent travel agents is OATS, or the Outside Agent Tracking System by TRAMS. OATS is designed specifically for home based travel agents and not only makes tracking sales and commissions easy, it will generate various reports by supplier, clients, or other data. OATS will allow you to generate client mailing labels as well. OATS is reasonably priced and is an extremely valuable tool for your business.

Chapter 8
YOUR HOME OFFICE OF THE NINETIES

If you are like most people who start a home based business you are entering an entirely new environment that has its own challenges, opportunities, and drawbacks. So challenging is operating a home based business that this chapter is dedicated to some of the demands you face as a home based travel entrepreneur. Following are considerations for operating your successful home based business.

HOME OR OFFICE, WHICH ONE IS IT?

One of the largest hurdles to overcome as a new home based travel entrepreneur is the continual temptation to integrate your home activities with your business activities. You start out in the morning fully intending to put a full days work in at your home office. The first thing you notice is it is a beautiful day and decide you will water the flowers for just a minute before you start to work. Then your neighbor happens by for a nice chat about your other neighbor and finally after one more cup of coffee you begin your daily work. Just as you sit down to get started your friend calls and wants to meet you for lunch and you figure, what the heck since it is almost noon anyway you agree to meet for lunch.

After lunch you stop by the post office to see if there is any mail and run into one of your past clients that wants to talk with you about their recent trip. You manage to shake the client but since you are driving right by the supermarket on the way home you stop to do some shopping. Finally when you get home and unload the groceries you notice that there are several messages on your voice mail. You listen to the messages and write them down one by one and decide to call the most urgent one first. A client needs immediate attention with their reservation so you pick up the phone and dial...."I am sorry, we are closed for the day can you call tomorrow?" is the response you get. You look at your watch and it is now 5:15 and you ask yourself, "Where did the day go?"

This is not an unlikely scenario for a new home based entrepreneur to experience. Separating your daily business from your home chores and personal activities is a very difficult transition to make. When we were employees we had to be at work promptly at nine and went home at five. Very few interruptions were allowed to take precedence over our work and you would never think of asking the boss for a few hours off to go grocery shopping. Maintaining the separation of home and office is critical to your success and following are some tips on how to do it.

CLEARLY DEFINE YOUR WORKPLACE

Whether your home office is in your basement, attic, spare bedroom, attached office, converted garage, or corner of your bedroom it should be clearly separate from the rest of your house. By clearly defining your workplace everyone will know where your office begins and home stops. By establishing clear demarcation of your office you and everyone else will know if you are work or not. If you can close your office off from view of the rest of the house so much the better. The best scenario is to add on a professional designed office to your home. The second best is to use an isolated room within your house that can be converted to your home office and used for nothing else.

CLEARLY DEFINE YOUR HOURS OF OPERATION

Even if your business is only part time you need to define when you will be open for business. By establishing definite working hours you will know when to start and when to stop working and you can schedule your time to accomplish the tasks you have allocated to the work period. By establishing definite work hours your family, friends, and clients will know when you are free to chat, telephone, or otherwise engage in leisure activities.

JUST SAY NO!

The very first time someone calls you for a personal conversation during business hours just say no. Explain that you work from home and that you are very busy and ask if they could call back after hours or could you call them back. People respect this kind of honesty and will respond by observing your work hours in the future.

INVOLVE YOUR FAMILY

Recruit your family's help in observing your hours of operation. Have them intercept phone calls and visitors with the explanation that you are working and won't be free until after business hours which begin whenever you have defined your work hours. You can signal your family that you are at work by some simple sign such as a shut door to your office space, an external light on or off, a small sign that you can hang somewhere that is clearly visible, and so on.

ISOLATE YOURSELF

Install separate business lines into your home based office for business use only. When you are open for business, answer the phone. When you are closed let your voicemail do the work. Install a solid core door to the entrance of your office to drastically cut down on noise from the rest of your home when children are about or other noises become a problem. Install more insulation above your ceiling to further cut down on distractions from external noises. Install a separate entrance to your home based office and remove internal entrances from within your home for true isolation from the rest of the house.

ORGANIZE YOURSELF

Keep all of your business materials within your designated office space. Spreading brochures, trade magazines, client files and other work materials all over the house only confuses the delineation of your work place. This leads to the eventual erosion of the separation of work place and home. You can imagine the difficulty your family might have if you are in the kitchen reviewing a client file when the phone rings. Are you at work or not? By consistently isolating your home office from your home you can establish clear boundaries for everyone to comply with.

YOUR HOME AS A BUSINESS MEETING PLACE

Another major concern most new home based travel businesses have is one of the suitability of their home as a place to meet clients and transact business. Most communities have local zoning laws that may restrict access by clients to a home based business and certainly most home owners associations restrict access. You should check with your local zoning department and review the Covenants, Conditions, and Restrictions (CC&Rs) for your home to see if home based businesses are restricted in any way. Most restrictions are designed to prohibit businesses that would be considered a nuisance by others in the neighborhood. Auto repairs, cabinet shops, light manufacturing, restaurants and so forth all involve issues of noise, parking and pollution that would clearly irritate neighbors and would be terminated if a zoning complaint were filed by neighbors.

Many businesses like real estate, insurance, direct marketing, securities, and travel are ideal cottage industries as they do not create the types of nuisances that are deemed undesirable to communities. In San Diego, as an example, all home businesses are prohibited by zoning statutes that have been on the books for years. San Diego's Mayor Golding was the keynote speaker for the City of San Diego Small Business Exposition in 1993 and opened her lecture by declaring small home based businesses as the cornerstone in San Diego's economic future. So convinced is Mayor Golding that the City of San Diego will annually sponsor the event which is focused solely on small home based business opportunities and services.

While the home business is certainly the growth business environment into the twenty first century, many new home based entrepreneurs are hesitant to meet clients in their own homes to transact business. Most of the communication with your clients will take place over the telephone, computer, or facsimile machine but sometimes meeting one on one is mandatory. Here are some ways to structure your business to handle the client.

OFFER FREE DELIVERY TO YOUR CLIENTS

Turn your hesitancy to meet your clients in your home to a positive by offering free delivery for tickets, documents, brochures and so forth. Your client will love the service and you can do it yourself or use traditional delivery services.

USE YOUR CLIENT'S MEETING FACILITIES

Don't make the client come to the travel agency, make the travel agency visit the client. Use your notebook computer to visit the client and handle the client's needs right in the comfort of their own home or office. Your client saves time, money, and energy and will appreciate the extra effort on your part.

ESTABLISH A "BRANCH" OFFICE

Use a friendly restaurant, club, hotel lobby, or host storefront agency to meet your clients. If you live near an airport join one of the airline's hospitality clubs and use the "club" for client meetings. Unless your client is a frequent flyer they probably do not belong and will be impressed by the setting and feeling of professionalism and travel that prevails in these airport hospitality suites. Hotels are another great place to meet people as they exude the excitement of travel. If you frequent a particular hotel enough to make the acquaintance of some of the staff they will make you look like a super star to your client. Hotel restaurants and bars are another great location to become a "regular".

ESTABLISH AN "EXECUTIVE MEETING" ROOM

Find a hotel in your area that has small meeting rooms and board rooms available and work a deal out on short notice rentals for meetings with potential clients. You can normally get just about any meeting room in a hotel for a few hours for a nominal amount of money. You may then schedule meetings with clients who will be impressed that you have gone to the trouble to rent a lavish meeting room for your presentation. The cost is nominal when compared to actually paying rent for a storefront and the impact is overwhelming for the client.

USE AN EXECUTIVE SUITE

Many executive suites offer services for home based entrepreneurs. For a modest fee they will offer you a limited number of hours per month to use their conference room, facsimile services, answering services, secretarial services and mailing services. You can use the address of the executive service as your primary business address and use the services only on an as needed basis. When it comes time for your clients to visit you can meet them in one of the boardrooms at the executive suite.

YOUR PROFESSIONAL IMAGE

Probably the most common concern that new home based travel entrepreneurs have is their credibility as a business. Many new agents feel that they will be considered somehow not as serious as their store front counterparts and that they may lack believability with their clients. While nothing could be further from the truth there are areas a home based travel entrepreneur can take positive steps to create credibility and a strong professional image.

YOUR TELEPHONE LINES

Definitely install a separate business telephone line into your home office. Always answer your business line with a professional greeting and clearly identify your business by name to your caller. Never let your children answer the business line and you should not allow your friends or your family's friends to call on your business line. By installing a business line your business will be listed in the phone directory and with operator assisted telephone number information. Even if you have a catchy name it is of little value if your telephone number cannot be found by the potential customer.

YOUR FEDERAL TAXPAYER I.D. NUMBER

By operating with a Federal Taxpayer I.D. number instead of your Social Security number you project an image of professionalism and credibility. It is an excellent idea to segregate your business income from your personal income using a Federal Taxpayer I.D. number. Contact the I.R.S. and simply request one for your use.

YOUR EQUIPMENT

The more state of the art your business equipment is the more believable you become. If you tout your ability to bring your travel services into your client's home, do so with a state of the art notebook computer. If you are heavily automated with state of the art personal computers your clients will be impressed when they visit your home office. Be sure you have all the trimmings of a mobile office such as a notebook computer, facsimile machine, cellular telephone, pager and so on.

IMPROVE YOUR PROFESSIONAL IMAGE BY INCORPORATING

Nothing shouts professional louder than having an Inc. behind your business name. For some reason incorporating your business cements a professional image. Be sure to consult with your attorney regarding the suitability of incorporating your business and to select from the many options you may have.

DRESS FOR SUCCESS

Just because you are working from home doesn't mean that you can stay in your bathrobe and slippers all day. By wearing professional clothing even when you are not expecting clients you will be ready for the day. Getting into the habit of dressing casually can even impede your own self image and undermine your personal credibility.

COMMUNICATE QUALITY

Communicate quality to your clients in every possible way. The constant image of quality is what impresses your clients. Answer your business telephone with finesse every time it rings....no matter how frazzled you may be. Use top quality papers for your business cards and stationary. Get a professional logo designed for your business, and use preprinted travel industry itinerary/invoices for your clients travel documents.

PROJECT YOUR FINANCIAL INTEGRITY

Be sure to operate your bank account as a trust fund even if your state does not require it. Simply have the words "Client Trust Account" put onto your your trust account and deposit your client's funds into the account pending deposit or final payment to the supplier or your host agency. Once final payment is made then transfer the commission to your "Operating Account" for disbursement as you see fit. Always purchase the most professional business checks possible. Never use your personal checking account for business matters.

PROJECT YOUR AUTOMATION EXPERTISE

Always use your E-Mail address on your stationery, business cards, brochures and business checks. Have your E-Mail address in the name of your travel business and use E-Mail to your advantage. If you are on the Internet consider a home page for your business on the World Wide Web. It is reasonably priced and will give you the professional image you are trying to project.

Chapter 9
YOUR HOME COMPUTER

Your personal computer is one of the primary reasons you can succeed at your home based travel agency. Personal computers have come through quite an evolution since the first days of the 8088 based systems. They have come so far that now even a novice can perform tasks that once required years of experience and specialization. All of the functions necessary to run a home based travel agency are available to the entrepreneur with an up-to-date personal computer. Word processing, contact management, accounting, desktop publishing, database management, fax broadcasting, E-Mail and many other sophisticated applications are now very affordable and easy to use.

You should integrate your personal computer into your home based travel agency immediately. If you have never owned or used a computer and are unfamiliar with the systems that are available you must develop your computer skills if you are going to take your business seriously. If you are just starting part time and intend to eventually build your business, now is the time to get involved with personal computers. You will find that your usage of personal computers will soon flow into your entire life as a natural outgrowth of your business usage and will greatly enhance your opportunities.

This information is written for individuals only slightly informed about computers and attempts to give basic information regarding the systems and software that would be the most appropriate choices for a home based travel agency. While this information is current at the time of this writing (Jan, 96) you should always contact a computer specialist or consultant for the latest information. Personal computer components change faster than the weather and "current" information grows stale faster than fresh fish or visiting relatives. Suffice it to say that you should purchase as much basic computer as you can afford, i.e. processor, hard disk, video card, and RAM and then add components as your need and budget allow. Do not run out and purchase a packaged personal computer at your local discount or electronics store as you are generally paying top dollar for outdated technology With that in mind, here are the basic components of personal computers.

NOTEBOOK COMPUTERS

One of the most fascinating events in the personal computer evolution has been the development of highly powerful but also highly portable computers. Known as notebook computers these P.C.s allow you to take your travel agency anywhere that you can find an electrical outlet or telephone jack. Notebook computers are equipped with huge hard drives, fast processors, and telecommunications capabilities. There are even models with full multi media capabilities. Virtually anything you can do on a desktop computer you can also do on a notebook.

Notebook computers are extremely viable for offering your clients "in-home" service. It is actually very simple to visit your clients with brochures, videos, and a notebook computer loaded with various travel related applications and access to one or more travel reservations databases. Clients are very impressed when you go on-line by simply plugging in their home phone line into your computer. It solidifies your professional image.

DESKTOP COMPUTERS

When we think of personal computers the more familiar desktop computer comes to mind. Today's desktops are more powerful than mainframe computers were just a few years ago. To fully understand the various components that make up today's desktop computer following is a discussion of the various parts that make up a computer. When you go to purchase your home based computer make notes about each of the components so you can let the salesman know what you want and how you intend to use it.

PROCESSOR (CPU)

The processor or "mother board" is the central processing unit, or "brains" of your computer. It is also referred to as the CPU. Processors come in different operating speeds and types. The operating speed of a processor is measured in megahertz which is expressed as Mhz. The higher the Mhz rating the faster the computer operates. Processors move information in "bytes" which are made up of 8 bits of information to a byte. One byte equals one character, number, or some other single piece of information. There are 8 bit (1 byte) processors (8088), 16 bit (2 byte) processors (80286), 24 bit (3 byte) processors (80386), 32 bit (4 byte) processors (80486), and 40 bit (5 byte) processors (Pentium). Processors that move more information at a time (32 bit and 40 bit) are much faster and also cost more.

For the home based travel agency speed is necessary because it will help run your newsletters and other graphic applications much faster. The minimum processor you should consider for your home computer is a 66 Mhz 80486DX2. The DX means that it is a true 32 bit processor. SX behind the number of the processor means that it really isn't what it says it is and will generally operate slower than its DX counterpart. There may be a math co-processor that enables a DX processor to operate at the higher performance standards. A better processor for your business would be an 100 Mhz 80486DX4 or even a Mhz 80846 X. Pentium processors are a bit more money but operate at faster speeds than the 80486 processors. The ideal CPU to purchase would be a 100 Mhz or 120 or 133 Mhz Pentium processor. These will cost about $500 more than their 486 kin but also are much more efficient.

RANDOM ACCESS MEMORY (RAM)

RAM is the memory where the actual work takes place in your computer. RAM is like your work table where you might take some work out of your filing cabinet, set on your work table and modify it in some way. There are two types of RAM, basic and extended. Basic RAM refers to the first 640 thousand bytes that is accessed by your computer when you turn it on and extended RAM is the balance of RAM you have installed in your computer. The operating system know as Windows can access all of a P.C.s extended RAM just like it was basic RAM. The minimum amount of RAM you will need for your P.C. is 8 million bytes (8Mb) with 16Mb a better selection. Be sure that the computer you are buying uses paean SIMMS RAM vs the older 30 pin RAM. As more and more people upgrade to faster 486 and Pentium computers there is little demand for 30 pin RAM and they are not interchangeable.

GRAPHIC OR VIDEO CARD

Your graphic card or adapter is the interface between your computer and your computer screen (monitor). The are various types of resolution you may use for your computer with SVGA, or Super Video Graphics Adapter, being the current choice. Older graphic cards such as CGA, EGA, and VGA are obsolete and should be avoided. Your SVGA graphics card should have memory all of its own for use in transferring information from your computer to your monitor. Normally these cards should have at least 1 Mb of memory with the upper end cards having 2 Mb. Upper end cards sell for $200.00 to $350.00 and are well worth the money when it comes to creating newsletters and graphics. Diamond Stealth, Orchid Fahrenheit, and Genoa are just some of the names of upper ended video cards.

These cards have a feature called accelerators and is one of the best investments you can make in a graphics or video card. The main benefit is the amount of time it will take your computer to respond to graphics. There are three types of data buses ISA, EISA and VESA. When you are discussing your video card with your computer expert be sure to tell him you want a VESA Local Bus (VLB) because you intend to do lots of graphics with your P.C..

HARD DRIVE

Your hard drive is where you store the vast majority of your programs, graphics files, clipart, text and other information that you want to retrieve for any reason. Hard drives come in a good assortment of sizes that are expressed in the number of megabytes (Mb), or one million characters of information, it can store. There has been tremendous advancement made in the construction of hard drives and where a few years ago a 10Mb hard drive was considered ample, today at least 540Mb is necessary. You should not purchase a hard drive with any less than 540Mb with a 1.2 gigabit (One Billion Two Hundred Million bytes) being better. Microsoft Office with Access will consume almost 70Mb just for the installation. As with your processor, you should buy as much hard drive as you can afford. Even with programs that "stack" the information on your hard drive so you can double its capacity you can run out of space.

DISK DRIVES

You will use the disk drives to load programs onto your computer's hard drive and also transfer files between computers. There are two types of disk drives, 5 1/4" and 3 1/2" and they come in both high density and low density. You should be sure both sizes are on your computer so that you can transfer to both notebook computers and other desktops. Only purchase high density 5 1/4 1.2 Mb and 3 1/2 1.4 Mb disks as low density are obsolete. By the way, when you buy floppy disks look for the HD in the title to be sure they are high density. Since 5 1/4" disk drives are almost obsolete this drive may be optional.

POWER SUPPLY AND CASE

There are a good number of configurations that cases for your home computer come in. The basic flat, rectangular desktop is known to everyone but there are several "tower" models as well. mini, mid, and full tower refers to the cabinet's height and configuration. There may be more than two disk drive bays for additional drives which would be desirable. Many full tower cases come with a total of six drive bays which allows for future expansion as personal computers evolve. If you intend to install multi media perhaps a full tower would be your best choice. Make sure there are enough "expansion slots" in the back of the cabinet for installing additional cards that you may want to add. Also there should be at least one high speed parallel and one serial port with two each being most desirable.

MONITOR

Again, SVGA is your best choice. Most monitors are 14" diagonal color monitors but if you can afford the upgrade to a larger monitor it will reward you ease of use and clarity of detail. The bigger the better is the rule with a 17" monitor being noticeably easier to use. The ultimate is a 20" or 21" monitor which will cost around $1,800.00. Sometimes you can find them for sale used if you keep a close eye on the newspapers. Large monitors really help you prepare professional quality graphics. Monitor clarity is measured by the number of pixels (dots) per inch. Resolution of 1280 X 1280 pixels is excellent SVGA clarity. The lower the pixel count the less clear the image on the screen.

FAX/MODEM

Be sure to have a good fax/modem installed in your computer. You can send and receive facsimiles through your fax board and set up fax broadcasts you can use in your marketing. You will use your modem to access the reservation system you choose to work with, the various on-line services and the internet. Currently, the standard fax speed is 14,400 BPS and most modem speeds are 9600 baud. Make sure the fax/modem you purchase is up-to-date as the increased transmission speed of 28,800 baud is being sold as the new standard.

MULTI MEDIA

Multi media is the term given a combination of P.C. components that allow for incredible graphics, text, and sound to be bought together for a whole new type of P.C. technology. Multi Media is made up of a sound card, CD ROM unit, and speakers. You should talk with your computer professional when considering multi media but here are some ideas. Only buy a quad speed CD ROM unit for your P.C.. An internal unit is more convenient than external and be sure to check on the average access time. Only purchase a 16 bit studio quality sound card that is compatible with all of the major standards like Sound Blaster Pro or Pro Audio Spectrum 16. Purchase the best speakers you can afford and make sure they are shielded for use with a computer. If you use regular speakers the magnets in the speakers may create havoc with your computer's storage media and RAM. With multi media watch your kids take an immediate interest in your computer.

While multi Media is still a stones throw from center stage in terms of travel information the CD ROM storage capacity of multi media has allowed unbelievable amounts of information to be kept in the small space of a compact disk. You can currently purchase 25,000 .WMF fully scalable color clip art images for under $30. 1,200 fonts on one CD for under $10. Telephone directories of the entire United States for under $20. 165,000 business fax numbers for under $15. A road map down to the smallest street for the entire United States for under $40....and so on.

MISCELLANEOUS ATTACHMENTS

Other considerations are the mouse, keyboard, joystick or any other attachments. Again, since you will spend a considerable amount of time with both your keyboard and mouse it is best to buy the most comfortable you can afford.

PRINTERS

There are several types of personal computer printers all of which are quite sophisticated for the home business. Most home based travel agents find that a personal laser printer meets their needs best. Personal lasers are quite inexpensive compared to their former cost and seem to continue their decline in price. The current standard for laser printers is 300 Dots Per Inch (DPI) with the upper end 1,200 DPI. The main advantage to 600 to 1,200 DPI printing is the increased resolution when printing graphics and clipart. If you can afford the additional upgrade to 600 or 1,200 DPI printers it is well worth the money. Since most publications are either subsequently faxed, printed, or copied there is not a particular need for color printers at this time. Color printers give you the opportunity to print in total color right from your document which is an excellent feature but rarely used in home based travel businesses. You may also obtain portable ink jet printers that are battery operated for your notebook computer. These ink jet printers simulate laser printers and offer 360 X 360 resolution for your graphic applications.

OPERATING SYSTEMS

The operating system is the software that controls your computer and makes it do what you want it to do. All of the applications software you purchase will operate under one system or another. Currently the leading operating system is Windows 3.1 and now Windows 95 soon to replace it.. Windows makes it extremely easy for anyone to operate a personal computer and eliminates the need to remember chains of commands to make your computer work. Unless you have experience in other operating systems, Windows 3.1 is the choice you should make. In order to install Windows 3.1 into your computer you will need to install DOS 6.2 as Windows currently works inside of DOS. Wherever you purchase your computer will be happy to load both DOS and Windows into your system so you can get going fast.

At the time of this writing Windows 95 is catching on quite nicely and appears to be a hit. If you are purchasing a new Pentium computer it will undoubtedly come with Windows 95 and lots of software written for it exclusively, you may want to consider it as your exclusive operating system.

WHAT KINDS OF OTHER SOFTWARE DO I NEED IN MY HOME BASED TRAVEL BUSINESS?

Once you have your computer and operating system it is time to consider the software you need to run your business. The most obvious is the reservations software but that will be looked at in depth in chapter eleven. You will need other types of software to do a number of things that will help you along and following is a list of some of the more common.

WORD PROCESSING SOFTWARE

Probably the most important software you will purchase is your word processor. There are numerous word processors on the market in all price ranges. The most professional are WordPerfect 6.0 and Microsoft Word 6.0. While many others exist that are excellent choices, compatibility is very important. Your word processor should have the ability to transfer information from your database and spreadsheet. It should also have the ability for you to use various graphics, fonts and clipart when you need simple desktop publishing features.

If your word processor operates under Windows your scalable fonts will be installed inside Windows so that you can access them from all of your applications. The term "scalable" refers to your ability to create the font in any point size you wish. You will need a laser printer to take full advantage of scalable fonts but they can make your work look very professional. Other features to look for in your word processor are spell check to help you correct any spelling errors; a grammar checker, to check your grammar and punctuation when you are done with a document; and a Thesaurus that offers the built in ability to find alternate words when stumped for words while writing correspondence.

Microsoft Word 6.0 has the advantage of being able to easily transfer information from Microsoft Access, a relational database for the purposes of creating mail merged letters and documents. This feature makes Word extremely attractive for a home based travel business.

DESKTOP PUBLISHING SOFTWARE

Desktop publishing refers to software that is designed to allow you to easily create newsletters, stationery, flyers, proposals, booklets, and so on. The key elements in desktop publishing are text, with a wide variety of scalable fonts, scalable clipart for use in the publication, and graphic features like borders, lines, backgrounds, shading, and other graphic enhancements.

There is a broad range of desktop publishing programs from inexpensive to very expensive. Most home based travel entrepreneurs find Microsoft Publisher 3.0 (Win 95, 2.0 Win 3.1) is perfect for their needs. Publisher is easy to use and is totally compatible with other Microsoft applications. Publisher's "page wizards" make layout and design a cinch for anyone and it focuses on the types of publications that travel agents use. Other desktop publisher programs are Pagemaker and Ventura Publishing which cost quite a bit more and really give you more power than you might need for your business. Print Artist is another excellent program for flyers and other light text publications. Be sure to start a clip art library for your publications once you get familiar with them.

DATABASE MANAGEMENT, CONTACT MANAGEMENT AND MAIL LIST MANAGEMENT PROGRAMS

A database program allows you to create lists of information and then sort it by various criteria. A mail list management program is simply a specialized database program that exists for the purpose of mail list management. It is very important for you to have the ability to keep track of your clients and their travel desires. A good mail list program is all you need to get going but be sure that it is compatible with DBase 4 which is the standard. If you are going to purchase a full feature database there are several good choices. Microsoft Access is compatible with the other Microsoft Office Programs and therefore is an excellent selection. Access allows you to input the information you acquire on your client profiles and then to sort the information by any item or number of items that can then be prepared for mailing labels, mail merge or special reports. Be sure to consult your computer specialist and let them know your specific needs before you purchase a database.

Another excellent program for pro active marketing is ACT. ACT is a contact management program that tracks your contacts in person, by phone and by mail. ACT is a very powerful tool when you are romancing larger accounts that depend on a well orchestrated series of exposures. ACT allows you to prepare mailing labels and will export information to most word processors and databases as well.

Avery Labels Plus is an excellent Mail List Management program that allows you to develop mailing list and then format them for any of Avery's label products.

SPREADSHEETS

A spreadsheet program allows you to keep track of numeric information. Whether it is your home expenses, business expenses, budgeting, planning, or tracking commissions, any information you need to add, subtract, multiply, or divide a spreadsheet is the proper tool. While the need for a sophisticated spreadsheet in your home travel business falls behind that for the above items, an excellent spreadsheet that is compatible with the other suggestions is Excel. Excel is easy to use and operates the same as other Microsoft Products and is included in the Microsoft Office package.

TRAVEL APPLICATIONS SOFTWARE

A trip to any software store will reveal numerous titles that are travel related. There are applications that offer maps of the U.S. and world, street atlases of the United States for your CD ROM, vacation planners, city travel planners with tons of information about maps, hotels, restaurants, sight-seeing, places of interest and so on. For international travelers, there are a good number of international destinations on CD for multi media that will dazzle even the most sophisticated traveller.

ON-LINE SERVICES SOFTWARE

On-line travel databases that exist in on-line services such as CompuServe, Prodigy, Gemini, America On-Line and so on are invaluable for the home based travel agent. If you have a client that is seeking information regarding cruises, exotic destinations, special interest sports, or any other specific topic of which you have no expertise, it is extremely easy to log onto one of the on-line services to access a wealth of information and "forums" in which to seek advice.

THE INTERNET

The World Wide Web has so many travel related sites now that it is almost certain to be one of the primary on-line sources for home based travel agencies. There are numerous web browsers available through the various on-line services and the price to use these services has become extremely reasonable. America On-Line, CompuServe and Microsoft Network (Win 95) all have instant access to the World Wide Web and are very easy to use. Simply click on the internet icon or choose internet connection from a menu and boom you are there.

Once at the WWW browser simply type in a word or series of words that describes where you want to go. Type "Cruise" and you will be presented with hundreds of home pages to choose from. Choose "CLIA" and you will enter CLIA's home page with tons of information and a consumer referral program that supports you! You can spend months here on the Wed and find so many interesting travel related topics that you can become lost. World wide weather forecasts, State Department advisories, maps of each island in Hawaii with detailed destination information you can print for your clients, ASTA's home page, on and on.

There are also Internet service providers that you can connect with in your area that offer competitive access rates and also housing for sites on the Web. Many home based travel agents have established their own presence on the World Wide Web and enjoy unbelievable exposure throughout the world. A home page makes a lot of sense if your niche specific enough that folks would be looking for information on the Web by a topic they can find your page without scrolling through hundreds of other pages first. At last count there were about 1,375 home pages that came up under the search "travel." I am sure you can see the challenge.

The World Wide Web is so important to the distribution of travel that you must enter this arena to survive in the long term unless you are so specialized as to be able to bypass it.

Chapter 10
SELECTING YOUR KEY TRAVEL SUPPLIERS

Now that you have established your business and office and are ready to start earning some income from your home based travel agency it is time to consider your key suppliers and make contact to establish yourself as a viable travel entrepreneur. By reviewing your business objectives it should be easy to see the direction you will need to pursue to initiate communication with the suppliers you will be working with closely.

It should be apparent that suppliers are not bound to work with you by virtue of the fact you have created your business but rather the marriage is one of mutual benefit and may take a period of time to arrange. Further, it is clear that you will need to locate an existing appointed retail travel agency to channel your miscellaneous sales through if you intend to offer "full service" to your clients. There are many different products and services you may choose to represent but following are some of the more important ones to consider. The method of negotiating and establishing one's credibility is the same for other suppliers not shown here.

CRUISES

Cruises represent the biggest opportunity for profits in the travel industry today for home based travel entrepreneurs. Besides having a huge yield per transaction a home based agent focused on marketing cruises can get commissions far in excess of 10% which really creates excellent profitability. If you are interested in selling primarily cruises be sure to read "*HOW TO START A CRUISE ONLY TRAVEL AGENCY*".

To join the Cruise Line International Association (CLIA) you must submit an application for CLIA endorsement. Upon receipt of your application, CLIA will review your application and if accepted by CLIA, you will receive a CLIA number. This CLIA number may entitle you to earn commissions from most of the CLIA member cruise lines which make up over 80% of the world's ships. Once you have joined CLIA you will be placed on CLIA's preferred mailing list and will begin receiving their newsletter and training materials. You will also receive the CLIA Cruise Manual which holds a wealth of information on ships, itineraries and more. ARC agencies that are non CLIA members may still earn commissions using their ARC number but are not on CLIA's preferred agency mailing list.

Once you have joined CLIA you may wish to shop around for a cruise consortium to join so that you may access some of the overrides and special commissions that are available through such organizations. The fee to join CLIA is nominal and the membership fees in cruise consortiums varies from organization to organization but are generally offset by the additional commissions you earn from your involvement. If you intend to work through a retail agent for your cruise sales make sure they are competitive in the marketplace. It is here that you need to evaluate whether or not you will join CLIA in your own business name or whether you will work with your host agency when selling cruises. Searching for and finding an agency that is a member of CLIA and a member of a cruise consortium may in fact be the route you decide to take. Some agencies have extremely favorable overrides and support from the cruise lines and their consortium partners. Thus, a host agency with a good override program and benefits, may be an option. If the agency does not receive overrides or other concessions it is very difficult for you to be competitive since you must also give up part of your commission to the agency. It is also important to mention here that a host agency with strong ties and good working relationships with the cruise lines can be very helpful when it comes time to negotiate group rates, promotional dollars, and of course to problem solve if need be.

Many of the cruise lines will require that you have a business telephone number listed with the information operator. They may also request a copy of your business license, fictitious business name statement or some other documentation to verify your authenticity as an agent.

PACKAGED TOURS

Many tour operators will work with you if they perceive your interest in their company to be beneficial to them. One way they entitle your business to a commission is by assigning a "pseudo ARC number" for your use. The number may be the last 4 digits of your Social Security number, your CLIA number, or some number they arbitrarily designate. At any rate, when you call to make a reservation you simply use your I.D. number when booking to be entitled to a commission. The tour operators are not obligated to issue these numbers. Generally, they are received from the operator's sales office after some dialogue between you and the sales department. Often times much documentation is necessary to again show them that you in fact are in the business of selling travel. You cannot call reservations and demand a pseudo ARC number as they will have no idea what you are speaking about. Many operators and vendors have cracked down hard on the issuance of such numbers and are carefully screening business's before they consider assigning such a number. Every operator or vendor has there own requirements and stipulations. In some instances the operator will require you to work through an ARC appointed agency. Others may even require that you work through an ARC appointed, store front agency. There are some that may not allow you to be home based and receive such a number. Again, as we mentioned when we spoke above of cruises, a host agency with a good support package as well as good commission overrides with vendors and suppliers may be a good choice. This is a decision, much like getting your CLIA appointment that rides on your overall business plan and budget.

Another way to be recognized by some operators is by joining a travel agency consortium that receives overrides from the various operators. The best way to contact operators you are interested in working with is to telephone their sales office and request a meeting with your sales representative.

INTERNATIONAL AIRLINE CONSOLIDATORS

Some consolidators will work directly with you after you have developed a relationship with them. Since there can be substantial amounts of money changing hands the consolidators want to get to know you before they open an account for your business. A visit to the consolidator's headquarters and a meeting with the principles will greatly enhance your possibilities as well as give you a clear picture of their operation. Many times the consolidator will require you to book through an ARC appointed agency.

HOTELS AND RESORTS

Most major corporate hotels will require an ARC number while many smaller resorts and leisure based hotels may not. Always check the commission policy before you make a reservation. If you are CLIA appointed, often times they will recognize that appointment and allow you to receive commissions.

DOMESTIC AIRLINE TICKETS AND MISCELLA-NEOUS SALES

Unless you intend to obtain your own travel agency airline appointments (see "*HOW TO START, BUY OR SELL A TRAVEL AGENCY*"), you will need to work with an appointed travel organization to fulfill your needs and there are several options to choose from.

You may want to work with a local retail store front agency to obtain your airline tickets and other services they may offer. This choice is an excellent one if you are brand new to the travel industry and want the security of having someone locally to talk with about your client's needs and need immediate response. They may also be a good choice as sometimes when one is new a little hand holding and guidance comes in handy. There are also larger agencies that have substantial outside sales forces that are primarily employees of the agency. Again, this might be a great choice if you are choosing an agency to get started in the travel industry and need a substantial amount of training and support. Agencies that specialize in working with independent contractors are known as independent contractor networks and are a great choice if you need to be more competitive in your marketplace and want a "turn key" program to establish all of your needs in your business.

The main differences between regular agencies and independent contractor networks is the relationship you have with the agency. As an outside sales person, you may be generating accounts for the agency and as a member of an independent contractor network, your accounts will be your own. One of the advantages of an independent contractor network is that this is their specialty and they are experienced at working with independents.

WHAT ARE KEY CONSIDERATIONS WHEN NEGOTIATING MY AGREEMENT WITH A HOST AGENCY?

COMMISSION SPLIT

Of course, your main concern is going to be who earns what from your sales. Agents universally split commissions and sometimes overrides. You should demand the best commission split that you can depending on the services you are requesting the agency to perform on behalf of your clients. Commission splits go anywhere from 90% for the house and 10% for the independent agent to 100% for the independent agent and 0% for the house. It simply depends on how effective a negotiator you are and the services you are requesting the agency perform on your behalf. If there is a standard "deal" it is a 50/50 split and the independent agent does all their own work. Many small agencies are hesitant to split commissions with either outside sales employees or independent contractors because they feel the cost of maintaining them is prohibitive. Others are excited to have you in their agency at any split. It is simply a matter of finding the right agency for you and your needs.

Independent contractor networks generally pay at least 70% of the commission generated from your sales to the independent agent and retain the balance in-house.

OVERRIDES

Again, if your agency or independent contractor network offers overrides, so much the better. The best way to participate in the override programs is on the same commission split that you enjoy for the regular commission amount. If you make 70% of the commission then you should make 70% of the override. Some 100% commission deals do not allow for overrides and that is where the agency makes their money. In order to be competitive you should access the overrides in your key markets and share in the productivity of your sales. If you need to discount a price to your client to make a sale, the discount should be deducted from the commission and override before you take your split so you do not carry an overwhelming burden of the discount on your portion of the commission. You should also participate in the overrides that are paid in arrears that your volume contributed to.

QUALITY CONTROL

The agency or independent contractor network should provide a complete quality control program for your reservations. If you have the security back up on every airline reservation, problems for your clients and yourself evaporate into thin air. If the agency simply tickets from your PNR then problems are common place. Be sure to check their quality control program thoroughly as this is one feature that will add to your success

EXPERIENCE

If your agency or independent contractor network has been around for years and years with a track record of successful performance and has worked with independent contractors successfully for years that is an excellent sign. On the other hand, if the agency has just started a program for outside sales be very wary. You do not want you and your clients to be the guinea pigs for some agent's attempt at developing an outside sales force. A record of successful integration of outside sales people and independent contractors is your best sign to jump. Always check references if at all possible.

TRAINING

What kind of training does the agency offer you and others like you? If they have an ongoing training program that is all the better.

AUTOMATION

Are the existing outside sales or independent contractors automated with dial up reservations software (see chapter 11)? What are the charges and what kind of contracts do you have to sign to obtain it? What kind of automation training is available and what kind of help if and when you get into trouble? Is the automation current and considered to be one of the better systems in the industry?

COMPATIBILITY

How compatible are you with the agency's owners? The actual agents that will be helping you? The other independent contractors or outside sales people? Compatibility is very important if you intend to develop a long term relationship with the agency.

BENEFITS

This should probably not be your number one priority but is the agency going to pass along travel benefits as they become available? Are they going to include you on the various airline registration lists if your sales qualify for such? Who has priority for the various familiarization tours, cruises, and airline tickets that come through the agency? Is it based on seniority or productivity?

CONVENIENCE

How convenient is the agency location to you? If you can simply walk to your agency in two minutes that is probably worth a bit off your commission. Conversely, if the agency is one located in another state or a good distance from you, yet this is what they specialize in doing then they may be a great choice. Most independent contractor networks that have an established program for working with agents have a ticket and document delivery procedure set up. Everyone has different comfort levels when it comes to working at a remote location and yours should be considered when making the decision to align yourself with an agency or independent contractor network.

Many independent agents have found that it is much easier to deal locally for many of the services they offer their clients.

COST

Many independent contractor networks charge up-front fees to join their networks. What do you get for your investment and how long will it take to recoup your investment because of additional commissions and overrides? Is the hardware, software, reference material, training and support all of interest to you or can you pick and choose what you want to participate in? Is the initial price adjusted for the items you do not want? Do not be afraid to spend a considerable amount to associate with an independent contractor network as long as they have a track record of successful independent contractors.

Conversely there are local agencies and agency networks that charge very little to join because they have perfected the skill of working with independents that require little or no training. Certainly someone that has completed a comprehensive travel curriculum would not require the same level of hand holding as someone absolutely new to the industry. Operating with a diverse group of independent contractors is very difficult and requires years to mature. The operation and in-house systems should be important to you. One perspective is that there are some networks that charge little or nothing to join yet they earn their money by taking little from large numbers of independents, rather than a large sum of money from only a few. New independent contractor networks should be carefully considered as the failure rate can be quite high if the operation is not streamlined and does not use time and resources effectively. You should be able to break the pricing into segments that make sense to you and justify the total price you pay based on the components you receive.

Many local agencies will not charge anything to put you on as "outside sales" but do not offer the myriad of services either. If you elect to work with a local agency be sure to understand the nature and extent of the agency's commitment to assist you in your business. Many local agencies are happy to have your business as long as you simply bring it in and don't ask questions, but is this what you want? Are you looking for some moral support? Discuss the issues that appear above with your proposed agency to help make a decision regarding their viability.

AGENCY SUPPORT

It is important to mention here that there is considerable inherent value in remaining loyal to your host agency. Of course as a true independent contractor you have the choice and option to deal with various vendors, however if the time arises where you need support and assistance with a problem your loyalty will likely be rewarded at that time. A host agency that has good, strong relationships with the various cruise lines, tour companies, airlines, etc. can really be a friend to you in time of need. This is something to be considered.

YOUR INDEPENDENT CONTRACTOR AGREEMENT

As you enter into a working relationship with either a retail travel agency or independent contractor network you must enter into a written agreement to perfect your independent contractor status. In the lack of a written agreement you will be considered an employee by the I.R.S.. If it is your intention to become an employee of the agency then you should also enter into a written agreement to clarify the many issues that may arise.

There are a good number of sample agreements for both employment by travel agencies and independent contractor agreements. Various contracts that can be used by independent contractors, agency owners, outside salespeople and rent-a-desk operations are included in the *NACTA INDEPENDENT AGENT'S HANDBOOK* which is given each new member. These contracts are worth the price of membership alone.

Regardless of where you obtain your written contract it should contain several items that will define your relationship and the duties of both parties to the contract. If the relationship into which you are entering is anticipated to lead to increasing involvement in the travel industry then every possibility should be considered and documented. It is much easier to agree in advance to potential dispute that may occur at a later time and your best negotiating position is at the onset of the relationship. In all instances you should seek the advice of a competent attorney familiar with independent contractor issues and the travel industry. Following are some of the more important issues you may want to appear in your contract.

PARTIES TO THE AGREEMENT

You should carefully identify all parties to the agreement and include formal mailing addresses and social security numbers. If you are entering into a contract with a corporation try to identify the key person with whom you should communicate.

PURPOSE OF THE AGREEMENT

Be as specific as possible when defining the actual purpose of the agreement being executed. The more definition here the better the agreement. Avoid ambiguous statements of purpose as they may be used to decide the intent of subsequent paragraphs in the agreement.

TERM OF THE AGREEMENT

An independent contractor agreement must have a specific term to be valid. You may want to incorporate a roll over clause so that the term is automatically renewed each time the term has elapsed or you may want to renegotiate at the completion of each term. Be sure the term is well defined.

DUTIES OF THE PARTIES OF THE AGREEMENT

You should spell out as many of the specific duties of both parties. If the agency has made a commitment to perform training, education, quality control, or some other special function on your behalf it should be detailed here as well.

INDEPENDENT CONTRACTOR STATEMENT

The agreement should state clearly that the working relationship between you and the agency is one between an independent contractor and the agency. Issues such as non-exclusivity, tools of the trade, control by the agency, risk of profit or loss, place of work, and so on should be detailed here. The more definition in the agreement of the perfection of your independent contractor status the better for both parties.

I.R.S. REPORTING

The agreement should clearly state that all commissions paid the independent contractor will be reported on an IRS form 1099 and that the independent contractor is responsible for reporting income on the appropriate IRS schedules and for making the appropriate federal, state, and local self employment tax deposits if necessary.

COMMISSION SPLIT OR OTHER REMUNERATION

The exact commission split, override split, and/or monthly rental charges should be detailed with examples. The timing of payment of the commissions and the method of payment should also be specified. Resolution of potential disputes over commissions should be considered here as well.

OWNERSHIP OF ACCOUNTS

A detailed statement of who owns the accounts bought into the agency by the independent contractor should be made here. One of the most common areas of dispute when an independent contractor decides to move on is the ownership of the clients the Independent contractor introduced to the agency. Agency owners feel that they have paid the independent contractor to develop the clients for the agency and the independent contractor feels that the clients are theirs to take with them. A clear and concise understanding of ownership in the agreement eliminates this issue down the road.

PAYMENT FOR SERVICES

Who is going to pay who for what? Is the agency going to require you to collect from your client and then issue your business check in return to pay the agency for services? This is sometimes the best way to go if you are dealing with multiple suppliers and you don't want to confuse your client by making checks out to several different entities for one vacation. If your agency is receiving checks directly from your clients what is their policy for holding client funds? Do they operate a trust account to protect your client's funds should they fail? If you are doing groups through the agency you should demand that the funds be held in a dual signature trust account so that you have some security the agency owner doesn't take off to Brazil with the group's funds.

Credit card sales should be processed thought the agency's ARC weekly report. What is the agency's policy on paying commissions on credit card sales? If a credit card charge is subsequently denied by a client what is the agency's policy on collecting the funds. Do they expect you to cover it and then collect from your client or are they willing to help you collect? All of the issues regarding payment should be considered as should the resolution of potential disputes.

INDEMNIFICATION

You should include an indemnification clause specifying in what instances each party will indemnify the other from loss created by their errors and omissions. If the agency issues an airline ticket with the wrong date surely the agency should correct the situation. Conversely, if you issue a reservation on the wrong date you should correct the situation. Dealing with the resolution of these issues in advance is a way to be sure both parties act in the best interest of the other.

MISCELLANEOUS OPERATING FEES

Both parties should try to agree in advance to miscellaneous operating fees that may kick in on certain types of transactions. Ticket reissues, voided tickets, special services like delivery, airport pick up, and courtesy reservations for hotels, frequent flyer awards and coupons. These all cost the agency plenty of money to perform but are not offset by revenue. Is there going to be a charge if the agency performs these tasks on behalf of the independent contractor and if so, how much?

TRAVEL BENEFITS

Is the travel agency going to include the independent contractor on their IATAN agency registration list and what is the criteria? A complete agreement regarding the extent of benefits the independent contractor can expect should be made as well as the procedure for obtaining the benefits.

COMPLIANCE WITH LOCAL, STATE AND FEDERAL LAWS

You should include a statement that both parties will comply and remain in compliance with all local, state, and federal laws during the lifetime of the agreement. Further, if your particular state has tour promoter or travel agent registration laws your compliance should be mentioned here.

MISCELLANEOUS CLAUSES

You should also include various legal clauses regarding the contract. If the agency is in another state than you are located, where will any disputes be heard and under which state's law will the agreement be interpreted? Do you wish to choose arbitration rather than going through the courts? If part of the agreement is unenforceable should the balance of the agreement be null and void or enforceable? Who pays attorney fees in case of a dispute? You attorney can inject phrases to deal with these issues to both parties mutual satisfaction.

Chapter 11
YOUR AUTOMATED TRAVEL RESERVATIONS SYSTEM

Nothing has driven the explosion of home based travel agents more than the rapid expansion of personal computers and dial up access into the various reservations systems of the travel industry. Not too long ago an agent had to maintain an ARC appointed store front travel agency to negotiate access into the travel industry reservations systems. The thought that an independent agent could take a notebook computer right into the client's home and set the travel agency up on the client's dining room table was unheard of.

This rapid expansion of access to the travel industry reservations systems has revolutionized the travel industry forever. The home based travel entrepreneur is in the best possible position to take advantage of the change.

There are several different opportunities to automate your reservations process but before we explore them let's first look at the current trends in the travel industry regarding the Computerized Reservations Systems (CRS) and Global Distribution Systems (GDS).

WHO OPERATES THE CRS/GDS?

There are basically four vendors of travel reservations systems in the industry. They all work the same way and access primarily the same databases for their information and charge other travel suppliers for the right to market their products and services through their systems. The charges other suppliers pay to market through the CRS/GDS are known as revenue segment fees and the charge is based on a per unit basis. If an airline markets through one of the CRS it will be charged approximately $3.00 per flight segment for the reservation and If a hotel markets through the CRS/GDS it may be charged $10.00 per night.

The CRS/GDS have been a major profit center for the carriers that have dominated the field. The consolidation of CRS into global distribution systems has seen the carriers giving up their specific control in favor of achieving global dominance. Following are the major vendors of travel reservation products within the travel industry.

WORLDSPAN

Worldspan is a partnership between Delta Airlines, TWA, and Northwest Airlines. Worldspan offers several products within the industry and their main agency reservation system is PARS. PARS is available in both a DOS and Windows environment. Delta Airlines system known as Datas 11 is all but obsolete at this time.

COVIA

Covia is owned primarily by United Airlines and offers two basic systems. Apollo is Covia's primary automation and Focal Point is their newer Windows based system. Focal Point is significant because it allows for multiple entries to be made within various windows all on one screen. A great amount of information is displayed at one time and the time taken to complete a reservation is significantly decreased. Covia's merger with Gallieo has created GDS stature for the system.

SABRE

Sabre is owned by American Airlines and offers only one agency level reservations product known as Sabre to the industry. Sabre is available in both DOS and Windows environments as well.

SYSTEM ONE

System One is owned by Continental Airlines and is a strong candidate in the lineup of CRS vendors. System One started out as Eastern Airlines internal reservations system and was originally marketed as System One Direct Access (SODA). It has recently merged with Amadeus to gain GDS status.

Virtually every automated travel agency in the United States uses one of these four systems and is bound by long term contracts. When you consider host agencies you will undoubtedly want to know which system they subscribed to so you can evaluate the dial up software that might be available. For more detailed information about travel agency automation see "*HOW TO START, BUY OR SELL A TRAVEL AGENCY*".

IS IT MANDATORY FOR A HOME BASED TRAVEL AGENCY TO AUTOMATE WITH A RESERVATION SYSTEM?

As discussed in previous chapters, domestic airline ticketing is one of the reasons traditional travel agencies are losing money. By embracing technology and the low overhead of a home base you may continue to sell airline tickets for profit. Unless you sell an isolated airline ticket every now and then you should look for dial up reservations access from your home personal computer.

Since the commission caps have taken effect the desirability of a professional level of CRS/GDS access has become even more important. The speed and efficiency in which you can conduct domestic airline reservations will determine your overall profitability. Since you must offer these services to your client to maintain their goodwill processing the information in the most professional fashion becomes mandatory.

The best way to get CRS/GDS training is either directly from the reservations system itself or from one of the schools that provide the training. While you can use consumer level reservations software as a relative good database only agency level dial up access will suffice in anything but the most modest venture.

WHAT KIND OF CONSUMER RESERVATIONS SOFTWARE IS THERE?

The CRS vendors all have developed consumer automation that allow the passenger to directly access their mainframe database and execute reservations. Many on-line services offer various consumer databases that can be used for both an informational database and actual reservations.

While these databases are designed for the casual consumer/user they can be very beneficial to you in your business as you first begin. When a client calls for information regarding an airfare you can immediately check the city pairs for the various airlines that offer service and do a low fare search to give your client the assurance that you are right on top of the situation. You can then suggest that you must research the fares to be sure you have obtained the lowest possible airfare consistent with your clients needs and call the various airlines for the final reservation. Of course this is not the most efficient way of conducting business as stated above but it will work in the beginning.

Many on-line services carry part or all of the following reservations systems but CompuServe seems to be the best choice. You can purchase a CompuServe starter kit at any software store and it basically self installs to get you on-line and going. The largest benefit of using CompuServe is their flat rate access. Currently it cost only $8.95 per month to access all of the data bases which is an excellent buy. Of course, there is an additional charge for usage of the OAG Electronic Edition. Following are key databases you can access for information.

You must remember that all of these databases are intended for consumer use and are designed to increase yields just by their nature and design. Only the most naive consumer would believe that these reservations services would give them the actual best airfare when making a reservation. Further, some of the CRS/GDS vendors have started charging "pick up" rates for reservations made in the consumer reservations systems and subsequently picked up by a travel agent for ticketing.

EASY SABRE

Easy Sabre is found just about everywhere you can log onto a bulletin board or on-line service. Easy Sabre is slow and cumbersome but is a relative inexpensive database for information about domestic and international flights. The big drawback with Easy Sabre is that you can only queue your reservation to a Sabre agency.

UNITED CONNECTION

United Connection is United Airline's entry into the personal reservations software field. United Connection is much the same as Easy Sabre in that it is slow and cumbersome. Covia (United Airlines) is currently releasing PERSONAL APOLLO which is touted to be the most advanced consumer software to date. While PERSONAL APOLLO will have many of the features of regular Apollo it remains to be seen how beneficial to consumers it will be.

TRAVEL SHOPPER

Travel Shopper is Worldspan's user friendly dial up reservations software. Travel Shopper is extremely easy to use and also allows you to string basic commands together to expedite the reservation process. In the realm of consumer software Travel Shopper is your best bet.

OAG ELECTRONIC EDITION

The OAG Electronic Edition is an excellent dial up reservations system but unfortunately OAG charges a per minute fee for access. While they advertise that it is free if you are either booking or canceling a reservation it still ends up costing you a good amount of money because the various databases in the system are difficult to resist.

WHAT AGENCY LEVEL SYSTEMS ARE AVAILABLE AND HOW DO THEY WORK?

All of the CRS vendors listed above offer dial up access into their systems that feature agency level language and speed. Unless you are ARC appointed you need to have your host agency negotiate an access code for your usage. While you would access the mainframe directly for reservations you are "bridged" to your host agency for ticketing. You would simply dial into the mainframe, make your reservations, seat assignments, and special requests, confirm the reservation and merely place the reservation (PNR) into a particular queue for quality control and ticketing by the host agency. Following are your choices for dial up access.

COVIA'S CORPORATE APOLLO AND LEISURE APOLLO

Corporate Apollo is slow and cumbersome and offers little if any meaningful support from the "help desk". While this would be acceptable if it were free, Corporate Apollo is expensive at approximately $6.75 per hour live time usage. Corporate Apollo offers both a user friendly mode and a bypass mode that communicates in traditional agency level Apollo format.

One of Covia's newest offerings is their "Leisure Apollo" access to Apollo's cruise and tour reservations database known as "Leisure Shopper". Non ARC appointed agents can purchase restricted access to Leisure Apollo for a one time fee of $150 and an hourly user's rate of $7 per hour. There is a two hour minimum, or $14 per month, user's fees as well. Leisure shopper currently features a good number of cruise lines and tour operators. While Leisure Apollo seems like a viable idea, make sure you can book cruises through Leisure Apollo and still claim your overrides and group concessions via your consortium.

COMMERCIAL SABRE

Again, Commercial Sabre is even more expensive than Corporate Apollo. At $6.95 per hour Commercial Sabre is the most expensive agency level system. Commercial Sabre offers user friendly access (Commercial Sabre) and bypass into regular Sabre agency format (Professional Sabre). Some Sabre agencies have automated with

"LanLink" that allows the home based agent to access Sabre at very reasonable rates and extreme efficiency. You should ask your Sabre agency if they have LanLink available.

WORLD DIAL LINK

World Dial Link (WDL) is Worldspan's dial up access into agency PARS. WDL is without question your best choice for reservation software as it is offered for a flat rate per month. WDL is fast and offers both domestic and international databases that rival anything on the market. Further WDL will allow you to print a travel agency formatted itinerary/invoice with one keystroke, something that neither Sabre or Apollo can offer. Your World Dial Link access code can be shared by your associates without the fear that one will run up a higher usage bill than the other because of the flat rate policy of Worldspan. Best of all World Dial Link is available on a productivity contract so you may be able to earn it for free by simply booking a specified number of reservations on it. Since price and the availability of productivity contracts must be negotiated with Worldspan, your host agency is in the best position to do this for you.

If your host agency is automated with anything other than Worldspan products, suggest they add World Dial Link as a back up system in those instances when the other vendors systems go down.

SYSTEMONE

Continental Airlines/Amadeus also offers dial up access into their database with a couple of products. There is a commercial dial up access similar to Apollo and Sabre that is available for a hourly rate called "Access". There is also a product called "Home Pro". Home Pro is actually terminal emulation software that allows you to take control of one of the terminals in your host travel agency's office to do your work. Home Pro is inexpensive (currently $45 per month) but unless you are within a local phone call of your agency you will pay for the phone calls between your computer and the agency location.

TERMINAL EMULATION SOFTWARE

This is probably your best bet if you live within a local call or reasonable toll charge distance from your host agency. You can install a variety of terminal emulation software on your personal computer and also on one of the terminals in the agency to gain access 24 hours per day, 7 days per week. Other than the cost of the software, there is no monthly user's fee associated with using the software. The only cost you would incur would be the telephone charges while on-line. If you purchase the unlimited local usage programs available from your telephone company this can really be the best way to go.

Terminal emulation programs are available at every computer store. Reach Out, PC Anywhere and Carbon Copy are the names of some of the programs that are being used successfully by home based travel agents for the most cost effective personal computer automation.

Your Automated Travel Reservation System

Chapter 12
SETTING UP YOUR SUPPLIER FILES

Now that you have your business started and your office equipped it is time to organize your supplier files so that you can locate information when your client requests it. Maintaining your supplier files is a job that requires daily attention and yields high dividends when your clients call for information. The difference between a good travel agent and a great one is simply the extent and effectiveness of their filing systems.

The key to maintaining a productive filing system is to divide the various areas of your specialty into key files with enough diversity so that you may quickly find any brochure you are looking in a minimum period of time. In your spare time you may tackle one or two areas of your filing system and request brochures from the various suppliers that you would like to make available to your clients if asked. Tour, hotel, sightseeing, and other brochures are almost always free to travel agents.

Always high grade your brochure files and update brochures that are no longer valid. If you invest enough time in your supplier files they can really establish you as an exceptional agent. Following are ideas for individual files that may appear in your system. Note that it may not be necessary for you to maintain all of these but certainly you will want to have the major files.

YOUR CRUISE FILES

If you sell cruises you should have a separate file for each cruise line. Included in the file should be a current brochure from the cruise line and all information you have gathered on each ship, cruise line and itinerary. If you specialize in just a few cruise lines then you would want to have a separate file on each ship....possibly each itinerary for each ship. Following are cruise lines you may want to create a file on.

ALASKA SIGHTSEEING/CRUISE WEST
AMERICAN FAMILY CRUISES
CARNIVAL CRUISE LINES
CELEBRITY CRUISES, Inc.
CLIPPER CRUISE LINE
CLUB MED
COMMODORE CRUISE LINE
COSTA CRUISE LINES

CRYSTAL CRUISES
CUNARD CROWN CRUISES
CUNARD EUROPAMERICA RIVER CRUISES
CUNARD QUEEN ELIZABETH II
CUNARD ROYAL VIKING
DELTA QUEEN STEAMBOAT COMPANY
DISNEY CRUISES
DOLPHIN CRUISE LINE
DOLPHIN HELLAR
EPIROTIKI CRUISES
EXPLORER SHIPPING CORPORATION
FAIRSTAR CRUISES
FANTASY CRUISES
HOLLAND AMERICA LINE
MAJESTY CRUISE LINE
MARQUEST
NORWEGIAN CRUISE LINE
OCEANIC CRUISES
ORIENT LINES
P&O CRUISES
PAQUET CRUISES
PEARL CRUISES
PREMIER CRUISE LINES
PRINCESS CRUISES
RADISSON SEVEN SEAS CRUISES
REGENCY CRUISES
RENAISSANCE CRUISES
ROYAL CRUISE LINE
ROYAL CARIBBEAN CRUISE LINE
ST. LAWRENCE CRUISE LINES
SEABOURN CRUISE LINE
SEAWIND CRUISE LINE
SILVERSEA CRUISES
SPECIAL EXPEDITIONS
STAR CLIPPERS
SUN LINE CRUISES
WINDJAMMER BAREFOOT CRUISES
WINDSTAR CRUISES
WORLD EXPLORER CRUISES

UNITED STATES - GENERAL INFORMATION

Domestic travel probably will not be your primary market but it is important to have substantial domestic files. Each file would contain hotel, sightseeing, an other information your clients would expect you to have. If you use a preferred supplier to a particular destination you would want several brochures of each property the operator offers in the destination to give your clients.

GENERAL INFORMATION
    MAPS OF THE USA
    MAPS OF INDIVIDUAL STATES
    GENERAL INFORMATION
ALASKA

CALIFORNIA
> SAN FRANCISCO
> LOS ANGELES
> SAN DIEGO
> DISNEYLAND
> ORANGE COUNTY
> WINE COUNTRY
> SANTA BARBARA
> PALM SPRINGS

NEVADA
> LAS VEGAS HOTELS
> LAS VEGAS BUS TOURS
> LAS VEGAS CHARTER FLIGHTS
> RENO HOTELS
> RENO PACKAGES
> LAKE TAHOE HOTELS
> LAKE TAHOE PACKAGES

ARIZONA
> SCOTTSDALE RESORTS
> PHOENIX HOTELS
> TUCSON HOTELS
> GRAND CANYON
> GOLF AND TENNIS
> DUDE RANCH RESORTS
> ARIZONA PACKAGES

FLORIDA
> GENERAL INFORMATION
> ORLANDO - DISNEY WORLD, EPCOT CENTER, UNIVERSAL STUDIOS
> MIAMI - SIGHTS, DECO ART DISTRICT, HOTELS
> FT. LAUDERDALE - HOTELS, SIGHTS
> PALM BEACH
> SARASOTA
> KEY WEST
> TAMPA/ST. PETERSBURG

WASHINGTON D.C.
> GENERAL INFORMATION
> SIGHTSEEING
> HOTELS
> LOCAL TOURS

NEW YORK
> HOTELS
> SIGHTSEEING
> TOURS
> NEW YORK STATE SIGHTS

TEXAS
> DALLAS/FT. WORTH AREA
> HOUSTON AREA
> AUSTIN
> OTHER TEXAS

ALL OTHER STATES ALPHABETICALLY
DOMESTIC TOURS AND PACKAGES BY OPERATOR

HAWAII - GENERAL INFORMATION

If you are located on the west coast or in the Midwestern states,

Hawaii will probably be a large market for you. For this reason your Hawaii files should be as complete as possible.

STATE OF HAWAII
    MAPS
    GENERAL INFORMATION
    SPECIAL INTEREST
MAUI
    KAANAPALI
    NAPILI
    KAPALUA
    WAILEA
    KIHEI
    MAUI SIGHTSEEING
    SPECIAL INTEREST
    MAUI TOURS
OAHU
    WAIKIKI HOTELS
    SIGHTSEEING
    SPECIAL INTEREST
    OAHU SIGHTSEEING
KAUAI
    HANALEI/PRINCEVILLE
    COCONUT PLANTATION AREA
    LIHUE
    NAWILWILI HARBOR
    POIPU BEACH
    KAUAI SIGHTSEEING
    SPECIAL INTEREST
HAWAII
    KAILUA/KONA
    HILO
    ANAEHOOMALU BAY
    WAIMEA/HAMAKUA COAST
    VOLCANO NATIONAL PARK
    HAWAII SIGHTSEEING
    SPECIAL INTEREST

MOLOKAI
    HOTELS
    MOLOKAI SIGHTSEEING
LANAI
    HOTELS

MEXICO - GENERAL INFORMATION

Mexico is another staple for west coast and midwest agents and should warrant detailed files.

MEXICO
    COUNTRY MAPS
    GENERAL INFORMATION
    SPECIAL INTEREST
ACAPULCO

PUERTO VALLARTA
MAZATLAN
BAJA CALIFORNIA NORTE
BAJA CALIFORNIA SUR
IXTAPA/ZIHUATANEJO
MANZANILLO
MEXICO CITY
YUCATAN
COZUMEL
CANCUN
OTHER MEXICO CITIES

CANADA - GENERAL INFORMATION

You should organize your Canada files around the destinations within Canada that you are likely to sell. This depends a great deal on where you are located and your interest in Canada as a destination.

VANCOUVER/VICTORIA
WESTERN CANADA
CANADIAN ROCKIES
    ALBERTA
    BRITISH COLUMBIA
    OTHER PROVINCES
EASTERN CANADA
    ONTARIO
    QUEBEC
    MARITIME PROVINCES

CARIBBEAN - GENERAL INFORMATION

Developing extensive Caribbean files will go far to helping you with your cruise sales. Most repeat Caribbean cruisers are looking for the offbeat destinations and want their travel agent to know about them. The Caribbean is difficult because of the diversity of each island's culture and heritage. One island may be beautiful and sophisticated and the very next desolate and unfriendly.

AGUILLA
ANTIGUA (BARBUDA AND REDONDA)
ARUBA
BAHAMAS
    ABACO
    BIMINI
    ELEUTHRA
    EXUMA
    NASSAU
    OUT ISLANDS
BARBADOS
CAYMAN ISLANDS
CUBA

DOMINICA
DOMINICAN REPUBLIC
GRANADA (CURRIACOU AND GRENADINES (MAYREAU))
GUADELOUPE (MARIE GALANTE)
HAITI
JAMAICA
      MONTEGO BAY
      OCHO RIOS
LEWARD ISLANDS - FRENCH (ST. MAARTIN, ST. BARTS)
LEWARD ISLANDS - NETHERLANDS (STATIA, SABA, ST. MARTIN)
MARTINIQUE
MONTSERRAT
NETHERLANDS ANTILLES (CURACAO & BONAIRE)
PUERTO RICO
SAN ANDRES & PROVIDENCIAS
ST. KITTS AND NEVIS
ST. LUCIA
ST. VINCENT (BEQUIA, CANOUAN GRENADINES)
TRINIDAD AND TOBAGO
TURKS AND CAICOS ISLANDS
VIRGIN ISLANDS - AMERICAN (ST. THOMAS, ST. JOHN, ST. CROIX)
VIRGIN ISLANDS - BRITISH (VIRGIN GORDA, TORTOLA)

EUROPE AND THE MEDITERRANEAN - GENERAL INFORMATION

Your Europe files will reflect your interest in the European market by their depth and definition. If Europe is your primary market then your files will be extensive if not, then you may only want the most popular destinations.

AUSTRIA
BALERIC ISLANDS (MALLORCA AND MINOREA)
BELGIUM
BOSNIA AND HERZEGOVINA
CORSICA
CRETE
CROATIA
CYPRUS
DENMARK
DODECANESE ISLANDS (RHODES)
ENGLAND
FINLAND
FRANCE
GERMANY
GILBRALTAR
GREECE
IONIAN ISLANDS (CORFU)
IRELAND
ITALY
JERSEY
LIECHTENSTEIN
LUXEMBOURG
MALTA

MONACO
NETHERLANDS
NORWAY
PORTUGAL
SCOTLAND
SERBIA (BELGRADE)
SICILY
SLOVENIA
SPAIN
SWEDEN
SWITZERLAND
WALES

EASTERN EUROPE AND RUSSIA - GENERAL INFORMATION

Since the fall of the Soviet Union more and more interest has been focused on the various countries of eastern Europe and Russia. If you specialty includes these wonderful countries then your files will reflect the depth necessary to sell these destinations.

BULGARIA
HUNGARY
POLAND
ROMANIA
RUSSIA (ST. PETERSBURG AND MOSCOW)
TURKEY
UKRAINE

THE MIDDLE EAST - GENERAL INFORMATION

Not many agents will specialize in the Middle East but those that do are rewarded with a rich and lucrative business. Following are files that those folks may use.

ABU DHABU
AJMAN
BAHRAIN
DUBAI
FUJEIRA
IRAN
IRAQ
ISRAEL
JORDAN
KUWAIT
LEBANON
OMAN
QATAR
RAS AL KHAIMA
SAUDI ARABIA
SHARJAH
SYRIA

UMM AL QIWAIN
YEMEN

ASIA · GENERAL INFORMATION

Asia is becoming more and more important to the travel industry. With the huge economic influance Asia has exercised over the western world, Asia deserves every agent's attention,

AFGHANISTAN
ARMENIA
AZERBAIJAN
BANGLADESH
BHUTAN
BRUNEI
CAMBODIA
CHINA
CHINA (TAIWAN)
GEORGIA
HAINAN ISLAND
HONG KONG
INDIA
INDONESIA
      JAVA
      BALI
      NIAS
JAPAN
KASHMIR
KOREA
LAOS
MACAO
MALAYSIA
MONGOLIA
NEPAL
PAKISTAN
PHILIPPINES
SINGAPORE
SRI LANKA
SULAWESI
THAILAND
TIBET
VIET NAM

PACIFIC OCEAN · GENERAL INFORMATION

The South Pacific is home to more daydreams than any other place on Earth and the Western Pacific is exotic and ripe with history of World War II. Maintaining detailed Pacific Ocean files sets you apart from other agents in your community.
AUSTRALIA
      SYDNEY
      MELBOURNE

     BRISBANE
     OUTBACK
     WEST COAST
     TASMANIA
COOK ISLANDS
EASTER ISLAND
FIJI ISLANDS
FRENCH POLYNESIA (TAHITI)
GALAPAGOS ISLAND
GUAM
MARSHALL ISLANDS (MAJURO & KWAJALEIN)
MICRONESIA (PONAPE, KOSRAE, TRUK, YAP, PALAU, CAROLINE ISLANDS)
NAURU
NEW CALEDONIA
NEW ZEALAND
     SOUTH ISLAND
     NORTH ISLAND
PAPUA NEW GUINEA
SAMOA
     AMERICAN
     WESTERN
SOLOMON ISLANDS
TONGA
VANUATU (NEW HEBRIDES ISLANDS)

ATLANTIC OCEAN - GENERAL INFORMATION

Many of the Atlantic Ocean destinations are difficult to find if contained in their mother country files so having a separate section for these wonderful islands is the best way to be sure you can get your fingertips on the information you need.

ASCENSION
AZORES ISLANDS
BERMUDA
CANARY ISLANDS
CAPE VERDE ISLANDS
FALKLAND ISLANDS
GREENLAND
ICELAND
MADEIRA

INDIAN OCEAN - GENERAL INFORMATION

The Indian Ocean is home to the most beautiful and exotic islands found anywhere on Earth. Most agents do not maintain files on the Indian Ocean and therefore miss out on opportunites to sell this wonderful destination.

MALAGASY REPUBLIC (MADAGASCAR)
MISCELLANEOUS ISLANDS
     ANDAMAN-NICOBAR ISLANDS

BRITISH INDIAN OCEAN TERRITORY (CHAGOS & DIEGO GARCIA)
CHRISTMAS ISLAND
COCOS ISLAND
COMORO ISLANDS
MAYOTTE
ZIL ELWANNYEN SESEL
MALDIVE ISLANDS
MAURITIUS
REUNION
SEYCHELLES

AFRICA - GENERAL INFORMATION

Africa is becoming more and mor popular each year as a destination. Africa's wildlife, culture, rain forests, and vast size have made it one of the travel industries' growth destinations.

ALGERIA
BOTSWANA
EGYPT
GAMBIA, THE
GHANA
IVORY COAST
KENYA
LIBERIA
LIBYA
MALI
MOROCCO
MOZAMBIQUE
NAMBIA
NIGER
NIGERIA
RWANDA
SENEGAL
SOUTH AFRICA
SUDAN
SWAZILAND
TANZANIA
TUNISIA
UGANDA
ZAIRE
ZAMBIA
ZIMBABWE (SOUTHERN RHODESIA)

CENTRAL AMERICA - GENERAL INFORMATION

Many Americans are finding that Costa Rica, Belize and Guatemala are excellent countries to retire to as the cost of living is so inexpensive and the governments are stable and friendly towards Americans. As a result of the migration to these Central American countries interest and travel has been on a constant upswing.

BELIZE (BRITISH HONDURAS)

COSTA RICA
EL SALVADORE
GUATEMALA
HONDURAS
NICARAGUA
PANAMA

SOUTH AMERICA - GENERAL INFOMATION

Your South America files will come in handy for that isolated client that is well traveled and is looking towards South America for a new frontier.

ARGENTINA
BOLIVIA
BRAZIL
COLUMBIA
ECUADOR
FRENCH GUIANA
GUYANA (BRITISH GUIANA)
PARAGUAY
PERU
SURINAM (NETHERLANDS GUIANA)
URAGUAY
VENEZUELA

ADVENTURE TOURS AND SPECIALTY TOURS

Here is where you would file your special interest tours and adventure tours.

ADVENTURE AND SOFT ADVENTURE TOURS
    BACKPACKING TRAVEL
    DUDE RANCHES
    ECOTOURISM
    FISHING TOURS
    GOLF TOURS
    HIKING TOURS
    HORSE CAMPS
    MOTOR HOME TRAVEL
    MOUNTAIN BIKING TOURS
    MOUNTAIN CLIMBING EXPEDITIONS
    SAILING TRAVEL
    SCUBA DIVING TOURS
    SKI TOURS
        CALIFORNIA
        COLORADO
        UTAH
        NEW ENGLAND
        CANADIAN ROCKIES
        EUROPE
    SURF TRAVEL
    TENNIS TOURS
    TREKS

WINDSURFING TRAVEL
SPECIAL INTEREST TRAVEL
ALL INCLUSIVE RESORTS
BED AND BREAKFAST INNS
CLUB MED
FOOD AND GARDEN TOURS
GAY AND LESBIAN TRAVEL
HEALTH SPAS
MUSIC AND THEATRICAL TOURS
SINGLES TOURS
STUDENT TOURS
RELIGIOUS TOURS AND PILGRIMAGES
WEIGHT LOSS TOURS
WINE TOURS

MISCELLANEOUS FILES

AIRLINE FREQUENT FLYER PROGRAMS/EXECUTIVE CLUB MEMBERSHIPS/
CREDIT CARDS
CAR RENTAL COMPANIES
EUROPEAN AUTOMOBILE DELIVERY
FOREIGN EXCHANGE
LIMOUSINES AND SHUTTLES
PASSPORT APPLICATIONS
TOURIST CARDS
TRAVEL INSURANCE
VISA APPLICATIONS

CORRESPONDENCE FILES

BUSINESS FILES AND CONTRACTS
CLIENT CORRESPONDENCE
SUPPLIER CORRESPONDENCE AND CONTRACTS

Chapter 13
SETTING UP YOUR TRAVEL REFERENCE LIBRARY

One of the most important resources in your home office will be your travel reference library. Be sure to have your reference materials handy to use so that you may find the answers to your client's questions right at your fingertips. The following publications are a good sampling of the materials available for your use and represent an excellent basic reference library. Spend a good amount of time researching what you feel you will need for your library as it is a key to your sales success.

C. L. I. A. CRUISE MANUAL

This is a must for your travel reference library. As a member of C.L.I.A. you receive the manual as part of your membership benefits. However, if you are not a member you may still purchase the manual and if you sell cruises you will find it invaluable. This manual is used by more than 25,000 travel agencies and is their primary reference guide on the cruise industry with over 600 pages of current information. The manual is designed with ease of use in mind and features easy to locate information about each C.L.I.A. member cruise line.

It is divided into three tables of contents with cruise company data being the first. This includes separate sections for each C.L.I.A. cruise line to delineate their sales policies, reduced rate policies, and names and phone contacts for sales personnel. Ship profiles on each vessel give quick reference information necessary to answer client's key questions. A few of the items covered here are nationality of crew, ship size and capacity, accommodation information and descriptions of the public rooms and their capacity. Other useful knowledge is given on meal seating, suggested dress, special diet availability, and tipping policies. Following the reference information on the ship you will find the ship's deck plan which may easily be photocopied for use in selling your client. Finishing the company data area you will find passenger information pages with assorted information for each cruise line. There are sample menus as well as sample newsletters that are distributed to each passenger's cabin daily showing the daily activities, meal times, and other fun and useful information. Once again, these pages are designed for you to photocopy and share with your client showing the services and activities they may enjoy on their cruise. For new cruisers, this information can assist them in knowing what to expect and it may even help them plan their wardrobe for the trip.

In the second table of contents you will find the Ship Data which is a cross reference of all ship profiles and deck plans prepared for you in alphabetical order. Many frequent cruisers will be looking for a new line to experience yet wanting to know how it will compare to what they have experienced before. Often times you will be able to share your own personal comparisons with your client and this guide will only enhance your intelligence.

Finally, in the third table of contents entitled General Information there is a wealth of data to use. There are comparative materials and promotional support items available to the travel agent such as 800 numbers, detailed embarkation port maps, glossaries, helpful checkoff lists, sample reservation forms and much more. For information about C.L.I.A. call 1-800-372-2542 for the fax retrieval system. Better yet, visit CLIA's home page on the World Wide Web located at http://TEN-I0.com/clia/.

GRAY LINE OFFICIAL SIGHT-SEEING GUIDE

This is a useful tool when planning motorcoach trips across the United States.

HOTEL & TRAVEL INDEX

This publication is distributed to subscribers on a quarterly basis and offers the latest up-to-date booking information on over 45,000 hotels, resorts, motels, and inns around the world. It includes rate information, accommodation details, representation companies, and reservation codes for CRS systems. It tells you what percentage of commission a particular hotel pays the travel agent which of course is very important information for the bottom line. Each hotel lists street and mailing addresses, phone and fax numbers, reference points and more.

In addition the books feature over 400 destination maps which pinpoint hotels, roads, airports, and major attractions in the area. There are over 30 full-color maps in each book as well as a worldwide geographic index. Over 7,000 ads are featured and many have 4-color detailed photos of the various hotels and resorts. In the front of each book there is a full list of worldwide Hotel Representatives and Reservations Services available for you to use. In addition, there is a worldwide Hotel and Motel Systems List, and International Telephone Dialing Guide. You will find valuable World time zone maps and air travel times for planning those complex itineraries. This year a new addition is entitled Hotel Programs and Policies-at-a-Glance. The Hotel & Travel Index is published for the USA, Canada, Mexico, Caribbean, Central & South America. For more information on ordering contact Reed Travel Group at 500 Plaza Drive, Secaucus, NJ 07096 or 1-800-360-0015.

HOTEL & TRAVEL INDEX/ABC INTERNATIONAL EDITION

As in the above edition this publication is also produced quarterly and a one years subscription includes four issues. The Hotel & Travel Index/ABC International Edition is published for travel professionals outside of the USA, Canada, Mexico, Caribbean & South America. This publication includes listings of 45,000 hotels, motels, resorts and inns worldwide. It also includes an International Reservation Section with 300 Locator Maps. Another helpful addition are the Public Holidays in over 36 countries, Time Zone Maps, as well as International Telephone Codes. For more information on ordering contact Reed Travel Group at 500 Plaza Drive, Secaucus, NJ 07096 or 1-800-360-0015.

MICHELIN GUIDES

These are sometimes known as the Green and Red Guides. They cover extensive sight-seeing and cultural information. They even offer suggested itineraries, maps, attractions and city plans. If you plan on selling a good amount of European travel the Red Series are famous annual guides with many hotel and restaurants listed. The guides can often be found at travel bookstores and some large luggage and travel stores.

OFFICIAL AIRLINE GUIDE - NORTH AMERICA

In lieu of an automated reservation system in your home office, this is a very useful tool of the trade. It is a rather large book somewhat like a phonebook in design and features flight schedules of scheduled carriers in the U.S., Canada and the Caribbean. It is circulated on a subscription basis in 12 monthly issues. For subscription information contact Official Airline Guides at 2000 Clearwater Dr., Oak Brook, IL 60521-9953.

OFFICIAL AIRLINE GUIDE - INTERNATIONAL

As in the North America edition, this is a complete city-by-city listing of all worldwide scheduled flights to points outside the North American Continent. This publication is circulated by subscription on a monthly basis. For subscription information contact Official Airline Guides at 2000 Clearwater Dr., Oak Brook, IL 60521-9953.

OAG WORLDWIDE CRUISE & STEAMSHIP GUIDE

This publication is issued quarterly and covers steamship and cruise schedules, ship profiles, booking procedures and reservation information. For subscription information contact Official Airline Guides at 2000 Clearwater Dr., Oak Brook, IL 60521.

OAG TRAVEL PLANNER & MOTEL/HOTEL GUIDE

This is a very handy reference guide to have in your library. There are actually three issues of this planner, the North American Travel Planner, the European Travel Planner, and the Pacific Asia Travel Planner. Each is a separate subscription and is published quarterly. They offer complete information and maps on airports as well as mileage information and times between various hotels, city centers and the airport. Airport transfer and limousine information also appears under each airport listing. An invaluable tool for the agent handling business travel. For subscription information contact Official Airline Guides at 2000 Clearwater Dr., Oak Brook, IL 60521.

OFFICIAL CRUISE GUIDE

This is yet another essential sales tool for the cruise agent. Published annually, this guide provides all the information you need to quickly find and book the right cruise for your clients. It is a comprehensive source of detailed cruise ship information with descriptions of over 300 cruise ships worldwide. Some cruise lines that may not be members of C.L.I.A. would likely be listed here yet not in the C.L.I.A. manual. The C.L.I.A. manual is really a must and this is and added bonus to your library.

It includes rates, accommodations, amenities, recreation, dining, toll-free numbers, commissions, and contact information. This is truly an unbiased classification system and it ranks ships from world class to popular showing the itineraries by ship all in one convenient volume. This issue features over 100 worldwide cruise lines, some with informative color ads showing deck plans and photos. There is a cross-reference by ship, date, and port of departure, ports-of-call, and itinerary. As in the other publications its unique page design makes it simple to photocopy deck plans and maps for your cruise clients. For subscription information contact Reed Travel Group at 500 Plaza Dr., Secaucus, NJ 07096 or 1-800-360-0015.

OFFICIAL HOTEL GUIDE

This in an incredibly comprehensive profile of 30,000 hotels and resorts around the world. This is published annually and comes complete with three volumes in a protective case. It includes detailed information on rates, locations, accommodations, dining, entertainment, amenities, commissions, and more.

In this publication you receive over 300 area maps pinpointing, attractions, hotels, and airports as well as facility locators listing the local attractions and recreational activities in a given area. There are over 50 Accommodation Planners with an area hotel analysis, hotel cost index, and alternative accommodations. Finally, it includes a complete listing of Hotel Representatives and Chains worldwide and the unique page design makes it easy to photocopy maps for your clients. For subscription information contact Reed Travel Group at 500 Plaza Drive, Secaucus, NJ 07096 or 1-800-360-0015.

OFFICIAL MEETING FACILITIES GUIDE

This is an essential reference for the travel professional involved in planning meetings and conventions. It features in-depth profiles of nearly 1,400 hotels and resorts that specialize in meetings and conventions. A one year subscription includes two issues and is updated semiannually.

In this publication you will find in-depth profiles of sites with pertinent facts on meeting facilities and equipment, accommodations, location, dining, entertainment, and rates. To assist you in reaching the right person for the job, they have included contact names, addresses, phone and the always helpful fax numbers. The issues feature over 70 destination reports, with facts about local attractions, transportation, museums, shopping, sports, climate and much more. To go hand in hand with the reports are 70 destination maps, pinpointing facilities, airports, highways, and other attractions in the various areas. There is an Index for easy reference and a listing of 350 Convention and Visitors Bureaus worldwide. In addition, there is a full list of Airlines and Car Rental Companies and editorial features about Convention and Visitors Bureaus destinations. For information contact Reed Travel Group at 1-800-662-7776.

OFFICIAL TOUR DIRECTORY

This directory has been called a travel professional's complete guide to worldwide vacation packages, cruises and destinations. The directory is published twice a year with a fall/winter issue and a spring/summer issue. The cost of the publication is very low in comparison to others of its type and is certainly a good handy book to have around.

It includes detailed information on just about every destination you can think of as well as tour operators that offer packages to those areas. Where would you go to find information on dog sledding tours? Well, page 647 of the Official Tour Directory features about 12 operators that offer packages to areas in Canada and Alaska with phone numbers and addresses for you to follow up on. All in all, you will certainly find it a useful tool for your home office reference library. Contact Thomas Publishing at One Penn Plaza, New York, NY 10119 or 1-212-290-7355.

THE INDEPENDENT TRAVEL AGENT DESKTOP GUIDE

This is a handy desktop guide with a multitude of references for your home office. This guide is a must as you begin your home based travel business. It features airline two-letter codes, three-letter airport codes domestic and international airports, and supplier contact information as well.

THE INTERNATIONAL ATLAS

Every good travel professional should have a current atlas. One of the best available is by Rand McNally. It features over 300 pages of full color maps and charts. This can be found at most large bookstore chains as well as at some travel bookstores.

TRAVEL INDUSTRY PERSONNEL DIRECTORY

This is a comprehensive listing of travel professionals throughout North America. To purchase a copy contact Fairchild Books at 7 West 34th St., New York, NY 10001.

WORLD TRAVEL DIRECTORY

This issue has been called a travel industry source book and is published annually. It features over 72,000 retail and wholesale travel agencies and tour operators worldwide.

The listings in this publication provide you with contact names, phone numbers, fax numbers, telex numbers, addresses, headquarter and branch office information as well as association memberships. Well over 4,500 wholesale tour operators are referenced with quick cross-checks by geographic specialty and special interest. Most co-ops, agency chains, and consortiums in the world are listed, as well as hard to find In-plant agencies. There is a listing of worldwide conferences, trade shows, and exhibitions for the travel industry.

Setting Up Your Travel Reference Library

Chapter 14
DEVELOPING A MARKETING PLAN

Now that you have established your agency, office, and organized your materials and files it is time to start marketing your products and services. It is very important that you clearly define your marketing efforts so that you achieve your stated objectives for growth and revenue in your business plan. Your marketing effort should be well defined so that each day, week, month, or year you can measure your efforts to your anticipated results and make any corrections as needed.

Developing a marketing plan is nothing more than deciding when, where and how you will expend your physical efforts and marketing budget. There are several considerations for opportunities to cultivate and grow your business and the ideal marketing plan would allow you to accomplish your objectives with a minimum investment of energy and expense. By mapping out your marketing endeavor you will continually plant the seeds that are necessary for continual growth that is conducive with your overall objectives.

Many home based entrepreneurs are so anxious to get revenue that they pursue any airline ticket that comes through the door and eventually forsake their original business purpose forever chasing more and more low yielding domestic airline tickets. During the initial weeks and months of your travel business you should spend the majority of time developing your primary business objective. If it is cruises, tours, groups, or whatever focus rather than jump at any piece of revenue that comes your way. You can clearly see the opportunity cost of abandoning your marketing plan in pursuit of short term revenue opportunities when you review your agency's performance. This and the following six chapters will look closely at various marketing opportunities you may incorporate into the growth of your business.

DEFINE YOUR MARKET

First and foremost you must define your market as conclusively as possible. There are a number of ways to do this and depending on your intended product or service specialization there are several sources of information. A quick trip to your public library's business reference section will unfold a wealth of reference material that will help you identify various markets. There are volumes of mailing lists that you can purchase from innumerable sources. If your market is cruises, you can purchase a list of folks who subscribe to *CRUISE MAGAZINE*" in your area. If your focus is the senior market, there are hundreds of publications centered on senior travellers where you may purchase a mailing list of their subscribers. Let's say you are interested in handling only small business travel you may find that some of the local business directories such as "*CONTACTS INFLUENTIAL*" may be just the ticket. Your public library is invaluable as a tool to help you identify your target market.

A visit to the newspapers in your marketplace that feature travel sections is another great resource. They have done substantial market research on the travel market within their domain and will be delighted to provide you with a wealth of information. The travel suppliers themselves are a cornucopia of intelligence and will eagerly share their knowledge with you. Industry associations, demographic studies, tax rolls, port authorities, local, regional and national chambers of commerce and other business associations, convention bureaus, and visitor organizations are all resources you can use.

QUANTIFY YOUR DESIRED MARKETING EXPOSURES

Marketing is nothing more than exposing your products and services to potential customers in the most positive and cost effective way possible. Marketing exposures may be quantified by reducing them to a meaningful number of exposures per a specific period of time. Then figure your conversion ratio from exposure to sale. Various types of exposures have had various types of conversion ratios and the challenge is to streamline your exposures and conversion ratio to result in the lowest cost per conversion possible.

Of course, each type of marketing exposure will have its inherent conversion ratio and cost per exposure vs cost per conversion. An advertisement in a regional newspaper may cost one thousand dollars and be exposed to a million potential clients at a cost of a fraction of a cent per exposure but if you only sell ten customers the cost per conversion is one hundred dollars. On the other hand if you did a seminar that cost a thousand dollars and attracted fifty people the cost per exposure is substantial higher at twenty dollars but if you sold twenty of the fifty your cost per conversion is lower at only fifty dollars. In this instance it would seem the prudent thing to do is pursue seminars in lieu of newspaper advertising.

Your marketing plan should be made up of locking in your existing clients, developing new clients, and prospecting for potential new clients. It should reflect a blend of marketing activity to achieve the lowest cost per exposure and the lowest cost per conversion that you can manage.

ESTABLISH A MARKETING BUDGET

First identify your potential market and establish the amount of money you will invest to develop the revenues necessary to achieve your profit objective as stated in your business plan. Allocate your annual marketing budget among the various elements that will make up your marketing plan. It is important to note that a successful marketing effort is administered consistently over the period of time for which the budget is allocated. Consistency in marketing is far more important than flamboyancy. Many home based entrepreneurs tend to spend the majority of their annual marketing budget in a few impressive but inconsistent exposures. Sure, it looks great to publish gorgeous printed material but without consistency it just doesn't work. Following are some of the elements that might make up your annual marketing plan.

NEWSLETTERS

Direct mail newsletters should be the number one priority in your marketing plan. They are the most cost effective way to retain existing clients and prospect for new ones. Chapter 15 deals with newsletters in depth.

DIRECT MAIL

In additional to your newsletters, nothing beats direct mail for stimulating sales and repeat business. Your direct mail program should also take priority in your marketing plan. Chapter 16 looks at direct mail in detail.

ADVERTISING

Most home based travel agencies are surprised to find that travel advertising opportunities are quite limited and need to be highly focused to become viable. Chapter 17 explores opportunities in travel advertising.

PROMOTIONS

Travel related promotions are an excellent way to develop new clients and offer the lowest cost per conversion of any prospecting effort the home based travel agent can pursue. Chapter 18 delves into travel promotions.

SPECIAL TRAVEL MARKETING TECHNIQUES

The nineties and personal computers have delivered substantial opportunity for marketing techniques that were beyond most home based entrepreneurs only a few years ago. Chapter 19 explores new opportunities on ways to kill your competition with your personal computer.

COLD CALLS, CANVASSING, TELEMARKETING, AND NETWORKING

Nothing beats a one on one salesman and the travel industry is no exception. Chapter 20 looks at direct sales as a method of developing your revenue.

GENERATING A WRITTEN MARKETING PLAN

Once you have explored the various opportunities for developing your business and identified your marketing budget, it is quite easy to sit down and develop an annual marketing plan.

ALLOCATE YOUR MARKETING BUDGET

Decide what elements of your marketing plan are going to receive what portion of your marketing budget. If direct mail newsletters are going to play a major part then how many mailings to how many clients? You can easily figure the cost to implement the effort. If promotions are a part of your budget, how much are they going to cost and how many?

By identifying all of the areas of cost in your marketing plan you can then allocate the portion of the annual budget allocated to the activity over the number of events in the element. Let's say you are going to do a total of six direct mail newsletters per year and you have allocated six hundred dollars total, then you could safely assume that each mailing should be budgeted one hundred dollars.

MAPPING OUT YOUR MARKETING PLAN

Once you have allocated your marketing budget for the specific events that are going to take place over the period of your budget, you can put each event on a calendar in pencil. If your marketing plan covers the period of one year then using a calendar that displays the entire year is best. Start by inserting each marketing event on the day of the month it should be completed. If you plan to mail your newsletters on the fifteenth day of every other month then you should enter the event on that day.

Each event should be recorded on the master calendar until all budgeted events appear. If there are any conflicts in activity you can easily change the dates to allow for uniformity of effort throughout the month. Next, budget time for the non-cost items in your marketing plan. Immediately set time aside for the review of your plan for effectiveness. At first, you should set an hour or so aside just for review and correction as often as once a month. During your review if you find that one thing doesn't seem to be working and another does you can simply reallocate your resources and change your calendar. If you find that your plan is too ambitious and you are having trouble keeping up, slice out some of the less productive activity so you can keep on track. Your marketing plan should be designed to maximize your marketing efforts and budget for your business, not bind you to activity.

Finally, the most important aspect of your marketing plan is the time you commit to the development of new clients. You should budget a certain number of hours each week for solicitation of new clients. For most people this is the last task they never get around to as there is always something else with a higher priority. Without the constant exploration for new clients your business will eventually become stalled and falter.

SAMPLE MARKETING PLAN

Remember our business plan from chapter 5? Following is a sample marketing plan for Mobile Cruise Source of San Diego, Inc. Note that the financial presentation has been eliminated and that much of the proprietary information removed. You can still see the intention of the plan and make certain decisions as to its viability.

Your plan doesn't need to be this inclusive but you should think about the various topics it presents. By quantifying your marketing efforts you can minimize waste and focus on result areas.

Marketing Plan for:

MOBILE CRUISE SOURCE OF SAN DIEGO, Inc.

Mobile Cruise Source of San Diego's marketing strategy is to enhance, promote and support the fact that our in home cruise sales are the most convenient, competitive and revolutionary way for consumers to purchase cruise vacations

The overall marketing plan for our product is based on the following fundamentals:

1. San Diego consumers do not currently have this service available to them

2. San Diego enjoys one of the highest per capital incomes in the nation and one of the highest densities of cruise oriented vacationers in the nation

3. Mobile Cruise Source of San Diego, Inc. will create a new and highly motivated sales force to reach these potential clients.

4. Within the first five years of business Mobile Cruise Source of San Diego, Inc. will capture 7 to 8% of the San Diego cruise market

Sales Strategy

Mobile Cruise Source of San Diego, Inc. will create demand for a whole new way for consumers to purchase cruises by offering complete in-home sales presentations that include in-home, on line reservations, multi media presentations, videos and brochures.

Positioning

1. Mobile Cruise Source of San Diego Inc. is perceived by consumers to be the premier mobile cruise agency in San Diego.

2. Mobile Cruise Source of San Diego, Inc. is recognized by the cruise industry as well as the travel industry in general as a revolutionary marketer offering clients services heretofore not available at competitive pricing. Mobile Cruise Source of San Diego is thought to be an aggressive marketer capable of moving distressed cruise product for the cruise suppliers.

3. Mobile Cruise Source of San Diego, Inc.'s enjoys a unique position in the market place because we are;

Meaningful: Not only do we offer highly competitive pricing but our service is beyond any travel organization in San Diego

Believable: As a part of a national franchise, Mobile Cruise Source of San Diego is already proven in the market place. All principles are Master Cruise Consultants (MCC), a professional designation of the Cruise Line International Association.

Motivating: Mobile Cruise Source of San Diego, Inc.'s unique in-home presentations create the thrill and desire for cruising right in the client's own home or office.

Memorable: Mobile Cruise Source of San Diego, Inc.'s mobile cruise travel agency vans are seen daily by more than 43,000 San Diego residents. The vans are designed for maximum consumer impact

Simple: The message is clear. Call Mobile Cruise Source for the most convenient and lowest price cruise shopping in San Diego.

Logical: Clients want to purchase leisure travel on their leisure time. Travel agencies are closed during normal leisure hours. Mobile Cruise Source of San Diego, Inc. will meet clients at their home, in their office, or anywhere, any time to make the most impressive presentations available.

Unique: Mobile cruise Source of San Diego is the only mobile travel company in existence and has pioneered the success of in-home presentations.

Pricing

Mobile Cruise Source of San Diego, Inc's pricing policy is simple. We will meet or beat any cruise price quoted by any competitor.

Mobile Cruise Source of San Diego, Inc. enjoys relationships with all of the major cruise lines that allow the same commissions and overrides as all other major cruise agencies in the United States.

Mobile Cruise Source of San Diego, Inc. belongs to two major cruise consortiums to be sure we access the very best commissions.

Current Selling Methods

Mobile Cruise Source of San Diego, Inc. offers clients in-home presentations on various cruise vacations. Clients respond to advertising in both the Los Angeles Times travel section and the San Diego Union travel section. The client responds to a toll free telephone number and the call is referred to the appropriate Mobile Cruise Source agent for a follow up appointment. Central operations is in contact via cellular telephone with the Associates who can respond immediately to the client's needs.

In addition to the major travel sections, Mobile Cruise Source of San Diego, Inc. uses direct mail, newsletters, fax broadcasting, and telemarketing to develop leads for the mobile Associates.

See attachment "C", our corporate brochure.

Distribution Channels

Mobile Cruise Source of San Diego, Inc.'s plans to sell cruises to consumers directly through the use of "Associates" who are controlled by Mobile Cruise Source of San Diego Inc. operations. These Associates operate as independent contractors and operate on a commission only basis. The Associates invest in their mobile cruise travel van and display the logo and artwork as prescribed by contract. Leads are generated by the advertising and promotion of Mobile Cruise Source of San Diego, Inc.. Associates enjoy an exclusive sales territory in which all sales activity falls within their responsibility.

Associate Sales

Customer profile: The typical cruise customer in San Diego falls between the ages of thirty-five and seventy. Mobile Cruise Source of San Diego, Inc. intends to target the mid to up scale cruise market.

Geography: Associate markets within San Diego County will be identified by a geographic boundary as defined in the Associate agreement.

Seasonal Variations: The purchase of cruises is cyclical. Sales tend to drop off in the Winter months and expand in the Summer months

Executive Sales

The successful recruitment of Associates will be accomplished by the executives of Mobile Cruise Source of San Diego, Inc. Because the success of our marketing depends upon the strength of our Associates, recruitment is one of our highest priorities.

Direct Sales

The majority of Mobile Cruise Source of San Diego, Inc. sales will be handled through direct sales by our Associates. Mobile Cruise Source of San Diego, Inc. anticipates contracting 12 Associates to cover the primary cruise markets in San Diego County within the first twelve months. Associate start up fees will be $12,500.00 plus the cost of the mobile cruise agent van.

We have chosen to use a direct sales force because cruises require considerable customer education and post-sales support directly from the company. Our price point, pricing structure and profits are such that our costs of sales warrants "person-to-person" selling strategy.

Direct Response Mail

We will be exploring the benefits of incremental, coordinated direct mail programs in each quarter of 1996. We anticipate a strong profit potential as we strengthen our direct response capabilities. We will be approaching this scientifically, as we improve our customer targeting ability. We propose four 50,000 piece campaigns, each preceded by a 5,000 piece test.

All direct mail activities this year will be directed to our existing customer base. In addition, we will use the subscriber list of _Cruise_ Magazine for San Diego County.

Telemarketing

We will use a contract telemarketing service to perform the following functions.

Provide sales support by soliciting appointments for Associates using telephone lists based on demographics developed by Data Quick of San Diego.

Concurrently, telephone contact will be used for the development of a direct mail mailing list.

Telemarketing will be used to consistently maintain contact with existing client base of Mobile Cruise Source of San Diego, Inc.

Fax Broadcasting

We will fax broadcast our customer database sorted by interest. All customers will be   maintained in a relational database. Mobile Cruise Source of San Diego, Inc. receives many last minute specials that are considerable bargains and will market these bargains via fax broadcast. Clients interested in offerings will be referred to the appropriate Associate.

Customer Service

Our customers emphasize that service and support is one of their major concerns. They are constantly impressed with the support we provide. Hot-line service is currently available to all customers enrolled in a support program.

We intend to provide free airport/dock transfers for customers in the San Diego area by using our own mobile cruise agency vans. The purpose for this service is to assure customer satisfaction and loyalty allowing us to increase sales as well as maintaining a high profile within our service area.

Advertising and Promotion

 Mobile Cruise Source of San Diego, Inc. recognizes the key to success at this time requires extensive promotion. This must be done aggressively on a wide scale. To accomplish our sales goals, we require an extremely capable advertising agency and public relations firm. Mobile Cruise Source of San Diego, Inc. plans to advertise in major newspapers with travel sections such as the San Diego Union. Upon funding, an agency shall be selected and, with their assistance, a comprehensive advertising and promotion plan will be drafted. Advertising will be done independently and cooperatively with Associates and cruise suppliers with whom Mobile Cruise Source of San Diego, Inc. has joint marketing relationships.

Objectives

Position Mobile Cruise Source of San Diego, Inc. as the leading mobile travel organization in the market.

Increase company awareness and brand name recognition among cruise customers. Generate qualified sales leads and potential new distributors for field sales organization.

Develop, through market research, significant information to create immediate and long-term marketing plans.

Create product advertising programs supporting our in-home positioning.

Coordinate sales literature, demonstration materials, telemarketing programs, and direct response promotions in order to maximize the image and impact of Mobile Cruise Source of San Diego, Inc..

Advertising Campaign

The best way to reach our potential customers is to develop an intense advertising campaign promoting our basic premise "Call Mobile Cruise Source of San Diego for the most convenient and cost effective way to purchase cruise vacations".

To establish and maintain our company image the delivery and tone of our statements will be hard driven excitement.

Ads will convey the look and feel of our ability to visit our clients with the lowest possible cruise vacation pricing.

Upon responding to the advertising our clients will;

Call our toll-free 800 number and place their order using their credit card, call for a brochure, or request an appointment with a Cruise Source of San Diego Associate to visit their home or office.

To eliminate the biggest objections to immediate action, our advertisements must address that our Associates are immediately dispatched and there is some urgency to respond to the advertisement because the offering is limited in availability and time.

Because our in-home presentations are so innovative and unique, it is important to develop a promotional campaign that is consistent and easy to understand.

Preliminary Media Schedule

Media	Circulation	Budget	Ad Size	Insertions
S.D.Union Tribune	350,000	$75,000	10 Inches	52
Various Radio Stations	Various	$18,000	30 Seconds	360
Total		**$93,000**		

Anticipated Response [ex: 1/1,000] 22,500 responses at $4.13 each.

Promotion

In addition to standard advertising practices, we will gain considerable recognition.

Mobile Cruise Source of San Diego, Inc. will participate in every fair, farmer's market, swap meet and outdoor gathering as possible. Our Associates will attend with their mobile cruise agency vans.

Mobile Cruise Source of San Diego, Inc. will issue weekly press releases via fax broadcast to travel desks of all newspapers and magazines within San Diego county.

Direct Mail

Mobile Cruise Source of San Diego, Inc. will engage in an ongoing direct mail program. We will publish and distribute quarterly a 24 page, 2 color newsletter featuring the best cruise rates and up to date cruise information and reviews.

In addition to using direct mail to distribute our newsletters, we will exercise our direct customer communications through the offering of distressed cruise inventory, and the formation of a direct mail based referral program. The direct mail objective is fully for profit.

List Management

Given the growing potential of electronic distribution, we are building our capabilities in database marketing. We have brought our customer list in house for this first phase, as we develop our database sophistication. Our registration cards and periodic customer surveys will help us understand our customer, and measure the success of our marketing, sales and product activities. Profile overlays or other lists that we buy will fill in our awareness gaps. This in-house presence will provide our sales and tech support teams with tools that streamline their operations, while they update our customer knowledge on a daily basis. We plan to develop a client profile format within Access that will aid sound decisions by providing historical answers to the marketing questions we pose.

Corporate Capabilities Brochure

To portray Mobile Cruise Source of San Diego, Inc as the leading supplier of cruise vacations we have developed a company brochure included in Supporting Documents. Note that the brochure includes Mobile Cruise Source of San Diego, Inc.'s introduction and background, operational facilities, unique in-home presentation concept and our mobile cruise agency vans. Our competitive pricing is also a main message in the presentation The brochure is designed to introduce our unique marketing concept and client benefits.

Developing a Marketing Plan

Chapter 15
DEVELOPING A NEWSLETTER

Direct mail newsletters are the single most effective way to make your business visible to your client base. An impressive but personalized communication will do wonders promoting your business as viable, competent and deserving of your client's attention. Your client's enjoyment of your publication on an ongoing basis will enhance your ability to obtain new customers and retain established clients. A well thought out newsletter will go a long way to establish the image and credibility so necessary to create new clients. With just a little effort you can project the specific image you would like your business to present.

A newsletter should have high priority in your marketing plan and may be one of your principle efforts and budget priority. There are several considerations to be made when planning your marketing effect with newsletters.

CONSISTENCY

If nothing else, your newsletters should be consistent. To be effective it should look the same, read the same and arrive at recurrent intervals. Receiving a well written newsletter is a constant reminder to your clients of your service and interest in their travel plans.

The frequency you choose to develop and distribute a newsletter should be given the utmost consideration. Just as consistency will pay huge rewards, a shabbily designed and executed newsletter that arrives sporadically can yield just the opposite results. The optimum frequency for a travel newsletter is every other month or quarterly. Lessor frequencies tend to lose the desired impact of familiarity.

A consistent design, typeface and size will enhance your newsletter's readability and intensify your image. Whatever style of newsletter you decide to pursue, maintaining it's general appearance will increase it's readership and impact.

DEVELOPMENT

To a certain extent your budget will dictate how snazzy and frequent your newsletter will be distributed. There are many ways to stretch your marketing dollars earmarked for this effort. Many home based businesses use a typewritten format that is produced on their home typewriter and simply copied at a self copy store in town. While this lacks the "Corporate Look" so many folks think necessary, typewritten newsletters appear extremely personalized and can be highly readable especially if enhanced with a personalized note or cover letter. It is very important to be sure a typewritten newsletter is formatted properly and that all words are spelled correctly. Any major grammatical errors might reflect poorly on your business skills.

Most home based travel businesses have developed a newsletter utilizing either the services of professional typesetter or by using one of the many software programs that can be run on a personal computer with a laser printer to produce professional quality text. Many word processors allow the user to format a document in columnar fashion and print the manuscript using any number of different fonts or typefaces. If you plan to make a major commitment to a monthly newsletter this is certainly something you should consider. A reasonable approach is to use your home based PC to keyboard the text and then take it to a typesetter, or imagesetter as some like to be called, and allow them to produce the camera ready copy. This saves the initial expense of a laser printer and lets you draw from their design and layout expertise.

WordPerfect 6.0 and Microsoft Word 6.0 are word processors that have the capacity to produce newsletter formats and are universally recognized by typesetters, imagesetters and graphic artists alike. There are many software programs that have been designed to enhance these product's capabilities. Numerous additional fonts or typefaces may be purchased as well as preplanned newsletter page formats and designs. With these programs you may simply choose a design and insert your text for camera ready and professional quality newsletters. There is unlimited clip art available for graphic images that both word processors can import.

No conversation about newsletter development can be complete without a discussion about desktop publishing. While a relatively new function of personal computers at the casual users level, there is sophisticated software available which will allow a home based travel entrepreneur to write, edit and produce camera ready text and graphics which rival the most professional of typesetters and graphic artists. These programs may be operated on either an IBM compatible personal computer or an Apple Macintosh.

The Macintosh computer is well known for it's graphics capabilities and is the easiest personal computer to use with desktop publishing, however anything a Macintosh can do, an IBM compatible can do and sometimes better. Depending on your level of commitment to a newsletter and other areas where desktop publishing may benefit you, considering a dedicated desktop publishing system may be the right approach.

Whether you choose IBM or Macintosh you will need at least 8 Megabytes of RAM and preferably 16 Megabytes. The fastest system you can afford will enhance your ability to process graphics and design as will a massive hard drive. Large monitors also enhance your ability to create more professional documents.

The three most sophisticated desktop publishing programs are Pagemaker by Adobe (formally Aldus), QuarkExpress and Corel Ventura Publisher. All three programs are highly refined and allow you to create text, graphics and art. You may import art and text files from other programs and have a maximum amount of flexibility of design, typefaces or fonts, and page layout. This book was designed in Pagemaker 5.0.

A less expensive and easier to use program is Microsoft Publisher 2.0 for Win 3.1 (3.0 for Win 95). This program allows you to get results fast without the long learning curve of the sophisticated desktop publishing programs. While there is less overall flexibility with Microsoft Publisher, the ease of use and results can be well worth it. Publisher can also import your clip art and various fonts for unlimited selections of design. One of the best features of Microsoft Publisher is the "Page Wizards". This unique feature allows even the most novice desktop publisher to create professional quality newsletter layouts in just seconds. There are several other inexpensive software programs available at most computer stores that all make the job of designing newsletters quite easy.

Another component of your desktop publishing work station is a laser printer. You should consider a laser printer from the start for all your home office needs as they have become very cost effective to purchase and operate. The results obtained from a laser printer are far superior to a letter quality printer and much easier to use. Most low end laser printers have the same resolution, presented as 300 DPI (Dots Per Inch) which remains the same even as prices of laser printers increase. Generally the only difference is the speed at which the printer works and the options which are included such as number of paper trays, fonts, etc. 600 DPI laser printers are available at a modest cost and offer twice the resolution of 300 DPI printers. 1200 DPI laser printers are also available which offer resolutions comparable to professional imagesetters. While 300 DPI is OK, 600 or 1200 is much better.

With your desktop publishing computer, software, and laser printer you may produce professional quality newsletters, flyers, brochures and correspondence.

YOUR NEWSLETTER'S CONTENT

What your newsletter says is the most important factor in it's execution. The most successful editions seem to focus on a number of topics.

DESTINATION INFORMATION

Focusing on a specific destination for each issue of your newsletter is an excellent way to generate immediate response and also have your clients save them for future use. Clients interested in Hawaii, Mexico, England or any other destination will likely save your newsletter for the information it contains. These issues may resurface when your customer becomes serious about planning their trip and will reward you with a phone call. Information about destinations can be compiled from trade magazines, newspaper travel sections, tour operators, travel books and publications, tourist boards and any number of other sources. Articles regarding special interest subjects such as skiing, scuba diving, square dancing, fishing and so on will enhance your presentation of a destination especially if introduced with general visitor material.

CRUISE INFORMATION

Articles focused on specific ships and itineraries that feature your chosen destination are extremely relevant. Information about new ships, itineraries, ports, events, theme cruises and so on are all of interest to your clients.

RESORT INFORMATION

New or refurbished hotels and resorts are always interesting to your clients. You may be able to generate new business by focusing on a specific resort which is located in the featured destination of your newsletter.

SPECIAL TRAVEL BARGAINS

Promotional airfares, frequent flyer promotions, discount cruises, inexpensive international vacations, off season promotional hotel and resort rates and so on are all desirable topics for your clients. You can find out about these special deals from researching the trade publications and from the Sunday travel section of major newspapers.

CLIENT TESTIMONIALS

Nothing works more to your benefit than to have one of your clients critique his or her recent vacation to a particular destination, cruise, or resort to which you sent him or her. This accomplishes a number of things at one time. It solidifies your relationship with the client who benefits from the stature of being able to share their experiences in a widely read publication. It benefits your newsletter recipients who are rewarded with unbiased and current information regarding a destination, cruise or resort they might be considering. This also lets them know that if they book their travel with you they may also be featured in a future issue. Most important, it benefits your image as a viable travel business with testimonials from satisfied clients.

LOCAL TRAVEL INFORMATION

Information about your local airport, train station or other conveyance is meaningful to your clients. Airport parking tips, local transfer companies, airline terminal maps, new air service or carriers are all worthy of consideration. So many times agents forget that their clients are not familiar with their local facilities and neglect to give them the information they need to efficiently make their flight or departure. Your newsletter is the vehicle that can establish you as the expert in your community for hassle free travel.

SPECIAL SERVICES

This is the opportunity for you to shout about your special services that are unique to your business alone. If you use a laptop and visit client's homes with travel reservations automation make a big deal about it in your newsletter. If you are available evenings and weekends this is the place to let people know. If you speak a second language, sign, or are equipped to communicate electronically be sure your clients get the message. By constantly reinforcing your unique services clients will build a dependence upon them.

VIDEO REVIEW

If you have a video available on the chosen destination, cruise or resort that is the focus of your newsletter be sure to review it and let clients know it is available for preview on their own VCR at home or they may enjoy it at your place of business. Always include the offer of the use of your video library in every newsletter and make mention of, or better yet review any, new videos you may have recently received.

COMMERCIAL ACCOUNTS

If your newsletter is distributed primarily to business travelers you may use the same format substituting destinations like New York, Chicago or Seattle and information about frequent flyer programs, new business oriented hotels and resorts or car rental companies. All of the travel trade publications feature sections on business travel that keep you abreast of current events and trends. A newsletter distributed to commercial accounts must be extremely professional and well organized to be an effective marketing tool.

CALL TO ACTION

Always be sure that your newsletter demands your client to do something to respond. Urge them to call for a video or to request a brochure. Include a reply card or a certificate redeemable for a discount on their next vacation or business trip. Whatever the reason, your publication should always spur the recipient to take immediate action.

TRAVEL NEWSLETTER COMPANIES

In every area there are individuals and companies that specialize in developing travel publications that feature articles on destinations, cruises, resorts, tour operators and so on. These newsletters are supplied so that your typesetter may simply overprint your business name, address, phone number and logo so that it appears the entire newsletter is published by your business. These can be a great time saver and can portray an excellent image. They may however, lack a certain level of personalization or they may focus on areas or products you or your clients are not particularly concerned with. The best newsletter companies will allow you to submit copy and photos to be integrated into their newsletter to overcome this drawback.

SAMPLE NEWSLETTER

Following is a sample newsletter for Mobile Cruise Source of San Diego, Inc. This newsletter was designed using a page wizard in Microsoft Publisher 2.0. The graphics came from "Click Art 25,000" CD collection. Note that the newsletter is professional and exudes a personal feeling as well. Anyone with a PC and this software and a laser printer can produce similar results almost immediately.

Mobile Cruise Source News

January 1996   Volume 1 Issue 1

Mobile Cruise Source of San Diego Wins Award!

Mobile Cruise Source of San Diego, Inc. wins an award of excellence from Mobile Cruise Source national for its innovative promotion with KCEO. Mobile Cruise Source of San Diego and KCEO had a promotion where consumers could win a free cruise by simply stopping any Mobile Cruise Source of San Diego van

and asking to draw from the "Free Cruise Box". Mobile Cruise Source registered 7,567 new cruise clients and awarded 12 free cruises aboard the "Fun Ship" Holiday out of Los Angeles.

Folks that did not win the free cruise were awarded discounts from $10 to $250 on their next cruise purchased from Mobile Cruise Source of San Diego, Inc.

San Diego's Only Travel Agency That Brings The Agency To Your Home!

Thats right! Mobile Cruise Source of San Diego, Inc. is the only cruise vacation company that is equipped to bring o u r travel agency right into your front room or office. O u r "Mobile Cruise Vacation Vans" are dispatched by cellular telephone and are available 24 hours a day, 7days a week to serve you! There is no need to drive anywhere simply call us and we will arrange an appointment!

1996 Cruise Bargains are here now!

If you are not on Mobile Cruise Source of San Diego, Inc.s mailing list for our quarterly discount cruise catalog you should call or fax us your request now. The 1996 discount catalog has just been published and there are so many values it is unbelievable. Our catalog has swollen to over 60 pages of outstanding values to choose from. Of special interest are Mobile Cruise Source of San Diego, Inc.'s Caribbean selections. Outstanding values are available on all itineraries. World cruises are also an extremely good bargain this year. Even if you have not made reservations

"Outstanding values are available on all itineraries ....there are more discounted cruises now than ever before"

there is still space available for this year's itineraries as well as next years. The Alaska cruises this year are also great bargains. There are more and more ships plying Alaskan waters this year than ever before and the choices are outstanding! Call us for more information or to arrange your own private presentation on the

DREAM CRUISE VACATIONS

1996 Cruise Bargains

CRYSTAL CRUISES

**SAVE UP TO $4,931
PER PERSON
AND RECEIVE A
2-CATEGORY UPGRADE**

February 8th, 1996

11-day cruise from Acapulco to San Juan

Space is very limited so call Mobile Cruise Source of San Diego, Inc. TODAY to reserve your dream cruise aboard the

CRYSTAL HARMONY

"2-For-1*" Fares Now Available! PANAMA CANAL

Princess Cruises
It's more than a cruise, it's the Love Boat

10 Days Sky Princess
March 7, 17, & 27, 1996

$1367.00

Sail Round-trip from Ft. Lauderdale
Fares are per person, cruise only, exclude suites & mini-suites.
Air add-ons apply.
*Prices subject to availability

CARNIVAL "FUN SHIP"

JUBILEE

7 day Mexican Riviera
$699 Oceanview Stateroom
February 4
$719 Oceanview Stateroom
February 11, 18, 25
March 3, 10
$769 Oceanview Stateroom
March 24, 31
April 7, 21, 28
May 5, 12, 19, 26

The above rates are cruise-only per person based on double occupancy. Port taxes are additional. Upgrades available for only $20 per guest per deck

SAVE 50% ON ALASKA CRUISES

It is not too late to take booking discounts avail-Alaskan cruises. All of ing discounts up to 65% and deposit 1996 cruises Following are some of various cruise lines. Be

ALASKA

advantage of the early able from many of the the cruise lines are offer-for individuals who book by February 1st, 1996. the discounts offered by sure to call Mobile Cruise

Source of San Diego, Inc. to find out more and make your reservations!

Cruise Discounts

Holland America	50%	N.C.L.	50%
Westours	50%	Radisson Seven Seas	20%
Regency Cruises	50%	Canadian Ferry Co.	30%
Carnival Cruise Lines	50%	Royal Cruise Lines	50%
Royal Caribbean Cruises	50%	Princess Cruises	50%

CALL MOBILE CRUISE SOURCE OF SAN DIEGO,

MOBILE CRUISE SOURCE ANSWERS

What clothes will we need?

That is the common question: What will I need to bring on a cruise? What kind of clothes should I pack? Here are some basic suggestions on what clothes one should pack for a cruise....

1. Where is your cruise going?

If you are cruising to New England, Canada, maybe Alaska or Europe, then a warm jacket, sweaters, turtlenecks, and as always comfortable walking shoes.

If you are cruising to the Caribbean, Hawaii, Mexico or Bermuda then comfortable cotton attire is best for on deck and shore excursions. Always carry that swimsuit along. Clothes made with polyester are not recommended as they tend to get sticky in warm humid climates.

2. What is the weather pattern in the areas you are visiting?

Ask your travel agent this important information. An experienced cruise associate at Mobile Cruise Source, Inc. of San Diego can provide you with details on past weather patterns and suggestions on wardrobe choices.

3. What kind of clothes will we need for days at sea?

Akways keep in mind that you are on vacation. If the weather will be warm, shorts, tee shirts, tennis shoes, and bathing suits are a must. Bathing attire and tank tops are generally not acceptable attire in the dining room and in some lounges. If the weather might be a bit chilly then jeans, slacks, sweaters and jackets would be suitable. Proper and always comfortable attire is a good rule of thumb. Your daily cruise long delivered to your cabin each night will help you with the next days wardrobe choices. Ask your Mobile Cruise Source of San Diego, Inc. cruise expert to suggest appropriate daily attire for your specific cruise.

4. Do we need to bring formal dress and a tux? And what about our kids, is it really necessary to buy them formal clothes?

In general 7 day cruises will offer two formal nights. The most formal is the captains dinner and the other night will be a more of a semi-formal attire. 3 & 4 day cruises will usually offer one formal night. Keep in mind that it is your vacation and do what feels right.

Gentlemen, should pack their tux if they have one and you will have the chance to wear it both nights. If you do not own one and wish to rent you may do so at any tux rental shop prior to your cruise or you might want to rent one from the cruise line. If the line you have chosen offers this service your cruise counselor will know. For convenience you can pre-order your tux with the line prior to your departure date to assure you will have your size and style. A dark suit is accepted on most lines. If that is not an option a pair of dress slacks and a dark blazer will usually

foot the bill. It is really apersonal choice. It is fun to dress up as most passengers do get into the swing of the formal nights.

Ladies...Have fun and dress up! Women will wear anything from long formal evening gowns or short cocktail dresses. There are some shops that rent evening attire. If you do not think you will be cruising again (that is highly unlikely) then a rental might be just the ticket. Try to avoid waiting to purchase that special dress until you are on board as the selections on the ship are large and the port you visit might not have what you are looking for. Remember to pack those matching shoes and evening purse to go with your special outfit.

Children...This depends on your children or teens. Some will love the chance to dress up as it is a bit of a novelty. However, some might just refuse. If that later is true then go with the flow. A nice pair of slacks for a young man and dress shirt with tie will be just fine. A nice dress for a young lady or a dressy pantsuit will be appropriate. If even that is a problem, do the best you can and know their will likely be others in the same boat. Some teens might just prefer to eat in the cabin that night which is always an option on a cruise. Remember, this is everyone's vacation and it should be fun for everyone. Relax and enjoy.....

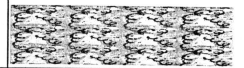

SHIP REVIEWS & NEWS

This upscale line offers "Pure Luxury & Comfort". The Crystal Harmony , a 960 passenger vessel has been a success for 5 years now. The Crystal Symphony a near-twin sister ship has now entered the luxury cruise fleet. Crystal Cruises now covers European, American, Asian and Australian waters.

Crystal's president and chief operat-ing officer since May of 1994 has said " Over the past five years, I have seen Crystal Cruises emerge as the new leader in luxury, large-ship cruising. This phenomenal success came about through an unswerving commitment to quality and a company-wide belief in superior quest service."

Since the lines inception it has at-tracted the best management executive in the cruise industry. These profession-als have skillfully taken the company t-the heights of achievement.

These vessels are known as refine-resorts at sea with a number of feature-that set them apart from the competition-With the largest penthouses afloat, tw-alternative dinner restaurants, a spectac-ular casino, glass stairways and lush greenery they certainly do set them-selves apart.

With all the attention to luxury many contented passengers will continue to cruise them year after year just for the joy of being treated as "royalty".

Be sure to look at our Mobile Cruise Source of San Diego, Inc. special fares on the Crystal Harmony on the February 8th, 11-day Panama Canal Cruise on page 2 of this newsletter....

MOBILE CRUISE SOURCE NEWS

**Mobile Cruise Source
Of San Diego, Inc.
P.O. Box 12345
San Diego, California 92120**

Bulk Rate
U.S. Postage
PAID
San Diego,
California

MOBILE CRUISE SOURCE OF SAN DIEGO, INC.

Chapter 16
USING DIRECT MAIL

Direct mail is the most cost effective way of communicating with your existing client base and potential clients. An effective direct mail effort will allow you to maintain a continuing relationship with your customers and selectively offer your clients product and services that meet their specific interests.

DEVELOPING YOUR MAILING LIST

Many home based travel entrepreneurs neglect to develop the full capacity of their mailing list by simply overlooking obvious opportunities. Following is a list of potential sources of people to whom you may want to initiate periodic mailings.

FAMILY

The number one source of quality names for your mailing list is your immediate family and their relations. Your parents, grandparents, sons, daughters, aunts, uncles, cousins, nephews, nieces, in-laws and their best friends should be included on the list. Even if you know they don't personally travel your constant bombardment of newsletters, flyers and offerings will be passed from your family member to their friends and acquaintances. In all probability, your relatives will endorse and support your services.

FRIENDS

Friends are also mandatory for your mailing list. They already know and like you and will endorse your services to their friends and acquaintances. Don't forget past friends as well. Using a list of your high school or college classmates is an excellent way to generate new business. If you think about it wouldn't you respond to someone contacting you from your past to offer a service that you are currently receiving from someone with whom you have no relationship?

NEIGHBORS

The people with whom you already have an existing relationships should be on your mailing list but so should those that are located near your home and would be interested in your service. Having a location close to these prospective clients and being available after hours or to deliver tickets to their home is a real leg up on the competition. Direct mail is the best way to let you neighborhood know of your business and services.

BUSINESS ASSOCIATES

Present and past business associates should be on your list especially if they are business travelers. People you know who have moved on to other organizations or individuals you have worked with in the past are logical for inclusion as well.

CLUB MEMBERS

If you belong to a private, social, business or other type of club, your fellow members should be included on your list. Often it is a good idea to join clubs with similar interests as you to access their membership mailing list. Seniors have access to clubs that travel consistently and there are many clubs of various ethnicity, interest and profiles.

ORGANIZATIONS

Members of your church are likely to be included if you know that they travel as should the person who handles your Church's travel arrangements. In your local community there are probably several business associations such as the Chamber of Commerce, Downtown Business Association or similar organizations with whom you may become involved. These business associations are always an excellent opportunity to meet new people and add them to your mailing list.

REFERRALS

Some of the best names for your mailing list will come from the referrals of your existing clients, family, friends, neighbors and other contacts.

YELLOW PAGES

The yellow pages can help you develop a quality mailing list by using them to jog your memory regarding past contacts with people you may have otherwise neglected on your mailing list. Often you may have met people while doing business on your personal account and may have established a rapport that would serve as the entree for a reciprocal business relationship.

Examples would be your accountant, attorney, automobile dealer, doctor, dentist, banker, broker, butcher, and so on. Simply start with the letter A in the Yellow Pages and work toward the letter Z making notes along the way. You will be surprised how many people you know that are obvious prospects for your mailing list.

GEOGRAPHICALLY DESIRABLE INDIVIDUALS

People who are logical clients based on their geographic location should be included on your list. Their proper names and addresses may be obtained at your local library from various directories listing individuals by their street address and so on. These directories can be very beneficial when expanding your mailing list with quality prospects who are logical targets.

DEMOGRAPHICALLY DESIRABLE INDIVIDUALS

Another approach for adding quality names to your mailing list is to qualify prospects by their income or another measure of purchasing power. There are many databases available that have recorded information from the state tax roles for real property owners. By using these databases you may find attractive prospects by qualifying them by zip code, home size or another desirable measure of the existence of discretionary income. Data Quick offers the Real Estate tax base you can access from your personal computer. Publications like Contacts Influential, Reverse Directories, Industrial Directories, and the various Cahner's Directories are invaluable tools for locating likely prospects.

MAILING LISTS

Mailing lists are available for every type of business, special interest, profession, and income. There are many mailing list companies that will sell you a list of names tailored to your specifications. While these lists tend to be expensive they may be an excellent way to prospect with exploratory mailings.

MANAGING YOUR MAILING LIST

While many home based travel agents use handwritten envelopes for controlling their mailing list, a more efficient way is to use photocopied labels. You can purchase sheets of gummed and cut labels and type or print your mailing list on the provided master. Whenever you need labels for a mailing simply take out the master and label sheets to a self copy store and have them copied.

USING YOUR PERSONAL COMPUTER TO MANAGE YOUR MAILING LIST

There are a number of software programs designed to help you manage your mailing list and print envelopes, mailing labels or merge the mailing list with your word processor. Avery Label Pro is one program that works quite well. You will find a good number of mail list management programs at your computer store and also available as share-ware. While these programs are good for the simple task of maintaining your list there are two other types of software that may be more comprehensive.

CONTACT MANAGEMENT SOFTWARE

This type of software allows you to maintain a good deal of information regarding your clients in a database that is set up so you may follow up efficiently with your clients. Contact management software allows you to manipulate the data into mailing lists and labels. You can also mail merge with your word processor and generate many types of special reports. This type of software is an excellent way for you to oversee the quantity and quality of contacts you make with your client base. ACT is one such program that has gained wide acceptance within the travel industry as being exceptionally effective for home based travel agencies.

DATABASE SOFTWARE

Without question, a database is the best way to control the information about your clients. Not only can you generate all of the above types of documents for direct mail purposes but you can arrange searches, or special reports, based on just about any information you would like. An excellent relational database for home based travel agents is Microsoft's Access. Access is compatible with Microsoft Office and acts in concert with Word and Excel which makes it very easy to use. Database marketing is the term coined for this type of information control and we will look more at it in chapter 19.

BULK MAIL VERSUS FIRST CLASS MAIL

Determining which mail service to use for your mailings is an important decision that may add tremendously to the effectiveness of you mailings. So many people throw mail in the trash can if they appear to be "junk" mailings and most people associate this type of mail with printed bulk mail permits and computerized labels. On the other hand mail sent via first class, addressed and stamped by hand gets read most often. Generally, newsletters and flyers are safe if sent via bulk mail if your customers can figure out their nature at first glance from the exterior of the mail piece. Though they may traditionally throw away most bulk mail they will read yours because of the existing relationship. Invitations, special offers on leisure product and announcements sent first class validate their significance.

Bulk mail permits allow the sender to take advantage of rates much lower than regular first class mail. When you first apply for a bulk mail permit the Post Office charges a fee that covers one year's use. Each time you complete a mailing you may then pay the lower rate. Bulk mail permit numbers may be printed right on your mail piece or you may buy precanceled stamps to affix to the mailing piece. These stamps may sometimes make the difference when doing exploratory mailings as they appear to be first class stamps at first glance. In order for a mailing to qualify for bulk rates it must be sorted by zip code and bundled in a fashion prescribed by the Post Office. A minimum amount of mail pieces must be met before the mailing will be granted bulk rates.

DEVELOPING A MAILING PROGRAM

Your direct mail program should be the base for your marketing strategy. Besides periodic newsletter mailings as described in Chapter 14 you should program other items as well. Some thoughts follow about the various types you may consider.

PERSONAL LETTERS

Probably the most effective way for a home based travel agency to market is by personalized correspondence. Lets say you have developed a data base on your clients and all of sudden you find that airfares to a destination or possibly a cruise line has lowered their fares. You can simply draft a personalized note in your word processor to that effect, sort your client list of those clients that would be interested in the new reduced fare and mail merge the two files. The result is a personalized letter addressed to your client advising them of new fares they would be interested in. Clients love this sort of approach and they will remember you for your thoughtfulness and proactive efforts.

FLYERS

Flyers on many topics can be designed and printed on your laser printer, copied, and sent to your clients when you find that airfares to a destination have plunged or possibly a tour operator has introduced a special discounted package to Hawaii. Lets say that there are some special airfares that you may want to let your clients know about. A quick flyer announcing the airfares and rules may stimúlate immediate phone calls. Designing a flyer around a special cruise, tour or resort discount deal will arouse your client's interest. They will call about the special and possibly book something else as a result. Flyers designed to pass along local information are also helpful. A map of your local airport arrival and departure terminals or a map and list of rates for off airport parking or any other information your clients are apt to keep and appreciate.

There is a good range of software capable of producing quality flyers for the offering of travel to clients. Microsoft Publisher 2.0 (Also good for newsletters) is an excellent choice and makes it very easy to produce excellent travel flyers for just about any purpose. Print Artist is another excellent product and allows you to do some outrageous things with type that no other program does. At the end of this chapter are flyers done in each of these programs so you may see their capacity. Again, there are several other programs that are very effective and are available from your computer store.

ADVERTISEMENTS AND ARTICLES

When you see an advertisement or article in the newspaper, trade publication, or any other source you can easily sort your mailing list for clients who have expressed an interest in the destination, cruise or other subject of the advertisement or article. Simply make a copy of the piece and personalize it with a note letting them know you are watching out for their best interest and send it to them first class mail. You will be amazed at the response with which this effort will reward you.

BROCHURES

Often times suppliers will share the cost of mailing their products or offerings to clients on your mailing list. This is a great opportunity to kill two birds with one stone. You will benefit from the reduced cost of the mailing to your selected clients and you also benefit from potential sales created by the endeavor.

GREETING CARDS

Christmas, Secretary's Week, New Years, Birthdays, and

Anniversaries all represent opportunities to touch base with your customers. A specially designed greeting card welcoming your clients home from their cruise, tour, or trip is an excellent way to start them talking about their next vacation or trip. The best time to schedule a "welcome home" letter or postcard is when you are finalizing the client's file and preparing to give the client documents. Simply fill out your letter or postcard, sign it and stamp it and file it in a tickler file to be mailed the week your client returns. Every Monday check your tickler file for correspondence that requires mailing that week. Your clients will love the attention.

CALL TO ACTION

Be sure every mailing you send has a direct call to action that prompts your client to pick up the phone or send something through the mail to you. Response cards and redeemable discount coupons are two effective ways to get client reaction. When using exploratory mailings always demand that your prospects either mail in a reply or call you on the telephone. When mailing a series of pieces to an exploratory list build in a mandatory response to continue receiving the mailing. If, after having sent an appropriate number of pieces, the recipient shows no interest and fails to reply to your call to action by not responding, you should remove them from your list.

SAMPLE TRAVEL FLYERS

Following are two sample travel flyers. The cruise flyer is done in Print Artist with clip art from the Corel Gallery CD. The Hawaii flyer is done in Microsoft Publisher 2.0 using the Click Art 25,000 CD collection.

Chapter 17
TRAVEL ADVERTISING

One of the most difficult tasks in marketing travel is to implement a viable advertising campaign. There are several reasons for this. The most common problem one encounters is that the products generally offered by a home based travel agency are the same that can be purchased from any travel agency. Whether you are advertising a cruise, tour, airfare, or resort your competition can intercept the demand created by your advertising and turn it into their sale. If you think about it, aren't you requested to call your travel agent in just about every travel advertisement you see?

Another difficult issue is one of penetration. If you place an advertisement in one of the major newspaper Sunday travel sections only one out of ten thousand readers might be considering your particular destination, cruise, or other product at that time. For these reasons, many home based travel entrepreneurs have opted for the cost efficiency of direct mail newsletters and correspondence instead.

There are many instances when consumer advertising can pay off and following is some discussion of the various advertising opportunities a home based travel agency has.

NEWSPAPER ADVERTISING

The best newspaper advertising for a home based travel agency is located in your local newspapers. If you are fortunate enough to be located in a community that has a local paper with circulation within a region that is similar to scope of your market area you might explore advertising on a weekly basis as a way to develop a continuous flow of new clients.

Local newspapers can work well if your advertising is consistent and dominates your field. Lets say your business specialty is sending folks to Hawaii and no other agent regularly advertises Hawaii as a destination. You may be able to dominate your local Hawaii business by establishing yourself as the Hawaii expert in the area through newspaper advertising. If there is a regional paper with a large Sunday travel section in it be sure to check for your specialization. If no agents are advertising your particular specialty you may again be able to dominate your specific market segment for a reasonably small investment.

Generally. the largest advertisement will dominate a particular market segment and if there is no competition you may be able to dominate with only 1 or 2 column inches. By reducing your market specialty down to one or two keys words you can let folks know what you do in a very small advertisement. After prolonged exposure to your advertisement week after week they will remember you and call when they have need for your specific services.

Advertisements that are general in nature or do not offer a specific call to action are not productive. Your advertising should say what you do or what your are offering in as bold, yet brief, a presentation as possible. You should give just enough information that the potential client will have to pick up the phone and call to get more details. The best travel advertisements consist of destination, price, business name, and phone number and not much more. A good exercise is to rapidly glance through your travel section and see what advertisements catch your eye and why. Pretend you want information about your specialty and see what your competition is doing.

You can negotiate with the newspaper for annual rates depending on how many column inches you intend to use during the year. Many times the newspaper will also throw in some editorial coverage of your business. Be sure to ask who you can send press releases and articles too. One of the oldest tricks in the world for travel agents is to purchase advertising on a bulk contract and then charge back the regular retail open contract rate to the supplier with whom you are cooperating on the advertisement.

MAGAZINES

Magazines that are focused on your specific market can be an excellent way to advertise. If your market is a special interest tour, sport, activity, or some other specific topic that either consumer or trade magazines are published about, you should pursue their advertising rates and policies to see if they are feasible. Obviously, if every Tom, Dick, and Harry is already advertising make sure you can dominate your particular market segment.

YELLOW PAGES

Yellow page advertising can be an excellent way to develop a continual flow of new client contacts. If you review the Yellow Pages in your area and the existing travel agencies are running generic advertisements that do not identify their various specialties you have an excellent opportunity of again dominating your specific market. Say your business plan is to establish yourself a an African Safari specialist and there is currently not an agent advertising this specialty at all. You may be able to direct every interested party to call you for their arrangements with a small but effective advertisement. Simply browse through the Yellow Pages pretending to be a client interested in the services that you offer. If there is no competition you may be able to dominate the Yellow Pages with a 1/15th page advertisement.

THROWAWAY PAPERS, PENNYSAVERS, CHURCH NEWSLETTERS, NEWSPAPERS WITHOUT TRAVEL SECTIONS

In our humble opinion, forget it. No matter how cheap the advertising sounds....it doesn't work and nothing is more expensive than advertising that doesn't produce sales.

ADVERTISING SPECIALTIES

An excellent way to promote your business to new clients and keep your name in front of existing clients is by using a wide variety of advertising specialties. Printing your business identity on pens, photo albums, flight schedules, paper clip holders, hats, tee shirts and so on can really pay off. Advertising specialties is an excellent way to invest in your future. Advertising specialty companies can be found in your yellow pages under "advertising specialties".

COOPERATIVE ADVERTISING

Many of the travel suppliers will cooperate on advertising in your local travel section and pick up half of the cost of the advertisement. This can be very advantageous especially if your identity is established in the market place. Contact the sales office of your suppliers to find out their cooperative advertising policies.

SAMPLE TRAVEL ADVERTISEMENTS

Following are some advertisements that have been put together for both newspaper advertising and yellow page advertising.

Chapter 18
TRAVEL PROMOTIONS

One of the best ways to gain exposure for your business is by entering into an aggressive promotional campaign. There are all sorts of different types of promotions a home based agency can cultivate and the results can be outstanding. By entering into a well planned crusade the home based travel entrepreneur can establish an identity within their community without having to carry the load of overhead demanded by a storefront location.

Promotional opportunities exist in all communities and present themselves frequently. To successfully take advantage of the opportunities you should have an ongoing plan of attack to exploit the promotions. Many folks think that becoming involved in various promotional activity will require substantial investment and nothing could be further from the truth.

Following are various types of promotions you may become involved in with excellent success.

WHAT KINDS OF TRAVEL PROMOTIONS ARE THERE?

T R A V E L S H O W S

Many communities put on formal consumer travel shows. They generally charge for a booth in the show portion and then charge the consumers to come into the event. Travel shows can be good but for the most part it is difficult to distinguish yourself from the rest of the crowd. Larger communities occasionally generate hundreds of exhibitors which makes it extremely difficult for a small agency to stand out in the crowd. If you have a specialty that would be of interest to a good number of the participants and the cost of the booth would be easily absorbed by the profit of new revenue that the show would generate, then participating in travel shows makes considerable sense. Local travel promotions hosted by shopping malls, Chambers of Commerce, and other business organizations are inclined to be more productive and are less expensive to participate in. If you intend to pursue travel shows as a method of meeting prospective clients you should investigate obtaining a professional trade show booth back drop or table top display to enhance your professionalism.

CRUISE NIGHTS

Cruise nights are a great way to turn new prospects into clients fast. There are a number of variations but a cruise night is a promotion you create for the purpose of meeting potential clients and selling cruises. You may involve one or more cruise lines who also host the event as well as other businesses with whom you may enjoy a symbiotic relationship. You need ample time to promote the event which will involve direct mail, advertising, and personal invitations.

First you would book a meeting room or rooms in a local hotel or other facility. Make sure you have abundant space for the exhibits of your partners the cruise lines. You can charge a nominal amount for clients to gain entrance into the cruise night and use the funds to offset potential costs for food, drinks and the like. You can start by inviting all of your existing clients by offering them free or discounted tickets and extending the offer to their immediate friends and neighbors. You can try purchasing a quality mailing list of potential cruisers and send direct mail invitations to the folks and follow up with discount tickets. You can advertise the event in your local newspaper three to four weeks in advance and make discount tickets available at the various businesses that are participating in the event. Luggage stores, formal wear rental businesses, wedding planners, photographers, and fine clothing stores all have business to be gained from exposure to potential cruisers. As your cruise night comes closer you may widen the invitation circle by advertising special cruise discounts participants can expect just for attending the cruise night. This will entice even your competitors clients into the event.

On the evening that you operate the cruise night be sure to have enough people on hand to circulate flyers offering special discounts for signing up right on the spot. Get every participant's name, address, and phone number for subsequent follow up and have lots of door prizes. Each cruise line that participates in the event will do presentations on their various ships and itineraries making your job that much easier.

TOUR/DESTINATION NIGHTS

Sponsoring a Hawaii night, Caribbean night, Mexico night or some other destination is an equally effective method of meeting new clients and securing old ones. The operation is basically the same as a cruise night but you can depend on newspaper advertising a little more heavily to produce potential clients. It is a bit more difficult to get people to pay to attend destination nights unless you offer a formal showing or presentation of the destination itself. Most tourist boards are not responsive and most hotels and tour operators are more interested in selling their own products instead.

TRAVEL SEMINARS

Assuming that you have narrowed your business focus down to an area of specialization it is easy to produce a 60 or 90 minute seminar that you can offer the various clubs, associations, special interest groups, schools, and other organizations that are continually looking for presentations. If your specialization is broad enough to run advertisements in the travel section offering fee or free seminars on your destination or specialization you may be able to pack an auditorium with prospective clients considering your products.

TRAVEL CLUBS

You may want to consider starting your own "Travel Club". By starting a travel club you can charge your clients an annual fee for the right of receiving your newsletters and offer them discounts on their future travel. Cruise clubs, senior travel clubs, ethnic travel clubs, alumni travel clubs, ski clubs, golf travel clubs, and SCUBA diving clubs are all examples of specialties that can be organized into travel clubs.

SPECIALIZED NEWSLETTERS AND BOOKS

If your specialization requires a good deal of extraordinary information you may be able to start a formal newsletter on the topic and feature your travel offerings as a part of the newsletter. The additional credibility that publishing a newsletter or book brings you, makes your travel offerings that much more enticing.

WHAT OPPORTUNITIES EXIST IN THE COMMUNITY TO PROMOTE TRAVEL?

While the above examples are primarily focused on travel promotions exclusively many opportunities exist for the home based travel entrepreneur to obtain great exposure to new potential clients by participating in community clubs, associations, and events. Following are some of the more obvious.

CHAMBER OF COMMERCE AND OTHER BUSINESS GROUPS

You can meet more people and make better contacts at a Chamber mixer or meeting than anywhere. Just about every business person in your community will show up at a Chamber function, meeting, or mixer at some point in time and the recognition you can achieve by maintaining a high profile is excellent. If there is a local business association in addition to the Chamber of Commerce explore the opportunity it offers.

LOCAL CHURCHES AND SERVICE CLUBS

All of the local service clubs like Rotary, Lions, Elks, Optimists, political clubs, parent/teacher clubs, garden clubs, and so on are a wealth of potential new clients. Your church is another opportunity to gain widespread exposure. Being involved in your community gives everyone a chance to get to know you and feel comfortable about calling you with their travel needs.

STREET FAIRS, FUND RAISERS, AND PARADES

Here is your opportunity to really show your stuff. If your community is having a street fair you can take out a booth and disseminate information about your specialty. Join a parade and go in the costume of your specialty. Get involved in fund raisers answering phones and give away an inexpensive prize for the exposure. These unselfish acts go very far in establishing your integrity in the community.

PRESS RELEASES AND TRAVEL ARTICLES

By entering into a program of consistently issuing press releases and travel articles about your business for your local papers you can get your name in print on a steady schedule. Your press releases can incorporate a story about one of your client's or one of the communities' leading citizens, recent trip, cruise, seminar, or whatever they purchased from you. Include a photograph or two from the trip that your client provides and the local papers are sure to publish it. This works to your advantage in two ways. First, your client will love the stroke of being seen by their peers in print and second other clients will respond positively to the fact that your clients are so notable. They may secretly desire to get into the newspaper as a result of purchasing their travel from you. Consistent exposure in your local paper as the agent who sends everyone on their vacation is proof positive of your credibility.

Whenever you pick up something in the trade publications that might be interesting to your community take a few minutes and write a brief article about the information. It could be a new carrier serving your market, a State Department advisory, a political event, promotional airfares, anything that could be of interest. Do a press release and send the press release and article to the various publications in your area and watch them get published. Don't give up if the first few aren't printed just keep sending them. Small newspaper keep "fillers" for months waiting for the need to fill space on a page and interesting travel articles written by local agents rate highest among publishers.

JOINT PROMOTIONS

Many businesses in your community share the same client list with travel agents, Sophisticated clothiers, photographers, SCUBA dive shops, wedding planners, formal clothing rental businesses, luxury car dealers, luggage stores, quality furniture dealers, boat brokers, small airplane brokers, ski stores, stock brokers, insurance agents, realtors, and a good number more are constantly looking for ways to increase their mailing list and business. Perhaps you could do a joint promotion with your local Mercedes Benz dealer, maybe offer a trip to the factory and offer a Europe pick up for new automobiles purchased through the local dealer. Perhaps you could use their facility for a cruise night or tour night. Maybe you could have a dive travel promotion selling a Caribbean cruise with diving at a local dive shop and you could give the dive shop owner an incentive to sell his clients as well as develop new dive clients through your joint advertising in the newspaper.

WELCOME WAGON PROMOTION

This is a great promotion if you are in an area that does not currently have a welcome wagon and are experiencing growth. Simply go to the same folks as mentioned above and get them to agree to pay you a nominal fee to expose their business in a one on one sales pitch under the favorable identity of the local welcome wagon. Of course, you pitch four or five other companies during the welcoming presentation but you also get to know the folks personally and have the opportunity to become their travel agent before they have had to search for one in a more traditional method. You make money representing the other businesses and derive credibility from the association with such companies and also get first choice of the newly arrived clients in town.

Chapter 19
TRAVEL MARKETING TECHNIQUES FOR THE NINETIES

Personal computers, telecommunications, networking, and the entrepreneurial era have ushered in new techniques of marketing and communication for business. These new concepts have allowed home based travel agents to expand their marketing activities into arenas once reserved for only the largest of travel organizations. Toll free 800 telephone numbers, E Mail, on-line services, the internet, fax broadcasting, voice mail, fax on demand and database marketing are just a few of the ideas that have changed the way we do business.

The home based travel entrepreneur is in an excellent position to take advantage of the technological revolution that has created great opportunity for small businesses all over the nation. By focusing your marketing energy on some of the more traditional efforts and some of the new technology that has become available you can guarantee success for your venture. Following are just some of the opportunities you may elect to exploit.

PORTABLE AUTOMATION, NOTEBOOK COMPUTERS

Nothing impresses a client more than offering to bring your travel agency into their home. By using a notebook computer and a portable printer you can offer the personal service to your clients of setting your travel agency up in their own home at their leisure. It is simple. Just load your travel reservations software onto the hard drive of your notebook computer. Be sure to keep a printout of the local access telephone numbers with you so you can dial into a toll free number wherever your client lives. You can simply visit your client, plug their telephone jack into the modem in your notebook computer and go on-line.

You will impress your client with your efficiency and ability to access huge amounts of information. When you book, confirm, obtain seat assignments and make special meal requests right on your client's dining room table your clients will applaud your service. When you have completed the reservation process you can simply press one key and generate a complete travel agency itinerary and invoice of the transaction for your client right on the spot.

You may also use notebook computers and portable printers to access on-line services. You may download testimonials about ships and destinations, or figure current currency exchange rates, up to the minute weather reports, snow conditions at various ski areas, State Department travel advisories, hotel information and destination information. Finally, a quick search of any computer software store will reveal numerous travel related titles for both your hard drive and CD ROM. Street maps for the entire United States and Europe, world atlases, city maps and virtually every detail about every country in the world is available. Travel planners for every major city worldwide are available that feature information about restaurants, golf courses, hotels, motels, resorts, shopping and sightseeing. Vacation planners, airfare databases, Bed and Breakfast directories, hotel directories, worldwide golf course guides are just some of the types of programs available.

TRAVEL VIDEOS

Nothing sells travel as videos can. There are hundreds of travel videos on every destination, ship and port that can help you sell travel faster and more efficiently. You should start your travel video library by acquiring videos that fall within your specific area of specialization and continually add to it every opportunity you get. You can use travel videos in a number of different ways. First, there is nothing better than a travel video coupled with a brochure of the cruise line, tour company or destination as a way for you to increase your own personal knowledge of a product or destination. By previewing the video, reviewing the brochure and then enjoying the video again, you get an excellent idea of the personality of the product or destination.

Your clients will appreciate the opportunity to take a travel video home to enjoy at their leisure when they are considering a specific itinerary, ship, port or destination for their vacation. The best part is that the videos generally answer the vast majority of their questions and make the task of completing the sale effortless. Your clients will be more satisfied with their arrangements after being exposed to a thorough video presentation of their vacation choice. They will perceive the information they have received as more valid than just a verbal presentation back up with the brochure. Many travel entrepreneurs offer the use of videos through the mail to prospective clients and often feature specific videos that have continuity with the cruises and destinations featured in their newsletters.

Many retail video rental businesses welcome travel videos provided by travel agencies for rental to their clients. You can have a short trailer made for each video you supply that features your agency and specialization with a call to action. You can also provide the video store with discount coupons for the cruise or destination featured on the video they rent. If a customer rents a Hawaii video, they see a 30 second commercial for your agency and are given a discount coupon for a Hawaii vacation they can redeem by simply calling you for information about Hawaii. Generally, the video store will keep the money generated from the rental but will provide you with the name and address of the customer for follow up. A large travel video library will set you apart from store front agencies that do not use video to sell their leisure products.

ON-LINE AND BULLETIN BOARD SERVICES

By simply purchasing an on-line starter kit for CompuServe, America On-Line, MSN, Prodigy, Gemini or many other on-line services you can access clients every day. These clients are looking for information and to make travel reservations for cruises, tours, airline tickets, hot- els and so forth. In addition to various reservations and informational databases, most on-line services promote live interactive "forums" where you can communicate with other forum members world wide. In CompuServe, as an example, there is a travel forum for every part of the world from Asia to Hawaii, from Africa to Japan, from Florida to Alaska. In every forum, members post messages to obtain information about their particular interest.

Let us say that your particular specialization is Hawaii. You could join CompuServe's travel forum and become active in the "Hawaii Help Line." Every day in this forum folks post messages looking for information on where to stay, what to do and where to go in Hawaii. Once you have picked up the message you can simply post your reply in the open forum for everyone to read. You can then E-mail your toll free telephone number and an offer of professional assistance to the person who posted the message. It is just that simple. Many home based travel entrepreneurs have made careers of working the on-line services and have built up quite nice businesses without every meeting even one of their clients in person.

If your specialization warrants an exceptional amount of electronic communication you can establish your own bulletin board and operate it as the system operator (SYSOP). Clients and individuals would dial into your system to access the multitude of information you offer and to communicate via E-mail with other members of the bulletin board. This direction is highly viable where your clients share a common interest or affinity and are located throughout the country. Another possibility is to create your own forum, open or hidden, on one of the main on-line services. Simply contact the SYSOP of the on-line service you are interested in to pursue the viability of your idea.

THE INTERNET

More than any other current marketing opportunity, the Internet is emerging as the most explosive distribution opportunity of the nineties. According to a survey by Nielsen Media Research for Commerce Net, one in six people that reside in the United States and Canada has used the internet. More than one in ten have used it during the last three months and about 2.6 million users have already made purchases on the World Wide Web.

The travel industry has flocked to the World Wide Web with virtually every major supplier in the industry establishing their own home page on the Web. The Internet is a wonderful place to obtain information and communicate with suppliers. It is also an extremely good place to find clients who are looking for information about your specific area of expertise. Many home based travel entrepreneurs are establishing their own home page and transacting business with people from all over the globe.

At the time of this writing (January 1996) America On-line and CompuServe are both refining their access to the World Wide Web simplifying passage onto the Web. They have also reduced their access fees to an affordable level and developed several types of flat fee access. The first cable TV access to the Net has been established in Sunnyvale, California and is expected to be the fastest growth area for new users. Download time using cable compared with telephone lines is nearly 500 times faster. Data is transferred via cable at an extraordinary rate of 10 to 27 million bits per second. For instance, computer users could download a movie off the Internet and onto their hard drives in nine seconds via cable. This would take approximately 27 minutes via telephone lines now.

The Internet is growing so fast and has so many applications for the travel industry that at least one travel trade publication, *Travel Weekly*, tracks all of the new World Wide Web home page sites established by travel organizations and reports them in their twice weekly publication.

NETWORKING

Networking seems to be the buzz word of the nineties. There are numerous networking organizations in every corner of the United States and they can be highly lucrative for the home based travel agent. To take advantage of these organizations simply look in your local newspaper business section for meetings taking place in your area. When you see organization meetings that sound interesting to you simply call them up and inquire about attending. The reason that they advertise in the first place is to encourage new members like yourself to join and broaden the sphere of influence of the organization.

Networking groups have the ability to pass along a good amount of relevant information regarding the possibilities of approaching new accounts and people connected to the group. Since a good number of the folks connected with the members of the networking group travel you are in a good position to gain valuable information at every meeting. You can join more than one networking group if they are dissimilar in the makeup of their membership and you may start your own if you really want to control the environment in which it operates.

VOICE MAIL

Let voice mail answer your telephone and handle all of your basic requests. Integrating voice mail into your operation will allow you to take extended leaves from your business to meet clients wherever you need to without the stigma of sounding like a one person operation. When you are either at home, or away from home, voice mail will answer your telephone with a professional greeting and offer your clients numerous options to choose from. If they want brochures, press two. If they want information regarding an upcoming tour, press three. To leave a message, press four. For a flyer on your fax on demand program, press five, and so on. Voice mail can qualify your inbound telephone calls even when you are home. Your first voice mail message could be, "If you would like to speak with.....push one. You can see how voice mail will help you streamline your communication.

FAX ON DEMAND AND FAX BACK PROGRAMS

Many telephone calls you receive from existing and potential clients alike are specific requests for information regarding travel. Tourist cards, state department advisories, discounted cruises, groups you are promoting, advertised specials and so on are likely reasons for people to call. It is very uncomplicated to have your clients call your voice mail and select an option for fax on demand where they can choose from a list of documents you have available for immediate transmission to their facsimile machines. The client simply chooses the document and prompts your computer to transmit the document. Fax on demand requires a facsimile modem and fax on demand software that is readily available through personal computer magazines or your computer software store.

A fax back program works like fax on demand except the client simply punches in their fax number and hangs up. The Fax back software then dials your client back and transmits the chosen documents. Fax back programs are less attractive as you must incur the cost of the call back to transmit the fax.

Both programs record the calling numbers so you may capture them for future fax blasts. Fax on demand and fax back programs can reduce your costs greatly by allowing your clients to access information that would normally require you to discuss it with your client and then mail it out to them.

MARKETING VIA FACSIMILE

Marketing via facsimile is one of the most efficient and cost effective ways to communicate with existing and potential clients. "Fax blast" or "fax broadcast" are the terms coined for the process of sending many facsimile transmissions to various clients in a single event. A typical fax broadcast may include five hundred transmissions. When the event is scheduled during the lowest long distance telephone rate period during a twenty-four hour day the cost per delivery may average only eleven cents each.

Facsimile broadcasting is accomplished using a personal computer equipped with a facsimile modem, usually operating at 14,400 or 28,800 bits per second. The appropriate facsimile management software is also needed to complete the package. The software allows you to enter your client's fax numbers into "phone books" by group. These groups then become the target of a facsimile event. The groups may be segregated by any criteria you would like. Say you want to broadcast everyone in the 213 area code, no problem. Winfax Pro 4.0 is an excellent choice for facsimile management software. It works just like your printer in Windows and is simply a print option on your printer menu. With Winfax Pro 4.0 you can do everything possible to effectively maintain an ongoing facsimile broadcast marketing program.

Lets say you have a group that is interested in Hawaii and another interested in domestic airfares. You simply create a flyer in one of your publishing programs, select Winfax Pro from your print menu, select the group you would like to broadcast and then schedule the event to start when the phone rates go down. It is that easy. The next morning when your clients arrive at their office there is a fax waiting for them with the latest information from you.

Facsimile broadcasts are extremely valuable in announcing airline pricing actions or airfare wars when time is of the essence for your clients to obtain the best fares and availability. When you hear of an airfare war simply broadcast your clients and watch the telephone ring off the hook. If the airfare war starts on a Friday night be sure to let your clients know that you will be available all day Saturday. Use your dial up reservation software to access your reservations system and process your client's requests right in the comfort of your own home while other travel agents are missing the boat. By the time Monday morning rolls around and your store front competitors finally open their doors to help their clients you have scooped the business. Most important you have made your clients extremely happy to be dealing with you.

DATABASE MARKETING

Database marketing is the term coined for using a relational database to control information about your client's travel patterns, desires, interest and other facts. By using an extensive database you can focus your communication with those clients that have expressed interest in whatever information you pass along. Your Hawaii clients are surely going to want to know when the airfares drop. Your cruise clients interested in doing the Southern Caribbean on a cruise ship are surely going to want to know of any special sailing. Your commercial accounts are going to want to know when an airfare war breaks out. These are all good examples of how database marketing can focus your efforts for maximum results.

Microsoft Access is an excellent relational database that is fully integrated with Microsoft Word and Excel. You can develop a client "survey" (see chapter 21) to obtain information from your clients to insert into your database. Once you have established your database you may sort the information in any number of ways. If you would like a list of all your clients that cruise, no problem. A list of clients that have visited Europe, are frequent flyers on United Airlines and also have shown an interest in skiing, is easy to compile. With a relational database you can build queries into the database that encompass any number of criteria. You can sort by the criteria and then print mailing labels, mail merge the list with Word, or create a phone book in your facsimile program.

CONTACT MANAGEMENT

One of the best ways to control the flow of communication between you and your client is with contact management software for your personal computer. Contact management software allows you to do a good number of things more effectively than a normal database.

First contact management software is a database in itself. You can generally create unlimited records with unlimited fields to sort by and you can maintain records of all contact history within each client record. You may also find all of your client contact data quickly and initiate a telephone call by simply autodialing your client's telephone number with one keystroke.

Contact management software also allows you to schedule meetings, telephone calls, things to do and just about any event well into the future. You can then view your calendar by the day, week or month to see the flow of your schedule. If there are items on your daily calendar that do not get accomplished your contact management software will automatically roll them over into the next day's activities.

You can generate reports on just about any of the information in your contact management program. Client lists sorted by various data, appointment schedules and contact activity by client, day, week or month are just some of the reports you can generate. Most contact management programs also include a word processor for mail merge with your client database. You can also print out mailing labels, envelopes and other information regarding your client list. One of the most important features to look for is the ability to create a fax merge with your facsimile management software so that you can sort your client base by whatever criteria you would like and then merge their fax numbers into a special group for a facsimile event.

ACT by Symentec is one contact management software program that meets all of the above qualifying factors for consideration. While there are many to choose from be sure the program you select is compatible with your word processor, database and facsimile programs.

Chapter 20
COLD CALLS, CANVASSING, AND TELEMARKETING

When most people think about making cold calls on prospective customers they think of the proverbial door to door salesman and get chills running up and down their spine. When people think of canvassers out mass distributing flyers door to door or telemarketers trying to sell printer ribbons to unsuspecting secretaries, less than desirable images ensue. In all actuality direct client contact is the very best way to meet potential new customers. A well executed program of direct sales to clients can reward the home based travel entrepreneur with substantial revenues and growth. Direct sales only requires a little effort and perseverance to yield huge rewards. Following are some ideas about direct client sales.

COLD CALLS, THE SECRET TO SUCCESS

Most people consider cold calls as the most difficult type of client development there is. Nothing could be further from the truth. When you think about it, all that cold calls represent is talking to people about something everyone loves to talk about....their next vacation or trip. Your approach to the subject is what is important and there are several ways to effectively break the ice.

DOOR TO DOOR COLD CALLS

This is without question the best way to develop new clients. Here is how you can do it and have fun. Design a two page newsletter in your Desktop Publisher and be sure to feature articles and offers everyone can relate to. Use a Hawaii program, a Caribbean cruise, a Mexico beach package, a 7 day Europe city package, a honeymoon resort program, and so on. On the bottom of page two put what appears to be a blank check with the amount and signature left blank. Pick an area where there are a number of businesses and start calling on every one in order. Set your objective in advance of say ten meaningful discussions so that you know when you are done. Continue your door to door effort until you have made ten meaningful contacts and then stop. You should carry your notebook computer with you in case someone needs immediate information on airfares or availability. This will absolutely dazzle them.

The door to door calls should go something like this: "Hi my name is....I own ABC Travel here in town. I was in the area delivering tickets and thought I would stop in and introduce myself.....Do you folks use a travel agent?" The response is either yes or no and either way will lead into a conversation about the next travel event the person you are talking with is planning. "Look, I would love to have the opportunity to work with you on that reservation." Of course by this time you have determined the potential value of the account or event. "Why don't you give me a chance to give you a competitive price on that tour, cruise or whatever. If you like my service and price I will give you the first fifty dollars towards your vacation just as a thank you for giving me the opportunity to handle your business." Now you simply write out the voucher in the amount of fifty dollars or whatever is appropriate and give the newsletter to your new client. Take one of their business cards to "register" the certificate in their name.

This method works every time and is an excellent way to qualify new business accounts and pick up the personal travel of the employees at the same time, Of course, once you "register" the voucher that you wrote you include the new client in your client database for future mailings and facsimile broadcasts. These "checks" will roll in for months after the initial contact and continually create new clients and referrals.

The key to success for this cold call sales strategy is to maintain a consistent level of activity. If you choose to make your goal ten quality communications a week then budget time to accomplish ten and no more. Keep going until you have achieved the ten you have committed to. If you make several calls on accounts where there is no possibility of travel or they are not in, do not count these in your ten meaningful calls. Only calls resulting in potential new business count.

MEETINGS, SEMINARS, CLASSES, AND OTHER EVENTS

An excellent way to contact potential new clients is by attending various public meetings, seminars, classes and so on. Wherever people get together is an excellent place to casually meet new people who are interested in travel. Keep an eye on your local newspaper for meetings that look interesting to you and that you think might attract people interested in travel. Take plenty of business cards and do not lose your focus. During breaks, before and after the events circulate and meet as many people as you can.

MEETING TRAVELERS WHILE TRAVELING

This is another excellent way to meet potential new clients. You should already budget time and money for cruises and trips to resort areas for your own familiarization why not make it a sales trip to boot. The best way to meet new clients while traveling is to budget time for the express purpose of making cold calls on your fellow travelers. It is as simple as climbing into the jacuzzi and starting a conversation about travel, or perhaps at the dinner table with your dinner partners, or maybe while on tour in a motorcoach. Wherever you make your connection it is easy to relate to someone experiencing the same ship, resort, or tour that you are and it is also easy to make a business connection. Be sure to carry lots of business cards and have a toll free telephone number for your new clients to call. Put them on your active mailing list and database as well.

CANVASSING, A QUICK WAY TO ESTABLISH YOUR BUSINESS

Canvassing differs from making cold calls because the objective in canvassing is to get as much information out about your business or offerings as fast as possible. While ten meaningful conversations a day is an excellent goal for cold calls you might want to distribute a thousand flyers to potential clients per day under an aggressive program.

Lets say you are located in a commercial area where there are factories and want to spread the word about an upcoming motorcoach tour. You might print some flyers up and post them on windshields of the employees cars or you might want to distribute a pile of flyers to each business to be put in the employees lounge for exposure. Door to door canvassing in residential areas is also effective if you are delivering general newsletters with some sort of call to action in them that would motivate consumers to register or some other response to express further interest. Canvassing can be done by yourself or you can hire people to canvas an area for hours, days, or weeks at a time. Canvassing can be very effective as long as you do not distribute anything offensive and obtain approval before you plaster all of the cars in a parking lot.

Canvassing is best done by you for a couple of reasons. First, you may run into people who immediately respond to your newsletter and want information on the spot. If you are relying on someone else they will probably not be able to answer questions that could lead into immediate sales. Second, by working a mobile home park, residential community, commercial district or apartment complex by yourself you have the opportunity to get the real feel of potential in a given canvassing area.

TELEMARKETING FOR THE NINETIES

Telemarketing is the buzzword for making cold calls via telephone rather than in person. Telemarketing travel can be very effective especially if you include instant fax in your approach. Basically, you can call a potential client and offer information regarding a specific product and offer to transmit a facsimile while speaking with the potential client. As you speak you can personalize a cover sheet to the client and send the fax over a separate phone line. During the time it takes for the transmittal to occur you can pursue the opening conversation. Once the fax has been sent you can allow the potential client a day or so to review the information and call back for any questions. This method works very well with commercial accounts and business where it is difficult to get an appointment with the appropriate party. After several phone calls and faxes, the potential client feels as if they know you and will grant an appointment at the first request.

Key to the success of a telemarketing program is the follow up with written material. Whether sent via mail or facsimile you must pursue the client past the original telephone communication. Of course, if you determine that the client has no potential business forget them and move on to the next. Many times you can use reverse directories at the library to identify possible customers and call with the reference of the local Chamber of Commerce or some other well known business group. By using this reference they are much more likely to speak with you the first time. Telemarketing can result in additional sales especially if you take the approach of establishing a long term relationship with the prospect.

Chapter 21
ORGANIZING YOUR MARKETING FILES

Your marketing files should be organized for action. The most effective way to maintain your existing clients and increase your new client list is by maintaining active and detailed marketing files. Your files should be easily accessed for use each and every day and should be kept current on a daily basis.

Simple is the name of the game when it comes to your client profile forms and action files. By integrating a proactive marketing campaign with these tools you may rest assured your clients will never stray to far without your knowing about it. There are numerous software programs that offer excellent sales follow up and contact management but for the purpose of this book here are some basic ways to guarantee an effective marketing program.

YOUR PASSENGER PROFILE FORM

The passenger profile form will become one of your most important tools of your trade. Don't we all feel special when someone remembers the correct way to spell our name and that we have a fond preference for seafood meals when on a flight? Little things go a long, long way. How about sending an anniversary card to the couple you sent on their honeymoon to Jamaica? These personal sales tactics are proven winners when selling travel.

The client profile form following these descriptions is only an example of one you may develop for your particular business and you may embellish on it in great detail. Most of the areas on the passenger profile are self explanatory. Following are some reasons why sections of the form can be so important to the success of your working relationship with your valued clients.

DATE

It is very important to date these profiles so that you can be assured the information is current. It is always a good idea to update the form every six months to be sure there are no changes that may affect the level of service you provide.

SPOUSE

Here is a helpful hint with the spouse's name. If your client Mr. Jones is married, don't assume his wife uses the name Mrs. Jones. Today so many ladies are maintaining their maiden names and or using a hyphenated name as in Mrs. Walker-Jones. Correct usage of names and spelling when arranging travel for your clients is one of the most important tasks requiring your expertise.

CHILDREN

Here is a great idea! Why not get the children's names and ages or birth dates for your form? If you date your form as mentioned above you can easily tell how old the children are each time you plan a trip where they will be traveling. It is important information for fares and prices as children sometimes pay a lessor fare than adults. It is equally important to be so on top of things that you need not even ask the parent the age of the child. Imagine how impressed you would be if your child just turned twelve last month and your agent said, "Well, it looks like little Andy just turned twelve, I will check to be sure we get the appropriate fare for your child. Be sure to wish him a belated Happy Birthday for me." Are you in touch with your clients or what?

RESIDENCE ADDRESS AND PHONE

If the only contact you have with the client is via a home phone or address you would not hesitate to use this information. On the other hand, if you are handling a business account for an individual, never assume that you should call him or her at home if they are unavailable at their office. Some folks do not mix business and pleasure and would be offended if you intruded in their personal lives. It is easy enough just to ask you client if they would like to be contacted at home and obtain their permission.

BUSINESS TITLE AND SECRETARY

These are two areas that may change frequently so it is recommended that you use a pencil. If Mr. Smith has just been promoted to Vice-President of his firm he certainly would not appreciate a letter addressed to him as Sales Consultant. Often times the secretary of your client will become your lifeline to the client's needs and desires. Creating a close and friendly relationship with the secretary or assistant will usually help serve your client more professionally. Sometimes you will never even have the opportunity to speak to the person who you send all over the world instead their secretary is your contact for all details. Therefore, remember him or her on special days and keep that line of communication open. Many times the secretary will become a client as well as they have become so dependent on your expertise and suggestions.

FAX NUMBER

In a previous chapter we discussed a marketing idea to send faxes to your business clients when an airfare has just dropped to a destination they frequent. Often times they can plan their trips in advance to save the company a little money and put a feather in their cap with the boss and the companies bottom line. Here you are the good guy again.

DELIVER TICKETS

As mentioned above under residence address, sometimes folks just don't mix work and home so be sure you are in tune to your client's needs and desires. Ticket delivery is a service and you will want to use it to achieve the optimum results for increased business.

PREFERRED CARRIER

Many folks have one or more airline that they prefer to fly with and here is the area to document that important information. You may even find that your client has a major pet peeve with a particular airline and may refuse to fly them. Be sure you don't ever book them on that carrier, or if they are the only one who flies to the needed destination be sure to let them know before you book them.

Beside the preferred carrier area you will see "ACCOUNT NAME AND MILEAGE#". Most of the airlines have some sort of frequent flyer program and it costs nothing to apply for an account number. Many travel agents offer the service of signing their clients up for these numbers if they do not already have one assigned. In most cases all you need is a name, address, and phone number to get an account set up. Once your client has a frequent flyer account number be sure to give it to the carrier every time your client flies on that airline so that they may begin to accumulate the mileage and earn the benefits. The benefits depend on the actual number of miles your client flies on a given carrier, and are awarded in the form of airfare discount certificates, class upgrades, car and hotel discounts, and even free tickets to domestic and international destinations.

An important item to remember is to have the airline ticket name field match the spelling on the clients account number with that carrier. A simple call to the airline supplying them with the number and name to check on the correct spelling will alleviate the potential problem of a client not receiving air credit on their flights because the name on the account did not match the name on the reservation and ticket. While this may be a small irritation for a less frequent flyer, it can mean the potential loss of a good client to one who travels frequently and enjoys the benefits earned from such.

CLASS OF SERVICE

While this is relatively self explanatory, some folks are very picky about airfares and the class of service they book. While a client may say they fly coach do they really mean coach fare or do they mean in the coach section of the aircraft? There is a big difference between these two points. The coach section of the plane is usually behind the first class and business section and is filled with folks paying all different fare levels.

Coach fare is usually called a "Y" class fare and indicates the client has no penalty restrictions on the fare and that they may change their reservation at will as long as a Y seat is available. The airline may impose a small change fee, but generally they are relatively unrestricted tickets. On the other hand, the man seated next to the fellow with the "Y" coach ticket is also in the coach section but is on a totally restricted ticket. His fare may be much lower than Mr. "Y" Coach, possibly as much as 75% or more, but he must travel on the date he is ticketed for and if he does not use it may forfeit the entire fare.

Many business travellers find it difficult to use these restricted fares because their plans change so frequently. It is usually someone like this who would use "Y" Coach fares because of the inherent flexibility.

SEATING PREFERENCE

This is a most important area of the form to provide good service to your client. Never assume your client will willingly accept a seat other than the one they normally request. Always check with them and advise them what you were able to secure and get their approval that the seat assignment will be acceptable. It may be a case of comfort which controls their preference or it may be a case of fear of flying and that they are better able to handle their feelings in a given area of the aircraft. These fears can be very real for folks and you must give credibility to the importance this may have on their travel plans.

SPECIAL REQUESTS

This is such a fun area from which to service your clients. Many travelers today do not realize that they can choose a special meal in advance. Of course, the meals are relatively limited in choice and are designed to accommodate those people on special dietary restrictions. There is an abbreviated list on the profile form and many more may be available when you contact the airline. A pre-reserved child's meal for your client may make the difference between your client's child eating or not on a flight. Most children get a real kick out of the Mickey Mouse cookies, hamburger, chips, fruit and jello meal. Remember to get the parent's approval first and then begin to win over yet another young client for your business. The "OTHER" area might be used for a client with a special need for a wheelchair or other special circumstance.

RENTAL CAR

Often times your clients will have a preferred company they choose to rent cars from as well as a preferred size. If they have an automobile rental corporate ID # or other membership number this will sometimes enable them to get a better rate on the car or a possible upgrade at a lessor cost.

HOTEL PREFERENCE

The hotel preference section is very similar to the car rental section. Be sure to request a clients preferred bed size and smoking or non smoking rooms if available. As with car rental companies, most larger hotel chains have membership clubs for guests. Once given the membership number it may entitle them to an upgraded room, discount, or other amenities. Many of the larger hotel chains offer airline frequent flyer mileage points for your client's stay so be sure to check when making the reservation.

PAYMENT INFORMATION

While the information here may change as frequently as the weather, it is always a good idea to have current information on file. Have more than one authorized credit card number available in case one is expired or the credit is maximized when you request an authorization code. The authorization area below is very important as it shows your clients willingness to allow you to use these credit cards on their behalf. It is a very good idea to obtain an actual imprint of the card for your files. While this signature will not satisfy the airline if your client decides to deny their charges, it will most certainly show good intent that they did authorize your use of their credit cards for travel in case you have to sue in small claims court. An original credit card imprint and signature on every credit card sale is always your best defense against denied charges.

EXAMPLE OF A CLIENT PROFILE FORM

The following page contains an example of a client profile form you can use to create your existing client files.

PASSENGER PROFILE

DATE_____

PASSENGER NAME(S): _____

SPOUSE/COMPANION: _____

CHILDREN (name(s) & age(s): _____

RESIDENCE ADDRESS: _____

RESIDENCE PHONE: _____ CALL AT HOME: YES   NO

BUSINESS NAME: _____

TITLE: _____ SECRETARY: _____

BUSINESS ADDRESS: _____

BUSINESS PHONE: _____ FAX NUMBER _____

DELIVER TICKETS:(circle one)   TO RESIDENCE   TO BUSINESS

PREFERRED CARRIER	ACCOUNT NAME	MILEAGE #

CLASS OF SERVICE	SEATING PREFERENCE	SPECIAL REQUESTS
FIRST CLASS_____	NON-SMOKING_____	VEGETARIAN_____
BUSINESS _____	SMOKING_____	LOW SALT_____
COACH_____	AISLE_____	LOW CAL_____
ECONOMY_____	WINDOW_____	KOSHER_____
RESTRICTED_____	BULKHEAD_____	CHILD'S_____
OTHER_____	FRONT/REAR _____	OTHER_____

RENTAL CAR COMPANY	CAR SIZE	CORPORATE ID # OR OTHER

HOTEL PREFERENCE	BED SIZE	CORPORATE ID# OR OTHER

PAYMENT INFORMATION

CLIENT USUALLY PAYS BY: (circle one or all) CASH   CHECK   CREDIT CARD

CREDIT CARD TYPE	ACCOUNT#	EXP. DATE	NAME ON CARD

I hereby authorize_____(your travel agency name) to charge airline tickets and travel services to the above credit cards upon my request to do so.

SIGNATURE OF CLIENT_____ **DATE**_____

YOUR CLIENT ACTION CARD FILE

Now that you have established a file with your client profile cards it is time to set up your client contact system by using client action cards. It is really very simple. You will need a metal file box in the size that you make your client action cards. You should have at least 52 different dividers or compartments....one for each week of the year. Your client action cards can be color coded by client, travel product, or whatever criteria you decide. Remember these cards are designed to make you effective so whatever size, design, and other parameters you decide to use are fine.

You should create a client action card for each active client that you have and start by calling your client to identify their immediate needs. A simple telephone call will reveal their latest travel plans, their future travel plans, and their overall potential as a client. Information from your initial telephone call should be recorded on the client action card as well as any specific requests the conversation uncovered.

Upon the conclusion the client action card should be filed in the next appropriate follow up period based on the client's request or inference. If the client commented that they were considering a ski trip to Aspen in December, then you would probably want to follow up on September 1st so you would file the action card in the appropriate slot for follow up. Let's say the client suggested you call when the next airfare war happened. Perhaps you could flag the card with a specific color marker to indicate a call should be made at the moment you learn of an airfare war that would affect your client's travel plans. Perhaps a different color could be used for clients interested in bargain cruises.

By continually working your client action cards your clients do not have a chance to think about calling another travel agent. When you stop to think about it, this is just the kind of proactive marketing campaign that you would appreciate from your travel professional. If your client gives you clear signals that they are not interested in your contacts simply remove them from your active client list. When you receive a referral or new client by way of exploratory mailing, advertising, canvassing, or cold calls simply create a new client profile and action card for them to start the follow up process.

A sample of a client action card appears on the following page for your use. Note that this example is 5" x 8" but any size will work. You can add any other information that you need in order to make the system more efficient for you.

CLIENT ACTION CARD

Client Names (s) _____

Home Phone _____
Work Phone _____
Home Fax _____
Work Fax _____
Address _____
City_____ State _____ Zip _____

FOLLOW UP DATE	**ACTION**

CLIENT QUESTIONNAIRE AND MARKET SUR-VEY

While your client profile form documents many of your client's travel preferences, operational details and history, a separate client questionnaire can be completed by your client to determine their travel interests and desires. By using a client questionnaire and market survey you can identify your client's interests and then transfer the information into a database. By using this information as various sort fields in your database you can identify clients who might be interested in certain travel specials or information that may arise.

Your questionnaire can be completed all at once or may be used every time you discuss travel with your clients. Lets say your client casually mentions that they would love to someday cruise Tahiti and her islands. That it has been a dream of theirs but they doubt they could ever afford it. If you receive information about a special sailing on Windstar Cruises that has been priced aggressively for whatever reason you can immediately sort your database for those clients that have mentioned a desire to cruise Tahiti and contact them via facsimile, mail or telephone to let them know they can realize their dreams at an affordable price.

This is just a simple example of how your client questionnaire and market survey can benefit both you and your client by quickly limiting correspondence to those folks potentially interested in such a product. By using this approach to disseminating information you can maintain a high quality of contact with your clients and a very cost effective campaign.

Sample Client Questionaire and Market Survey

Following is a sample client questionnaire and market survey. You would certainly want to modify this sample with information that relates to your specialty.

CLIENT QUESTIONNAIRE & MARKET SURVEY

DATE_____

NAME:_____

RESIDENCE ADDRESS_____

RES. PHONE:_____BUS. PHONE:_____FAX_____

We appreciate your taking the time to complete our brief travel questionnaire. It is our sincere hope that the time spent completing this form will be rewarded with the perfect travel arrangements for your next vacation. With this information we are able to imput your preferences in our database. With your past travel information we are able to see your travel trends so that we will be able to offer you just those type of vacations you love. With your travel dreams we are able to search for travel specials that may become available to the destinations where you would like to travel.

LAND BASED PAST TRAVELS

YEAR VISITED		DESTINATION	YEAR VISITED		DESTINATION
_____	___	AFRICA	_____	___	EUROPE
_____	___	ALASKA	_____	___	HAWAII
_____	___	ASIA	_____	___	MEXICO
_____	___	CANADA	_____	___	MIDDLE EAST
_____	___	CARIBBEAN	_____	___	SOUTH AMERICA
_____	___	CENTRAL AMERICA	_____	___	SOUTH PACIFIC
_____		OTHERS_____			

PAST CRUISE TRAVEL

YEAR	CRUISE LINE	CRUISE DESTINATION
_____	_____	_____
_____	_____	_____
_____	_____	_____
_____	_____	_____
_____	_____	_____

FUTURE LAND BASED TRAVEL PLANS

WHEN		DESTINATION	WHEN		DESTINATION
_____	___	AFRICA	_____	___	EUROPE
_____	___	ALASKA	_____	___	HAWAII
_____	___	ASIA	_____	___	MEXICO
_____	___	CANADA	_____	___	MIDDLE EAST
_____	___	CARIBBEAN	_____	___	SOUTH AMERICA
_____	___	CENTRAL AMERICA	_____	___	SOUTH PACIFIC
_____		OTHERS_____			

FUTURE CRUISE TRAVEL PLANS

WHEN	DESTINATION	CRUISE LINES	SHIPS
_____	_____	_____	_____
_____	_____	_____	_____
_____	_____	_____	_____
_____	_____	_____	_____

CLIENT QUESTIONNAIRE & MARKET SURVEY
continued

WHEN I TRAVEL I PREFER THE FOLLOWING:

AIRLINES   **REASONS**

_____   _____
_____   _____
_____   _____
_____   _____

RENTAL CAR COMPANIES   **REASONS**   **CAR SIZE**

_____   _____   _____
_____   _____   _____

HOTEL CHAINS   **REASONS**

_____   _____
_____   _____
_____   _____

HOTEL TYPES & AMENITIES (check preferences or add additional information)

_____ DELUXE ALL INCLUSIVE RESORTS   _____ BED & BREAKFASTS
_____ DELUXE HOTELS   _____ RESTAURANT AT HOTEL
_____ FIRST CLASS HOTELS   _____ MEETING FACILITIES
_____ BUDGET HOTELS/MOTELS   _____ TENNIS COURTS
_____ HIGH RISE HOTELS   _____ GYM/SAUNA
_____ SMALL INTIMATE HOTELS   _____ POOL
_____ CONDOS & ALL SUITE HOTELS   _____ HANDICAP FACILITIES
ADDITIONAL INFORMATION_____
_____

CRUISE SHIP PREFERENCES (check preferences or add additional information)

_____ MEGA SHIPS   _____ MANY ACTIVITIES ON BOARD
_____ LARGE SHIPS   _____ QUIET SHIP, FEW ACTIVITIES
_____ MEDIUM SIZE SHIPS   _____ SENIOR ORIENTED CRUISES
_____ SMALL INTIMATE SHIPS   _____ FORMAL CRUISES
_____ SAILING SHIPS   _____ CASUAL CRUISES
_____ DELUXE 5-STAR SHIPS   _____ 7 - DAY CRUISES
_____ FAMILY ORIENTED SHIPS   _____ 10 DAY CRUISES
_____ OLDER SHIPS   _____ 14 DAYS OR LONGER CRUISES
_____ NEWER SHIPS   OTHER_____
_____ THEME CRUISES (type)_____ _____
_____ MANY PORTS   _____
_____ MORE DAYS AT SEA   _____

THANK YOU FOR YOUR TIME & EFFORT

Chapter 22
DEVELOPING YOUR PRO-FESSIONAL KNOWLEDGE AND SKILLS

Developing your knowledge of the travel industry's various products and services will take years of research and exposure. While there are several options you may elect to expedite the process, your choice to start your travel career in a home based location is one of the best approaches to take. Since the business of retailing travel takes years to develop, a slow growth approach is the best course to pursue. Jumping into a full time store front travel agency can be devastating as there is so much knowledge needed to successfully operate the venture.

One of the major benefits derived from starting your home based business is the opportunity to establish your professional knowledge and skills slowly as you grow in your business. By starting slowly you can spend an abundant amount of time on each transaction to be sure you have researched every possible detail. This is probably the very best way to learn the intricacies of the travel business.

Travel schools, correspondence courses, industry certification programs, supplier seminars, familiarization tours and cruises are all ways to increase your professional knowledge and skills while learning the industry at the same time. Remember that the travel industry is involved in the continuing evolution from an operations based business to a sales and marketing based business. Where once a travel agent needed to study complex tariffs and handwrite tickets that required substantial skills now having personal selling skills coupled with modern marketing techniques are the ingredients for success Following are some of the more common options you have available to you.

SHOULD I ATTEND A TRAVEL SCHOOL?

The most common question asked by individuals new to their home based travel business is "should I attend a travel school?" This is indeed a difficult question to answer with a blanket statement as everyone has different business specializations, objectives, and expectations. There are a good number of different types of travel schools and we can take each one individually

INDEPENDENT TRAVEL SCHOOLS

Independent travel schools have sprung up all over the United States and offer a variety of curriculum. Most of the independent travel schools offer four to six week classes with an optional forty or eighty hour class on a particular computerized reservations system (CRS). While any training and information is valuable you must clearly understand the nature of the school's curriculum. If the school is focused on training for salaried travel agency positions you must consider it very carefully.

The information in the curriculum is probably designed for the individual that would like to obtain employment as a beginning agent in a retail store front travel agency. One excellent approach is to attend some of the one semester training programs offered nationally at one of the colleges or universities listed in Chapter 23. The price tag for attending one of these programs is inexpensive, especially when you consider the quality of the content.

Of major concern to the home based travel entrepreneur is the lack of focus on product information and marketing and sales techniques. Most of the private travel schools rely on a heavy amount of processing of accountable documents as the meat of their curriculum which really isn't of benefit to the home based travel agent.

STATE AND LOCAL COLLEGES

Many state and local colleges offer travel curriculums and Associates degrees. Since the unit cost of the college's courses is generally quite inexpensive this is a great way to obtain an education in the travel industry. Most schools offer classes like ticketing, geography, selling tours and cruises, and a myriad of other courses. Many home based agents are in a hurry to get their education and elect the higher priced private travel schools and really miss the boat.

REGIONAL OCCUPATION PROGRAMS (ROP)

Now this is a great way to go if your are both in a hurry and short on funds. Many communities offer regional occupation programs for free or close to it. The typical travel ROP offers just the same information as the private travel schools and are generally several weeks long. Most ROP programs are offered with outstanding instructors that also work in the travel industry by day.

SUPPLIER SPONSORED TRAVEL SCHOOLS

Many of the airlines sponsor travel schools and academies. The most famous is the TWA Travel Academy which has trained many travel agents who swear by the program. Again, review the curriculum carefully to see if it is focused on selling travel or learning how to write tickets. If your business specialty is selling cruises it is doubtful that the TWA Academy will help much and these types of schools tend to be quite expensive.

CAN TRAVEL VIDEO TRAINING HELP?

There are outstanding videos available for you to use to familiarize yourself with the travel industry. For the most part they are extremely effective and will serve you well as you enjoy them. There are several types of videos you may purchase and following are some of the more important.

DESTINATION VIDEOS

If you stop and think about it, when people ask you about a particular destination they are really asking why they should go there and what it will cost. Destination videos can expose you to the best that each individual destination has to offer. By watching destination videos you not only see the important sights of the destination but you also get to hear the proper pronunciation of the various cities, sights, and names of important hotels as well. This is the knowledge most folks want when they talk with their travel agent.

CRUISE VIDEO TAPES

Vacations on Video in Arizona produces virtually all of the cruise line's video presentations and they are available to travel agents at a very reasonable cost. Cruise videos make selling cruises exceptionally easy. While the videos vary in quality they all offer an excellent rendition of the ship's personality, decor, public areas and cabins. The videos always give wonderful information regarding their ports of call and overall itineraries.

Using cruise videos with the cruise lines own brochures is an excellent way to become acquainted with the ships, itineraries, pricing, and brochures themselves.

TRAINING VIDEOS

The Cruise Line International Association (CLIA) offers a good number of training video tapes on selling groups, cruises, and industry professionalism which are all great! Royal Cruise Line's Cruise Sales Seminar is available on VHS and is a four hour seminar that will greatly enhance your understanding of the cruise market. Many tour operators offer training tapes on selling their destination and products as well.

SOFTWARE TRAINING TAPES

One of the best ways to get started with any new software that you purchase is by purchasing a VHS training tape to get you going. Training tapes are available for many different software titles. WordPerfect, Excel, Microsoft Word, Pagemaker, DOS, Windows and just about every popular application has a training video available.

WHAT TRAVEL INDUSTRY TRAINING IS AVAILABLE?

A good way to learn how to sell specific travel products is to get the training on how to sell them directly from the suppliers themselves. Following are the different types of industry training opportunities that are available to the travel agency community.

SUPPLIER SEMINARS

Virtually every day one supplier or another is training and entertaining travel agents in major cities throughout the nation. Hotels, airlines, tour operators, government tourist bureaus, and cruise lines host breakfast, lunch, or evening functions to expose their products to the travel community. Most of the seminars are published in the trade magazines and extend an open invitation to the travel industry, outside sales and independent contractors included.

Many times suppliers will host in-depth destination and product seminars for a modest fee. These seminars are always taught by active industry gurus that will both educate and motivate you to higher achievement in your business.

TRADE SHOWS AND CONVENTIONS

One of the best ways to increase your knowledge of the travel industry is by attending one of the many trade shows or conventions that take place frequently. Many of the trade shows feature hours of seminars on various topics by industry speakers that are designed to increase your effectiveness in your business. The trade shows occur' all over the country and many of the industry conventions convene in foreign countries. All of the industry conferences offer pre and post conference travel agency tours of the region. The personal travel experience gained by attending the events and the content of the seminars make this one of the best ways to get rapid exposure in the industry.

INDUSTRY ASSOCIATION FAMILIARIZATION TOUR AND CRUISE SEMINARS

Many of the industry associations offer a full agenda of seminars, meetings, familiarization trips, and other opportunities to learn. The National Association of Commissioned Travel Agents (NACTA) operates a good number of Fam/Cruise/Seminars per year for outside sales people and independent contractors like yourself. The American Society of Travel Agents (ASTA) sponsors a number of regional and national meetings throughout the year. The Grand Daddy of travel industry functions is the ASTA World Congress that takes place once a year and includes travel agents, suppliers, and other interested people from around the globe.

Many destination oriented associations also offer substantial opportunity for learning through seminars and travel. The Pacific Area Travel Association (PATA) offers off shore meetings frequently that focus on one of the PATA member countries. PATA trade shows are a great way to pick up information on Pacific Rim nations.

TRAVEL INDUSTRY ORGANIZATIONS THAT OFFER TRAVEL AGENT TRAINING

Many of the organizations that operate in the travel industry offer substantial training. The Cruise Line International Association (CLIA) offers a certification program for travel agents that want to present themselves as professionals in the industry. You may become a Accredited Cruise Consultant (ACC) or a Master Cruise Consultant (MCC) by fulfilling the criteria to qualify. The Institute of Certified Travel Agents (ICTA) offers several opportunities to gain professional level designations in the industry. Upon completing ICTA's criteria you may become a "Destination Specialist" (DS) and use ICTA's DS professional designation behind your name. ICTA also offers the Certified Travel Consultant (CTC) professional designation as well.

One of the best correspondence travel courses available is published by ICTA and costs a nominal amount of money. Once you have completed the course and been in the industry for one year 'ICTA will issue you a Certificate of Professionalism. The Airline Reporting Corp. (ARC) offers a number of courses on ticketing and reporting that are available for agents for a small fee. Many airlines and government tourist offices offer destination oriented specialization certifificates you may earn by simply attending seminars or completing a test on the destination itself. Each one of these certificates entitles you to hold yourself as a professional agent serving clients.

Chapter 23
LEGAL ISSUES AND PROTECTING YOUR BUSINESS

While the travel industry is relatively free of the kinds of liability most businesses face in today's litigious society there are several concerns that you will need to address to ensure a trouble free operation. As a travel agent you may face certain issues that deal with the disclosure of information to your client, representation of the quality of the various products and services, accomplishing due diligence necessary to offer a particular tour company, airline, cruise line or other travel supplier, and of course, the general liability of meeting a client either at your home or theirs.

Many publications have been written regarding travel industry law. Alexander Anolik is probably the most recognized travel attorney in the industry and has written a number of books on preventative legal care for travel agents that are well worth the price. Mr. Anolik has also developed a cassette tape series for independent contractors that considers legal issues and answers. The National Association of Commissioned Travel Agents (NACTA) Handbook is an invaluable tool to obtain advice and sample contracts, disclosures and other legal material. It is worth the price of NACTA membership alone. You should always consult an attorney regarding legal issues and advice as this chapter is not designed to substitute for the professional advice of an attorney.

Areas for consideration and discussion with your attorney are as follows.

INSURANCE

Insurance is a part of every business person's protection and certainly a home based travel entrepreneur needs the security of various types of insurance as well.

HOMEOWNER'S INSURANCE POLICY

Your homeowner's or apartment dweller's policy will offer you considerable protection for most problems that may arise from your home based business. Make sure you have a complete list of your business assets as well as your personal assets in case a robbery, fire, or some other loss occurs. Check the liability portion of your policy and increase the coverage if you will be meeting clients in your home or apartment. You never know when a client could slip and fall on your doorstep picking up a ticket.

ERRORS AND OMISSIONS AND GENERAL LIABILITY INSURANCE

If you do make a mistake on one of your client's trips and they return only to sue you for negligence or worse, you need errors and omissions insurance to take care of the lawsuit and settlement. Errors and Omissions insurance is mandatory for independent contractors that stand the risk of being sued separately from their host agencies that may or may not be named in the suit. The reason is that the chain of liability identifies the independent contractor as a separate legal entity that must be held accountable for their actions. While this is good news to the host agency as there is great relief in their liability, the independent contractor must be able to answer any lawsuits on their own behalf.

Outside sales people who are employees of the agency may be covered by the agency's E & O policy by simply signing a rider and paying the additional premium for the coverage. Some Independent Contractor Networks offer this type of blanket E & O insurance at premiums below that which the agent could obtain separately. Also some of the industry associations (NACTA, NACOA, ARTA) offer individual E & O policies at competitive rates.

CREDIT CARD SALES

Travel agents are in the unenviable position of having the responsibility of processing credit cards sales, obtaining signatures, authorization codes, and card imprints, yet lack the control to dispute any charge backs by the airlines. Since the airline is the actual vendor as recognized by the credit card company and the travel agent is simply a sub-agent of the vendor (the airline), the travel agent is bound by a separate agreement with the airline and without legal standing to take action against the credit card company.

This is a very difficult concern as every airline will accept credit card numbers over the telephone and then issue the ticket via mail to the client directly. The clients expect that you will offer this same service and have made "telephone order" credit card transactions common place. The problem for the independent contractor appears when a client disputes a charge to their credit card. The credit card company immediately debits the airline, who in turn sends a debit memo to the ARC travel agency for the charge back. At this point the agent can either produce a fully executed Universal Credit Card Charge Form (UCCF) or pay the debit. If the agency has not obtained an original signature and credit card imprint on the UCCF they must pay the debit memo.

If the sale was originated by an independent contractor the agency will collect for the debit from the independent contractor who is left without recourse against the credit card company, airline, or travel agency and must pursue the client for satisfaction. This is generally difficult if the client has denied or disputed the original charge and usually involves a small claims action to try and recover the funds. A few credit card charge backs can ruin an otherwise profitable year for an independent contractor.

LIMITED POWER OF ATTORNEY

By using a limited power of attorney as authorization to process phone orders for airline tickets on your client's credit card you may recover any disputed charges in small claims court by using this authority as proof of your client's intent. Unfortunately it will not satisfy the credit card companies' demand for a fully executed Universal Credit Card Charge Form (UCCF).

UNIVERSAL CREDIT CARD CHARGE FORMS

The UCCFs provided by the Airline Reporting Corporation for the purpose of processing credit card charge airline ticket sales must be completed with the following information to be considered acceptable by the airline processing the charge. It must have an original signature of the cardholder (no second party signatures will be accepted), an original imprint of the valid credit card (handwritten information will not be acceptable), and a valid authorization code issued by the appropriate credit card company.

Without the above information a credit card company is not bound to accept the form of payment. It is mandatory that independent contractors obtain a credit card validator to process credit card sales for their clients. The UCCF should be validated with the credit card and signed by the client for self protection in case of credit card charge backs. Even if the validation and signing take place after the ticket is issued to the client it is imperative the independent contractor maintain a file of these processed UCCFs for their own protection.

DISCLOSURES

One of the most important jobs a travel agent has is to research each detail of a transaction and disclose their findings to the client. If a tour company seems financially risky the travel agent should tell their client, if an airline ticket has penalties if changed or refunded the travel agent should tell their client before the ticket is purchased, if a destination is affected by a State Department advisory the travel agent should tell their client.

Many of the issues that find their way into small claims court are based on the client's claim that their travel agent failed to disclose information or misrepresented information. These claims are very easy to avoid by using written disclosures with your client and obtaining their signature upon disclosing the information. Even if you have verbally disclosed that an airline ticket was non-refundable, it is your word against your client's in small claims court and there is always a 50/50 risk that the judge will rule in your client's favor.

Following are some of the more important things to disclose in writing to your client that will resolve the vast majority of small claims matters that may arise without written disclosure.

RECEIPT OF DOCUMENTS

This is a basic issue that is better resolved in writing. Let us say you deliver an airline ticket to a client who subsequently loses the ticket and calls you to replace it and claims you never delivered it in the first place. The only way you can actually prove that you did deliver the ticket is to obtain your client's signature upon executing the delivery. Airline tickets are just like cash. Can you imagine handing your client one thousand dollars in cash without getting a receipt for the money?

AGENCY DISCLOSURE

By disclosing the fact that you are the agent of the supplier you represent in the transaction the client is engaged in they may not later claim that you failed to disclose your relationship with the supplier was one of agency. You have a fiduciary obligation to your principle, the supplier, and only a responsibility to be fair and honest with your client. Failure to disclose your agency relationship may result in creating a fiduciary responsibility to your client who then can hold you responsible for many things. As an agent of the supplier the obligation of performing the service contracted for in the transaction clearly lies with the supplier.

RESPONSIBILITY OF AGENT

You may want to further clarify your responsibility by indicating that you do not guarantee fares, guarantee the operation of the flight, tour, cruise, hotel or any other part of the transaction. You may want to state that you are not responsible for the cancellation, substitution, or change of any ingredient of the transaction. That you act simply as an agent of the supplier and assume no other responsibility.

RECEIPT OF BROCHURE

If your client has purchased a tour, cruise, or any other travel product that is offered in a brochure you want to be sure he signs that he has received a copy of the brochure and is familiar with the change, cancellation, and various refund policies that may be imposed by the supplier. Many times even though a client may have a brochure they may claim they didn't know there would be a cancellation fee once they deposited a tour. By obtaining a signature from your client for the supplier's brochure it becomes crystal clear that it has become their responsibility to familiarize themselves with the various policies of the supplier. Besides a signature, it is best to have your client initial the "Terms and Conditions" section of the brochure used as a file copy in your client file.

CANCELLATION, CHANGE, AND REFUND POLICIES

You should obtain your client's signature or initials that they have been told and that they understand the various cancellation penalties, change fees, and refund policies associated with their transaction.

TRIP CANCELLATION INSURANCE

You should offer every client trip cancellation insurance even if they refuse it time and time again. If you fail to offer it and the client subsequently loses their payments they could claim that you never told them they would lose their money and never offered them trip cancellation insurance. By obtaining their initials or signature of acceptance or rejection there is little doubt that you did your job.

LOST BAGGAGE INSURANCE

Once again it is in your best interest to offer your client lost baggage insurance especially if they are going on a cruise or extended vacation. If they decline, a simple initial or signature will get you off the hook should they have a loss.

MEDICAL INSURANCE

Medical trip insurance should always be offered to your clients especially if they are going out of the country. If your client refuses the insurance you should once again get their initials or signature documenting your effort.

LICENSING AND REGISTERING YOUR BUSI·NESS

While each state is has different requirements you will probably have to file a fictitious Business Name Statement, obtain a business license and possibly register your business as a seller of travel with the state attorney general or appropriate authority.

FILING A FICTITIOUS BUSINESS NAME STATE·MENT

To file a Fictitious Business Name Statement you will need to contact either your local newspaper or your local County Recorder's office. If you use your local newspaper they will file your statement for you and do the necessary publishing that you are establishing a DBA. If you are in a hurry to get your bank accounts open you can go directly to the county recorder's office and file it directly with the County Recorder. The actual form that you fill out is very simple. You still must publish your statement in a newspaper of general circulation for the prescribed period but the County Recorder will give you your recorded Fictitious Business Name Statement upon recordation and you can use this to open your bank account.

OBTAINING A BUSINESS LICENSE

Once you have recorded your business name you should visit your city hall or local county official that issues business licenses for your area. You will need to fill out a simple form and pay whatever the appropriate charge is to obtain your business license. Once you have received your license you are officially in business. If your county doesn't require a license you may have to get some sort of document from the county to satisfy suppliers.

REGISTERING YOUR BUSINESS WITH YOUR STATE

Some states have laws that require sellers of travel to register their business with the Attorney General's office and to pay an annual registration fee. You should contact your state Attorney General's office to find out if your state has such a law. Currently some 15 or so states do have registration laws and more are expected to follow. If you cannot find out from your attorney general's office you should contact one of the trade associations in your area. Failing that you may contact NACTA for a current list of states that have registration laws.

RECEIPT OF TRAVEL DOCUMENTS, NOTICE TO ALL CLIENTS, AGENCY DISCLOSURE AND AGREEMENT OF SALE

You may want to incorporate all of the disclosure items into one single form that you use for all of your clients. Your client would simply sign the form when you deliver their travel documents. Disclosure notices will vary from state to state and from agency to agency depending on the type of disclosure your state requires and the type of business you are involved in. Disclosure forms will go a long way in preventing legal problems....but only if you obtain and keep your client's signature.

On the next page is a sample of a disclosure form. Please do not use this form without consulting a travel attorney or representative in your state of one of the industry associations. This sample disclosure from is simply meant to give you an idea of what your's might look like.

RECEIPT FOR TRAVEL DOCUMENTS, NOTICE TO ALL CLIENTS, AGENCY DISCLOSURE AND AGREEMENT OF SALE

AGENCY DISCLOSURE

(Your travel agency name here) issues these traffic documents in the sole capacity as Agent for the airline, tour company, cruise line or other supplier as indicated in the traffic documents, brochures, correspondence or other communication. As the agent of the supplier (Your travel agency name here) does not assume the responsibility for the cancellation or substitution of service by the supplier, financial default of the supplier, refunds for unused services to be provided by the supplier, or any other obligation, service, or moneys not the specific responsibility of (Your travel agency name here)

INSURANCE

(Your travel agency name here) recommends that you purchase insurance to protect yourself from any unforeseen event.

_____ I wish to accept/decline trip cancellation insurance (circle one)
_____ I wish to accept/decline trip medical insurance (circle one)
_____ I wish to accept/decline lost/damaged baggage insurance (circle one)

REFUNDS, CHANGES, CANCELLATIONS

(Your travel agency name here) has advised me of the supplier's refund change and cancellation fees and penalties. I am aware that the airline ticket may be subject to the loss of some or all of the fare should I elect to change or cancel this reservation.

_____ I have been advised that cancellation, change, or refund penalties do apply to these documents and I fully understand the terms and conditions of such penalties.

I have read the above paragraphs, checked the applicable spaces and agree to the terms as stated

Name_____Date_____

Chapter 24
HOME BASED TRAVEL AGENCY TRAVEL BENEFITS

When most folks think of the travel industry the first thing that comes to mind are the wonderful benefits that travel agents must receive. People are under the impression that travel agents get to travel anywhere they want in the world as guests of the airlines, hotels, tour companies and so on. While travel agents do receive some benefits from their association with the travel industry, for the most part, these benefits are partially dependent on the agent's productivity. Simply being a travel agent and having a travel agent's business card does not entitle an individual to any discounts whatsoever and many folks have been duped into buying phoney travel agent identification cards with the belief that they will be the beneficiary of substantial discounts and free trips.

While travel benefits are just one of the reasons most travel agents stay in the industry the benefits seem to pursue those agents that are the most productive. One reason this is true is the hands on approach most suppliers have to travel marketing. If an agent is selling travel in a given market the supplier's sales representative is likely to be involved with the agent. This is true whether the agent is home based, works from a store front location, or is the owner of a large store front agency. It is the supplier sales representative's responsibility to know what is going on in their specific territory and to also know what agents are selling their products and what agents are not. For this reason, you will find some productive home based agents with numerous invitations to join various familiarizations trips and others that never get invited.

Like any business, those that produce meaningful revenues for their vendors get the advantages of their production while those that do not produce only have aspirations of the privileges. While the many advantages of being in the travel industry are available to all, the various travel companies are not careless in their award of the discounts and invitations that make being in the travel industry appealing to many. One way to view the benefits as a home based entrepreneur is to perceive the potential incentives and discounts available for viable travel agents as a reward for an occupation well performed. Surely, if everyone were invited on a familiarization trip it would lose all value to those agents that are highly productive.

Understanding the relationship between the seller of retail travel products and the vendors requires a sophisticated understanding of the cost/benefit correlation to the supplier. If the discount offered an agent is still profitable to a supplier because of low retail utilization of their products then the supplier is likely to view the travel agent as a separate productive revenue segment of the consuming public and allow the discount to be offered as a profit center. On the other hand, if the supplier is thinking of travel agents as a dilution of consumer revenues they are predisposed to only offering discount rates to their most productive and coveted agents.

On the other hand, many travel suppliers consider the travel agent sector of the consuming public as a viable extension of their marketing efforts and a meaningful portion of their overall revenue. As an example, a hotel may elect to offer a "travel agent's" rate that is substantially lower than their normal rate. This offer may be made only during periods of historic weak utilization of the property's rooms when the hotel knows that they expect extremely low occupancy rates. The revenue derived from the sale of rooms to travel agents, while discounted, is desirable income to the property. Of course, they offer other excellent rates to different market segments as well during these periods such as senior rates, special corporate rates, and so on. While these special travel agency discounts are very motivating and create demand from the agency community they also create revenues for the property where none existed before.

Nothing is more perishable than a hotel room night gone unused, a vacant cabin sailing on a cruise ship, or an empty airline seat. The entire cost of operating the hotel, cruise ship, or airline is amortized over the number of actual guests or passengers and revenues created by discounting to various market segments has a dramatic impact on the bottom line of these companies. Of course, the suppliers are going to set the travel agent discount rate at a level they perceive to maximize profitability from the sale without diluting the motivation created by the offer. Travel agents casually involved in the travel industry are the likely target of such marketing and the travel suppliers often allow one or more non industry companions at these special "travel agent rates".

On the other hand, many travel suppliers offer complimentary stays, cruises, or airline seats to agents for promotional purposes. They hand pick the agents who receive the invitations and generally impose stiff qualification criteria the agents must meet. It is highly doubtful that these types of discounts would be made available to casual agents but would favor full time seasoned professionals. Many times suppliers will offer free travel for agents meeting a minimum level of productivity which is measured by actual sales of a specified product to qualify. These incentives work for both the agent and the supplier as only those agents producing results enjoy the benefit of free or substantially reduced travel. Many suppliers give away free trips, cruises and airline tickets at travel agent séminars. Some cruise lines offer every agent in attendance a free cruise.

TRAVEL AGENT REGISTRATION PROGRAMS

Because of the alleged abuse of travel privileges and misrepresentation of agent's qualifications by a few travel agencies, some industry associations and more orthodox agents have demanded a program to document travel agent's eligibility. This is done by recognizing their gross earnings from the industry. These programs have been around for a long time but only now are they gaining the support from the industry at large.

Following are the travel agent registration procedures as they currently exist at the time of this writing (January, 1996), Note that the industry is changing quite rapidly with regard to its acceptance of these forms of verification. In the final analysis it is the supplier's decision to honor a request for travel agency reduced rates and decide what they will require as documentation. It would seem the supplier is the one most competent to make the decision, not the travel agency community.

INTERNATIONAL AIRLINE TRAVEL AGENCY NETWORK (IATAN)

The International Airline Travel Agent Network is an organization that has taken on the task of registering travel agents and issuing travel agent I.D. cards to the industry. IATAN has gained the support of the industry associations and various groups and is emerging as the preferred travel agency I.D. card by the industry and suppliers alike. At the time of this writing (January, 1996) IATAN has announced their intention to offer the IATAN ID cards to qualified cruise oriented agencies as well. This should finally establish the IATAN ID card as the industry standard for all trqvel agents.

To qualify for an IATAN travel agent I.D. card you must have been paid at least $4,080.00 in commissions by an IATAN endorsed entity and work at least 5 to 19 hours per week in the industry. This could be your host agency, one of your IATAN endorsed suppliers, or possibly a consolidator that is IATAN endorsed. The cost of the card itself is nominal (currently $15.00) but the catch is the cost of endorsement by IATAN which is several hundred dollars. Non ARC appointed agencies can gain IATAN endorsement but must post a bond to do so.

If you are an independent contractor doing business with multiple suppliers and did not get paid $4,080.00 by any one IATAN endorsed supplier, don't worry. You may file an application for an IATAN I.D. Card by submitting an income statement showing the cumulative totals of your sales and commissions from all sources. As long as you have earned a total of $4,080.00 from all of the sources you will still qualify for the card. You must, however, submit the application through an IATAN endorsed location to be considered and some independent contractors feel this is an invasion of privacy. Regardless, the IATAN I.D. Card is rapidly becoming the I.D. card of the travel industry.

AIRLINE REPORTING CORPORATION "ARC LIST"

At one time the ARC list was the standard for agent documentation but ceased to exist in January 1994. It is possible that the ARC may get back into the travel agency registration business if IATAN does not receive universal support from the industry.

FORMAL AGENCY LETTERS OF REQUEST

Many tour companies, cruise lines, hotels and other travel suppliers will honor a formal letter of request made by the agency's owner or manager as sufficient documentation to confirm travel agency reduced rates. Generally, if an agency is known to be productive and viable a formal request is all that is needed to authenticate the agent's identity to the vendor.

TYPICAL TRAVEL AGENCY BENEFITS

While there is no set discount established for travel agents by supplier type and every supplier sets their own policies regarding travel agent incentives, there are some trends that occur when travel agent discounts are made available. Following are some of the more common offerings by supplier type.

DOMESTIC AIRLINES

Most domestic airlines offer discounts or free transportation to agents based on productivity. Unfortunately, the carriers do not perceive an outside sales person or independent contractor as in the mainstream of distribution. Generally, the owner or manager of an ARC appointed location is awarded the reduced rate transportation based on the agency's productivity and is then free to distribute the passes as they see fit. If you are doing a fair amount of domestic airline travel you should discuss access to productivity passes with your host agency.

Promotional airfares are offered on occasion and may require an IATAN I.D. card before the fare is granted. Normal travel agent promotional airfares occur off season and are considered to be revenue productive by the airlines and ordinarily allow one or more companions at the agent's airfare as well. You may find out about promotional agency airfares from your host agency or the airline's sales office. Many times airlines will present agents attending seminars free system passes or award a few passes as door prizes. These passes are not as restricted as most of the promotional airfares are.

If you are negotiating and moving groups the airlines have free passes right in the tariff. They will award a site inspection pass so that you may visit the destination to negotiate hotel rooms, land arrangements, or other services necessary to accommodate the group. There are tour conductor passes right in the tariff, usually one for fifteen paid or two for forty paid, so that you or your tour conductor can travel with the group.

INTERNATIONAL AIRLINES

Most international airlines will offer discounts of 50% positive space or 75% space available for IATAN agents. Again, the international airlines offer numerous promotional airfares during shoulder and off peak seasons that usually allow for one or more companions. The international carriers also have group site inspection passes and tour conductor passes as well.

CRUISE LINES

All CLIA member cruise lines and most other lines offer cabins at substantial savings to CLIA member travel agents. Most cabins sell for $25 to $50 per person, per day and include every feature of the cruise a normal paying passenger would expect. Generally the cruise line will confirm requests two to three weeks before departure and will confirm the highest available cabin category available. Many times the cruise lines will invite cruise agents on special sailings as their guest and also include agents on inaugural sailings.

HOTELS

Most individual hotels, resorts, and major hotel chains alike, offer discounts of varying levels to the travel industry. A normal discount would be 50% off whatever the normal, or rack, rate is for the specific room that you have requested. You must book the room in advance and the availability of the rate is subject to occupancy levels at the hotel during your requested stay. Sometimes hotels and resorts will offer free or substantially discounted rooms to agents during their off season period. This gives them exposure with the agency community and generates whatever miscellaneous sales the agents produce while staying at the property.

CAR RENTALS

Most car rental companies offer discounts to travel agents during periods of low utilization of their fleet. The rates may be daily, weekly or some other special value. Proper advance reservations are a must to obtain confirmation of these special rates. You may also be required to produce valid travel agent identification when checking in for your car rental.

SIGHTSEEING ATTRACTIONS

Many sightseeing attractions and events offer travel agents special rates. Some offer free admission while others offer a special rate upon proper industry documentation.

FAMILIARIZATION TOURS

"Fam" trips, as they are known within the travel industry, are operated by tour operators, hotels, airlines, government tourist bureaus or some other entity or group of entities. The purpose of a fam trip is to host travel agents to a short and all inclusive trip to a destination to expose the agents to the supplier's products and services. Some of the better fams are extremely attractive values and other widely promoted fams may not be as attractive. Many fam trips are operated for profit and therefore are not as selective as to the agent's qualifications.

TRADE ASSOCIATIONS

Most trade associations feature monthly meetings, off shore work shops, and annual conventions with trade shows. Industry conventions occur worldwide and offer agents the opportunity to travel not only to the conventions site but on one of the many pre and post conventions tours that are offered. The ASTA World Congress is the travel industry's premier international convention. It changes location each year and showcases the region of the world it is located in.

INDUSTRY TRADE SHOWS AND CONVENTIONS

Numerous industry trade shows and conventions transpire worldwide. Some trade shows have as many as 800 exhibitors and last several days while others are focused on special industry segments and destinations. Many of the trade shows and conventions allow agents to take advantage of reduced rate air transportation to and from the event.

TRAINING SEMINARS

Many of the trade associations and private companies offer travel agent training seminars designed to train travel agents in areas critical to their success in business. NACTA alone, operates many fam/cruise/seminars for outside sales people and independent contractors. Many of the destination associations also offer off shore travel experience coupled with destination seminars and education.

Chapter 25
TAX BENEFITS FOR HOME BASED TRAVEL AGENCIES

You must seek the advice of a Certified Public Accountant, tax specialist, or some other accounting and/or income tax professional to structure the taxation of your business. The details contained in this chapter are strictly for informational purposes only and should not be taken as advice or used without authenticating the material with your accounting and/or tax professional. Further, this information is deemed reliable at the time of the writing of this book (January 1996) but may have changed without notice since this date. Use this data simply as ideas for discussion with your accounting and/or tax professional who will document the suitability of this information for your personal and unique tax situation.

Many entrepreneurs have found the potential tax advantages of operating a home based travel agency extremely desirable and one of their primary motivations for entering the business. There are many applications of creating tax savings by operating a home based travel business that may be broken down into several categories. Your home office will create new deductions for dollars you may already be spending. Using your automobile in your daily business activity may result in outstanding tax benefits. The travel you do as part of your normal business may be deductible and all of your normal business expenses are deductible.

Following is a closer look at some of the tax benefits you may be able to generate by operating your own home based travel business.

YOUR HOME OFFICE DEDUCTION

Much has been said and written about the deductibility of a home office and there is bound to be even more controversy as the increase of home offices creates a decrease in IRS revenue. As the federal budget deficit and trade deficits continue to increase the IRS is very likely to try and reduce deductions for home offices and self employment. This action would probably be counterproductive and result in even further deterioration of tax revenues. One of the main reasons for the evolution of home based businesses is the favorable tax structure a small entrepreneur can create while growing their business.

The IRS has been extremely specific in describing the criteria for qualifying for a home office deduction and as long as you meet this criteria are entitled to the full deduction as allowed by the tax code. The major criteria for a home office deduction are as follows.

EXCLUSIVE BUSINESS USE

You may deduct your home office that is for the "exclusive use" of your business. This means that if your office is in a spare bedroom and the spare bedroom is only used for your office it may be deductible. If you use the kitchen table for an office and then clear your materials away to enjoy dinner, this may not be deemed "exclusive use". For income tax purposes, think of your home office as a separate space and entity from the rest of your home and treat it as you would your office away from home. Exclusivity of use is critical to substantiating the deductibility of your home office.

PRINCIPAL PLACE OF BUSINESS

Your home office must also be your principal place of business. If your agency provides you with a desk and computer it is very likely that your deduction for a home office will be disallowed. You must be dependent on your home office to conduct business and have no other location from which you conduct business. Your business telephone and address must be your home office.

REGULAR BUSINESS USE

Regular business use is mandatory to determine the deductibility of your home office. Even if your dedicated space is exclusive it is probably not deductible if you only use it for business occasionally. If you use your home to meet clients this further perfects the deductibility of your home office.

DEDUCTIBLE HOME OFFICE EXPENSES

There is a wide variety of deductible expenses you may incur operating a home office. Following are some of the more common.

Business Allocation of Deductible Mortgage Interest
Business Allocation of Depreciation on Home

Business Allocation of Home Owner's or Renter's Insurance
Business Allocation of Real Estate Taxes
Business Allocation of Utilities
Casualty Losses
Cleaning
Furniture and Equipment Used For Business
Maintenance and Repair of Business Portion of Home
Premises Rent (Portion Allocated to Business Use)
Refuse Collection
Telephone (Except local service for your personal residence line)

I.R.S. FORM 8829 "EXPENSES FOR BUSINESS USE OF YOUR HOME"

The appropriate form on which to determine and report your home office expenses is the IRS form 8829. Following is a sample of this form as it appears for the tax year 1995. Expenses documented on IRS Form 8829 would be transferred to your Schedule C as an operating expense of the business. Again, be sure to consult your tax specialist to verify the deductibility of your specific situation.

Form **8829**

Department of the Treasury
Internal Revenue Service (99)

Expenses for Business Use of Your Home

▶ File only with Schedule C (Form 1040).
Use a separate Form 8829 for each home you used for business during the year.
▶ See separate instructions.

OMB No. 1545-1266

1995

66

Name(s) of proprietor(s)

Your Social Security Number

Part I — Part of Your Home Used for Business

1	Area used regularly and exclusively for business, regularly for day care, or for inventory storage	**1**	
2	Total area of home	**2**	
3	Divide line 1 by line 2. Enter the result as a percentage	**3**	%

• **For day-care facilities not used exclusively for business, also complete lines 4 - 6.**
• **All others, skip lines 4 - 6 and enter the amount from line 3 on line 7.**

4	Multiply days used for day care during year by hours used per day	**4**		hr
5	Total hours available for use during the year (365 days x 24 hours)	**5**	8,760	hr
6	Divide line 4 by line 5. Enter the result as a decimal amount	**6**		

7	Business percentage. For day-care facilities not used exclusively for business, multiply line 6 by line 3 (enter the result as a percentage). All others, enter the amount from line 3 . . . . ▶	**7**	%

Part II — Figure Your Allowable Deduction

8	Enter the amount from Schedule C, line 29, **plus** any net gain or (loss) derived from the business use of your home and shown on Schedule D or Form 4797. If more than one place of business, see instructions	**8**	

See instrs for columns (a) & (b) before completing lines 9-20		**(a)** Direct expenses	**(b)** Indirect expenses		
9	Casualty losses	**9**			
10	Deductible mortgage interest	**10**			
11	Real estate taxes	**11**			
12	Add lines 9, 10, and 11	**12**			
13	Multiply line 12, column (b) by line 7		**13**		
14	Add line 12, column (a) and line 13			**14**	
15	Subtract line 14 from line 8. If zero or less, enter -0-			**15**	
16	Excess mortgage interest	**16**			
17	Insurance	**17**			
18	Repairs and maintenance	**18**			
19	Utilities	**19**			
20	Other expenses	**20**			
21	Add lines 16 through 20	**21**			
22	Multiply line 21, column (b) by line 7		**22**		
23	Carryover of operating expenses from 1994 Form 8829, line 41		**23**		
24	Add line 21 in column (a), line 22, and line 23			**24**	
25	Allowable operating expenses. Enter the **smaller** of line 15 or line 24			**25**	
26	Limit on excess casualty losses and depreciation. Subtract line 25 from line 15			**26**	
27	Excess casualty losses		**27**		
28	Depreciation of your home from Part III below		**28**		
29	Carryover of excess casualty losses and depreciation from 1994 Form 8829, line 42		**29**		
30	Add lines 27 through 29			**30**	
31	Allowable excess casualty losses and depreciation. Enter the **smaller** of line 26 or line 30			**31**	
32	Add lines 14, 25, and 31			**32**	
33	Casualty loss portion, if any, from lines 14 and 31. Carry amount to **Form 4684**, Section B			**33**	
34	Allowable expenses for business use of your home. Subtract line 33 from line 32. Enter here and on Schedule C, line 30. If your home was used for more than one business, see instructions . . . . ▶			**34**	

Part III — Depreciation of Your Home

35	Enter the **smaller** of your home's adjusted basis or its fair market value	**35**	
36	Value of land included on line 35	**36**	
37	Basis of building. Subtract line 36 from line 35	**37**	
38	Business basis of building. Multiply line 37 by line 7	**38**	
39	Depreciation percentage	**39**	%
40	Depreciation allowable. Multiply line 38 by line 39. Enter here and on line 28.	**40**	

Part IV — Carryover of Unallowed Expenses to 1996

41	Operating expenses. Subtract line 25 from line 24. If less than zero, enter -0-	**41**	
42	Excess casualty losses and depreciation. Subtract line 31 from line 30. If less than zero, enter -0-	**42**	

D181 For Paperwork Reduction Act Notice, see instructions.

Form **8829** (1995

FDIA6901 09/20/95

YOUR DEDUCTIBLE AUTOMOBILE EXPENSES

Here again you may be able to recapture some of the money you are already spending on your automobile by simply using it in the normal course of your home based travel business. You will need your automobile to meet with clients to discuss travel plans, deliver tickets and travel documents, attend seminars and training classes and so on. Virtually all of your direct automotive expenses are deductible as are a good number of other costs.

Depending on the percentage of business use that you utilize your automobile you may elect to simply use the IRS Standard Mileage Rate or Actual Expenses.

STANDARD MILEAGE RATE

The IRS determines yearly the average cost per mile of operating a normal automobile for business purposes. Each tax year the IRS will set the allowable amount per mile that may be deducted . If you have used your automobile in your home based travel agency business simply multiply the number of miles by the IRS multiplier to arrive at your allowable deduction. You must have written documentation for the deduction to be taken but this is an easy way to determine your expense.

ACTUAL AUTOMOBILE EXPENSES

You may deduct all of your actual expenses of operating your automobile for your business purposes including the acquisition price of the car itself! Following are just some of the expenses you may recover by deducting your actual expenses of operation. There is a minimum percentage of business usage you must maintain in order to depreciate the purchase price of your car so you must check with your accountant or tax specialist.

Depreciation (See IRS Form 4562)
Garage Rent or Business Allocation of Garage Expense to House a Business Asset
Gasoline
Insurance
Interest (Only Self Employed Independent Contractors)
Lease Fees and Payments
Licenses
Oil
Parking Fees
Personal Property Taxes

Rental Fees
Repairs
Tires
Tolls and Fees

I.R.S. FORM 4562 "DEPRECIATION AND AMOR-TIZATION"

The appropriate form on which to set up the depreciation for the business usage of your automobile is the IRS form 4562. Again the amount of allowable depreciation is then transferred to your Schedule C as an operational expense of your home based travel business.

Form **4562**	**Depreciation and Amortization** **(Including Information on Listed Property)**	OMB No. 1545-0172 **1995**
Department of the Treasury Internal Revenue Service (10)	▶ **See separate instructions.** ▶ **Attach this form to your return.**	Attachment Sequence No. **67**

Name(s) shown on return | Business or activity to which this form relates | Identifying number

Part I Election To Expense Certain Tangible Property (Section 179) (Note: *If you have any "Listed Property," complete Part V before you complete Part I.*)

1	Maximum dollar limitation. If an enterprise zone business, see page 1 of the instructions . .	**1**	$17,500
2	Total cost of section 179 property placed in service during the tax year. See page 2 of the instructions	**2**	
3	Threshold cost of section 179 property before reduction in limitation	**3**	$200,000
4	Reduction in limitation. Subtract line 3 from line 2. If zero or less, enter -0-	**4**	
5	Dollar limitation for tax year. Subtract line 4 from line 1. If zero or less, enter -0-. If married filing separately, see page 2 of the instructions	**5**	

(a) Description of property	(b) Cost	(c) Elected cost	
6			

7	Listed property. Enter amount from line 27	**7**	
8	Total elected cost of section 179 property. Add amounts in column (c), lines 6 and 7 . . .	**8**	
9	Tentative deduction. Enter the smaller of line 5 or line 8	**9**	
10	Carryover of disallowed deduction from 1994. See page 2 of the instructions	**10**	
11	Taxable income limitation. Enter the smaller of taxable income (not less than zero) or line 5 (see instructions)	**11**	
12	Section 179 expense deduction. Add lines 9 and 10, but do not enter more than line 11 . .	**12**	
13	Carryover of disallowed deduction to 1996. Add lines 9 and 10, less line 12 ▶	**13**	

Note: *Do not use Part II or Part III below for listed property (automobiles, certain other vehicles, cellular telephones, certain computers, or property used for entertainment, recreation, or amusement). Instead, use Part V for listed property.*

Part II MACRS Depreciation For Assets Placed in Service ONLY During Your 1995 Tax Year (Do Not Include Listed Property.)

Section A—General Asset Account Election

14   If you are making the election under section 168(i)(4) to group any assets placed in service during the tax year into one or more general asset accounts, check this box. See page 2 of the instructions . . . . ▶ ☐

(a) Classification of property	(b) Month and year placed in service	(c) Basis for depreciation (business/investment use only—see instructions)	(d) Recovery period	(e) Convention	(f) Method	(g) Depreciation deduction
Section B—General Depreciation System (GDS) (See page 2 of the instructions.)						
15a 3-year property						
b 5-year property						
c 7-year property						
d 10-year property						
e 15-year property						
f 20-year property						
g Residential rental property			27.5 yrs.	MM	S/L	
			27.5 yrs.	MM	S/L	
h Nonresidential real property			39 yrs.	MM	S/L	
				MM	S/L	
Section C—Alternative Depreciation System (ADS) (See page 4 of the instructions.)						
16a Class life					S/L	
b 12-year			12 yrs.		S/L	
c 40-year			40 yrs.	MM	S/L	

Part III Other Depreciation (Do Not Include Listed Property.) (See page 4 of the instructions.)

17	GDS and ADS deductions for assets placed in service in tax years beginning before 1995	**17**	
18	Property subject to section 168(f)(1) election	**18**	
19	ACRS and other depreciation	**19**	

Part IV Summary (See page 4 of the instructions.)

20	Listed property. Enter amount from line 26	**20**	
21	**Total.** Add deductions on line 12, lines 15 and 16 in column (g), and lines 17 through 20. Enter here and on the appropriate lines of your return. Partnerships and S corporations—see instructions . .	**21**	
22	For assets shown above and placed in service during the current year, enter the portion of the basis attributable to section 263A costs	**22**	

For Paperwork Reduction Act Notice, see page 1 of the separate instructions.   Cat. No. 12906N   Form **4562** (1995)

Part V — Listed Property—Automobiles, Certain Other Vehicles, Cellular Telephones, Certain Computers, an[d] Property Used for Entertainment, Recreation, or Amusement

Note: *For any vehicle for which you are using the standard mileage rate or deducting lease expense, complete only 23a, 23b, columns (a) through (c) of Section A, all of Section B, and Section C if applicable.*

Section A—Depreciation and Other Information (Caution: *See page 5 of the instructions for limitations for automobiles.*)

23a Do you have evidence to support the business/investment use claimed? ☐ Yes ☐ No **23b** If "Yes," is the evidence written? ☐ Yes ☐ N[o]

(a) Type of property (list vehicles first)	(b) Date placed in service	(c) Business/ investment use percentage	(d) Cost or other basis	(e) Basis for depreciation (business/investment use only)	(f) Recovery period	(g) Method/ Convention	(h) Depreciation deduction	(i) Elected section 179 cost
24 Property used more than 50% in a qualified business use (See page 5 of the instructions.):								
		%						
		%						
		%						
25 Property used 50% or less in a qualified business use (See page 5 of the instructions.):								
		%				S/L –		
		%				S/L –		
		%				S/L –		

26 Add amounts in column (h). Enter the total here and on line 20, page 1. . . . . . **26**

27 Add amounts in column (i). Enter the total here and on line 7, page 1 . . . . **27**

Section B—Information on Use of Vehicles

Complete this section for vehicles used by a sole proprietor, partner, or other "more than 5% owner," or related person.

If you provided vehicles to your employees, first answer the questions in Section C to see if you meet an exception to completing this section for those vehicles.

	(a) Vehicle 1		(b) Vehicle 2		(c) Vehicle 3		(d) Vehicle 4		(e) Vehicle 5		(f) Vehicle 6	
28 Total business/investment miles driven during the year (DO NOT include commuting miles)												
29 Total commuting miles driven during the year												
30 Total other personal (noncommuting) miles driven												
31 Total miles driven during the year. Add lines 28 through 30.												
	Yes	No	Yes	No	Yes	No	Yes	No	Yes	No	Yes	No
32 Was the vehicle available for personal use during off-duty hours?												
33 Was the vehicle used primarily by a more than 5% owner or related person?												
34 Is another vehicle available for personal use?												

Section C—Questions for Employers Who Provide Vehicles for Use by Their Employees

*Answer these questions to determine if you meet an exception to completing Section B for vehicles used by employees who **are not** more than 5% owners or related persons.*

		Yes	No
35	Do you maintain a written policy statement that prohibits all personal use of vehicles, including commuting, by your employees?		
36	Do you maintain a written policy statement that prohibits personal use of vehicles, except commuting, by your employees? See page 6 of the instructions for vehicles used by corporate officers, directors, or 1% or more owners		
37	Do you treat all use of vehicles by employees as personal use?		
38	Do you provide more than five vehicles to your employees, obtain information from your employees about the use of the vehicles, and retain the information received?		
39	Do you meet the requirements concerning qualified automobile demonstration use? See page 6 of the instructions . .		

Note: *If your answer to 35, 36, 37, 38, or 39 is "Yes," you need not complete Section B for the covered vehicles.*

Part VI — Amortization

(a) Description of costs	(b) Date amortization begins	(c) Amortizable amount	(d) Code section	(e) Amortization period or percentage	(f) Amortization for this year
40 Amortization of costs that begins during your 1995 tax year:					
41 Amortization of costs that began before 1995 . . . . **41**					
42 **Total.** Enter here and on "Other Deductions" or "Other Expenses" line of your return . . . **42**					

TRAVEL AND ENTERTAINMENT EXPENSES

Here is an area many folks find extremely attractive while operating a home based travel agency. Many times your client may well be your best friend and that lunch you enjoyed while delivering your friend's airline tickets may well be a deductible expense. Your trip to Hawaii may well be deductible as might your Caribbean cruise.

You certainly need the advice and support of a tax professional when documenting these types of expenses but the tax code allows valid deductions for business travel and entertainment and as a self employed business person you are entitled to claim these deductions.

TRAVEL EXPENSES

The IRS allows all expenses directly related to business travel to be deducted as a normal business cost. Transportation, lodging, car rental, tips, meals, telephone calls, laundry, parking fees, and so on may all be deducted. Fees for attending industry conventions and trade shows, seminars, and familiarizations tours may all be deductible. You must document the business purpose of the travel and it must meet with IRS approval.

If you have received a free tour as a group organizer and act as the volunteer group leader you must claim the fair market value of the tour as income on your Schedule C. Further, as a volunteer group leader, your travel expenses cannot be deducted.

ENTERTAINMENT

Entertainment done for business purposes is partially deductible under certain circumstances. You must document the business purpose of the entertainment, as well as the participants, cost, and how the entertainment was directly related to your business. The percentage that you may write off has changed considerably over the past few years so you will want to check with the IRS or your tax professional for the applicable IRS multiplier.

GENERAL BUSINESS EXPENSES

In addition to the above deductions you may also deduct all of your normal business expenses that you incur in the day to day operation of your home based travel business. Some of these would include the following.

Accounting and Bookkeeping Fees
Advertising Expenses, Prizes and Contests
Attorney Fees
Automated Reservation System Fees
Automobile Expenses as Described Above
Bank Service Charges
Business Start Up Expenses
Commissions Paid Other Independent Contractors
Consultant Fees
Corporate Organization Expenses
Depreciation On Your Business Usage of Your Home and Automobile
Dues and Subscriptions
Education Expenses For Maintaining or Improving Your Required Skills
Furniture and Equipment (Office)
Gifts (Limited to $25 Per Person Per Year)
Home Office Deduction (As Mentioned Above)
Insurance Expenses
Interest on Business Loans (Includes Car Loan for Self Employed)
IRA, Keogh, or Other Pension Plan Contributions
License and Registration Fees
Office Maintenance and Repair
Office Supplies
Passport and Visa Fees
Postage and Delivery Fees
Printing and Copying
Professional Association Fees and Dues
Tax Preparation and Advice
Telephone, Facsimile, E-Mail and Other Communication Costs
Travel Expenses (As Mentioned Above)
Uncollectible Accounts
Utilities

THE IRS SCHEDULE C "PROFIT OR LOSS FROM BUSINESS"

This is the appropriate schedule to report your business profits or losses and to also record the impact of your home office deductions (Form 8829) and automobile depreciation and expenses (Form 4562). Following is a sample Schedule C.

SCHEDULE C (Form 1040)	Profit or Loss From Business	OMB No. 1545-0074

SCHEDULE C (Form 1040)

Department of the Treasury
Internal Revenue Service (10)

Profit or Loss From Business
(Sole Proprietorship)
▶ Partnerships, joint ventures, etc., must file Form 1065.
▶ Attach to Form 1040 or Form 1041.   ▶ See Instructions for Schedule C (Form 1040).

OMB No. 1545-0074

1995

Attachment
Sequence No. **09**

Name of proprietor

Social security number (SSN)

A Principal business or profession, including product or service (see page C-1)

B Enter principal business code (see page C-6) ▶

C Business name. If no separate business name, leave blank.

D Employer ID number (EIN), if any

E Business address (including suite or room no.) ▶
City, town or post office, state, and ZIP code

F Accounting method: (1) ☐ Cash   (2) ☐ Accrual   (3) ☐ Other (specify) ▶

G Method(s) used to value closing inventory: (1) ☐ Cost   (2) ☐ Lower of cost or market   (3) ☐ Other (attach explanation)   (4) ☐ Does not apply (if checked, skip line H) | Yes | No |

H Was there any change in determining quantities, costs, or valuations between opening and closing inventory? If "Yes," attach explanation

I Did you "materially participate" in the operation of this business during 1995? If "No," see page C-2 for limit on losses.   ▶ ☐

J If you started or acquired this business during 1995, check here

Part I — Income

1	Gross receipts or sales. **Caution:** *If this income was reported to you on Form W-2 and the "Statutory employee" box on that form was checked, see page C-2 and check here* ▶ ☐	**1**
2	Returns and allowances	**2**
3	Subtract line 2 from line 1	**3**
4	Cost of goods sold (from line 40 on page 2)	**4**
5	**Gross profit.** Subtract line 4 from line 3	**5**
6	Other income, including Federal and state gasoline or fuel tax credit or refund (see page C-2) ▶	**6**
7	**Gross income.** Add lines 5 and 6	**7**

Part II — Expenses. Enter expenses for business use of your home **only** on line 30.

8	Advertising	**8**	19	Pension and profit-sharing plans	**19**
9	Bad debts from sales or services (see page C-3)	**9**	20	Rent or lease (see page C-4):	
10	Car and truck expenses (see page C-3)	**10**		a Vehicles, machinery, and equipment	**20a**
11	Commissions and fees.	**11**		b Other business property	**20b**
12	Depletion.	**12**	21	Repairs and maintenance	**21**
13	Depreciation and section 179 expense deduction (not included in Part III) (see page C-3)	**13**	22	Supplies (not included in Part III)	**22**
			23	Taxes and licenses	**23**
			24	Travel, meals, and entertainment:	
14	Employee benefit programs (other than on line 19)	**14**		a Travel	**24a**
15	Insurance (other than health)	**15**		b Meals and entertainment	
16	Interest:			c Enter 50% of line 24b subject to limitations (see page C-4)	
	a Mortgage (paid to banks, etc.)	**16a**		d Subtract line 24c from line 24b	**24d**
	b Other	**16b**	25	Utilities	**25**
17	Legal and professional services	**17**	26	Wages (less employment credits)	**26**
18	Office expense	**18**	27	Other expenses (from line 46 on page 2)	**27**

28	**Total expenses** before expenses for business use of home. Add lines 8 through 27 in columns. ▶	**28**
29	Tentative profit (loss). Subtract line 28 from line 7	**29**
30	Expenses for business use of your home. Attach **Form 8829**	**30**
31	**Net profit or (loss).** Subtract line 30 from line 29.	**31**

31 **Net profit or (loss).** Subtract line 30 from line 29.
- If a profit, enter on **Form 1040, line 12,** and ALSO on **Schedule SE, line 2** (statutory employees, see page C-5). Estates and trusts, enter on Form 1041, line 3.
- If a loss, you MUST go on to line 32.

32 If you have a loss, check the box that describes your investment in this activity (see page C-5).
- If you checked 32a, enter the loss on **Form 1040, line 12,** and ALSO on **Schedule SE, line 2** (statutory employees, see page C-5). Estates and trusts, enter on Form 1041, line 3.
- If you checked 32b, you MUST attach **Form 6198.**

32a ☐ All investment is at risk.
32b ☐ Some investment is not at risk.

For Paperwork Reduction Act Notice, see Form 1040 instructions.   Cat. No. 11334P   Schedule C (Form 1040) 1995

Chapter 26

THE NATIONAL ASSOCIA-TION OF COMMISSIONED TRAVEL AGENTS (NACTA)

The National Association of Commissioned Travel Agents

The National Association of Commissioned Travel Agents is the national association of travel industry outside sales agents, independent contractors, cruise only travel agencies, and ARC appointed agencies that work with outside sales forces and independent contractors. NACTA was established in 1986 to represent the interest of independent entrepreneurs within the travel industry and to facilitate a national organization to promote professionalism and create a forum for open communication. NACTA offers many benefits to its members and membership is open to those entering the industry as well as those already established.

You should consider joining this valuable industry association as one of the first things that you do when establishing your home based travel business. NACTA offers just about everything you need to establish yourself with credibility and is well worth the cost of membership. Following are some of the member benefits you will receive.

NACTA "INDEPENDENT TRAVEL AGENT's HANDBOOK"

Written by Tom and Joanie Ogg, this handbook is the very latest word on issues confronting independent contractors and outside sales people in the travel industry. It is bulging with hard core information you need to successfully set up your business. The NACTA agreement for Independent Agents are worth the price of membership alone. The manual gives great insight into issues confronting the new entrepreneur and is an invaluable working tool. A copy of the "NACTA INDEPENDENT TRAVEL AGENT HANDBOOK" is included with each new membership.

NACTA "INDEPENDENT TRAVEL AGENT NEWS"

For over ten years independent travel agents have relied upon the NACTA newsletter for the latest information on suppliers friendly to independent agents, legal issues, industry trends, consortiums, marketing ideas, income opportunities, new automation, home office issues, cruises, destinations and much more. The magazine style newsletter is issued four times a year and is worth the price of membership alone.

NACTA ON-LINE

NACTA operates its own section in the Travel Professional's Forum in CompuServe.   This section is for travel industry personnel only and is open to all NACTA members. If you are not yet on-line NACTA will provide you with CompuServe software as part of your membership benefits and instructions to get you up and running. You can use the forum to communicate with industry leaders and other NACTA members. You will also access NACTA E-Mail updates as they occur. If you already are in CompuServe just type "GONACTA" to visit NACTA's forum.

NACTA is also active on America On-Line in the Travel Professional's forum. If you prefer AOL over CompuServe, NACTA is available to you by logging on to the Travel Professional's Forum and scrolling down to the "Ask NACTA" section. Simply choose Travel, then Travel Forum, then click on Travel Boards, then the Travel Professional's Board, then scroll to "Ask NACTA." If you are not yet on-line with AOL, your NACTA membership entitles you to free software and ten free hours of access. Let NACTA know you are interested in AOL!

NACTA's presence on the internet is in the form of its own domain on the World Wide Web, "NACTA.com."   NACTA also offers NACTA members both home page design and hosting as well as E-mail services within the NACTA domain. You can E-mail NACTA at NACTA@NACTA.com if you are interested in their internet services. Visit NACTA's home page at http://www.NACTA.com.

ERRORS AND OMISSIONS INSURANCE

NACTA offers an excellent individual errors and omissions insurance program for independent contractors and travel industry outside sales. The policy is designed for maximum protection and includes general liability insurance as well. NACTA offers a very competitive rate for members.

NACTA INDEPENDENT CONTRACTOR LIBRARY

NACTA offers up to the minute information on publications, videos and tapes of interest to independent contractors and outside sales agents within the travel industry. Publications and seminars on tapes from industry gurus are offered in a manner that is easy to access so that you acquire just the information you need. NACTA maintains an ongoing search for topics of interest to its membership

NACTA FAMILIARIZATION CRUISES AND TOURS

NACTA offers cruise seminars each year that feature the world's top cruise ships with seminar speakers that are considered the best in the industry. The seminars are focused on issues of importance to independent contractors and outside sales as well as agency owners interested in the independent contractor evolution in the travel industry. NACTA also operates land based familiarization tours to various parts of the world that are focused on destination orientation and issues of importance to independent contractors and outside sales agents.

NACTA's "OUTSIDE AGENT TRACKING SOFT-WARE'

As a NACTA member you receive "OATS" commission tracking software for outside and independent agents at a substantial discount. OATS makes the task of staying on top of commissions extremely easy and uncomplicated. OATS allows you to gain instant access to your sales data and eliminate the need for unnecessary paperwork and bulky paper files.

NACTA DISCOUNTS ON TRADE PUBLICATIONS AND INDUSTRY SOFTWARE

As a NACTA member you are entitled to either free or special subscription rates to the following trade publications _The Wholesale Source Book_, _Porthole Magazine_, _Cruise Travel Magazine_, _Cruise Week/Cruise Observer Newsletter_, _Travel World News_ and more. NACTA members also receive substantial discounts on _CD ROM Travel Planner_ and _CruiseBase_, a software program to help you select just the perfect cruise itinerary and ship for every situation. In addition to the above discounts on publications, NACTA members receive discounted rates on two extremely good familiarization trip publications. Both _GTC Fam Facts_ and _The Fam Connection_ feature hundreds of listings offering reduced rate and agent discounts to qualified travel professionals

NACTA's Supplier Guide

As a NACTA member and an independent contractor you may acquire NACTA's Supplier's Guide. This catalog links independent contractors to suppliers and host agencies throughout the world. You may book directly with hundreds of travel industry suppliers as a Supplier guide subscriber and member of NACTA! What would take an individual months to accomplish is done in just minutes with the NACTA Suppliers Guide. For only $49.95 and your NACTA membership you are in touch with the travel community in minutes.

NACTA MEMBERSHIP APPLICATION

For the sake of making it easy for you to get involved in the travel industry here is a membership application for NACTA. You do not have to designate an agency affiliation to join but may advise NACTA after you have aligned yourself with your host agency. If you are interested in joining NACTA simply complete the following application and forward it for immediate processing.

National Association of Commissioned Travel Agents

Membership Application

Name _____
First   Middle I.   Last

Title _____ Agency Name _____

Address _____
Street   City   State   Zip

Home Phone_____ Work Phone_____
Area Code   Area Code

24 Hour Fax_____ AOL E-Mail Address _____
Area Code

CompuServe E-Mail_____ Birthdate ___/___/___ Today's Date ___/___/___

Circle any of the following descriptions that apply:

ARC Agency Owner   Inside Agent   Outside Agent   Independent Contractor   Cruise Oriented Agent
Full Time   Part Time   New to Industry   1-2 Years   3-5 Years   5-10 Years   10 Years or More
Please list any seminar topics you would be interested in _____

Statement of Liability and NACTA Membership Agreement

This NACTA membership is valid for one year from the date noted below. NACTA membership price is $95.00 for the first year and $55.00 per year thereafter. New members receive the NACTA's "Independent Travel Agent's Handbook" and a subscription to NACTA's "Independent Travel Agent News" quarterly newsletter upon receipt of application and fees. Membership fees are non-refundable. The National Association of Commissioned Travel Agents neither guarantees nor insures that the service provided any officer, employee or member and shall assume no responsibility or liability for actions or events beyond its control in connection with services provided. Further members agree to hold NACTA harmless for any act, error, omission, injury, loss, accident, nonperformance, financial failure, or any other irregularity, or any consequences resulting therefrom, which may be caused from the neglect, default, or any other action of association, company, carrier, independent contractor or person engaged in the service of NACTA.

Signature_____Date____/____/____

Please charge $95 to my Visa/Mastercard #_____Expiration Date___/___/___

Name as it appears on the card_____Check enclosed$_____

Please make check payable to NACTA and mail to: **NACTA**
P.O. Box 2398
Valley Center, California 92082-2398
619-751-1197   Fax 619-751-1309   CServe GONACTA   AOL NACTA

Chapter 27
TRADE GROUPS AND ASSOCIATIONS

Beyond this book, there are numerous sources for further information and assistance. Several trade associations have developed seminars, video tapes, cassettes and publications which deal with the organization and operation of retail travel agencies and most colleges, universities, and travel trade schools offer additional training and information. The following are sources within the industry for information, support, and assistance in developing your knowledge of the travel industry and while there are many other organizations performing similar functions, these are the most prominent:

APPOINTING ORGANIZATIONS

AIRLINE REPORTING CORPORATION   703-816-8000
1530 Wilson Blvd. #800   Applications   703-816-8085
Arlington, VA 22209-2448   Bond & L.C. Info   703-875-0796
    Fax   703-816-8104

Represents domestic carriers and appoints travel agents to issue traffic documents for these carriers.

CRUISE LINE INTERNATIONAL ASSOCIATION
500 Fifth Avenue #1407   212-921-0066
New York, New York 10110 Fax   212-921-0549
    Applications & Fax Back Info 800-372-2542

Represents most cruise lines throughout the world and designates agents as official CLIA members. The organization provides training and educational seminars.

INTERNATIONAL AIRLINES TRAVEL AGENCY NETWORK
Suite 4060, 2000 Peel Street   514-844-2877
Montreal, Quebec, Canada   Fax   514-844-5286

Represents most international carriers and lists travel agencies for industry identification. IATAN issues an industry identification card to qualified agents.

TRADE ASSOCIATIONS

AIR TRANSPORT ASSOCIATION OF AMERICA (ATA)
1301 Pennsylvania Avenue NW, Suite 1100   202-626-4000
Washington, DC 20004-1707   Fax   202-626-4181

ATA is an all airline member trade organization representing the airline industry.

ALLIANCE OF CANADIAN TRAVEL ASSOCIATIONS (ACTA)
1729 Bank Street, Suite 201   513-521-0474
Ottawa, Ontario,   Fax   513-521-0805
Canada

An association representing the interests of agents, suppliers, and wholesalers to the public, government and other bodies.

ALLIANCE OF WESTCHESTER TRAVEL AGENTS (AWTA)
232 N. Highland Ave.   914-762-2229
Ossining, NY 10562   Fax   914-762-2608

An association of retail travel agents in a geographic area.

AMERICAN HOTEL & MOTEL ASSOCIATION (AHMA)
1201 New York Avenue NW, Suite 600   202-289-3100
Washington, DC 20005-3917   Fax   202-289-3199

An association representing the hotel and motel industry's position to the government and the public. A directory of membership is available.

AMERICAN SOCIETY OF TRAVEL AGENTS (ASTA)
1101 King Street, Suite 200   703-739-2782
Alexandria, Virginia 22314   Fax   703-684-8319

ASTA is an international association of retail agents, suppliers, and other affiliated industry members numbering over 23,000 worldwide. Members enjoy conventions, seminars, training classes, educational materials, and effective representation in industry affairs and government legislation. They offer a comprehensive consumer affairs department.

ASSOCIATION FOR THE PROMOTION OF TOURISM TO AFRICA
289 S. Robertson Blvd., Suite 266   310-659-8480
Beverly Hills, CA 90211   Fax   310-659-8569

An association of travel professionals promoting tourism and travel to Africa.

ASSOCIATION OF BRITISH TRAVEL AGENTS (ABTA)

55-57 Newman Street   071-637-2444
London, England WIP 4AH

An association of retail travel agents in a geographic area.

ASSOCIATION OF RETAIL TRAVEL AGENTS (ARTA)

845 Sir Thomas Court #3   717-545-9548
Harrisburg, PA 17109   Fax   717-545-9613

ARTA enjoys over 3600 members and helps agencies through presenting on-going training classes, developing training material, industry representation on government legislation and regulation, and offers continuing phone support.

ASSOCIATION OF TRAVEL MARKETING EXECUTIVES (ATME)

P. O. Box 43563   202-232-7107
Washington, DC 20010

A national association of sales and marketing executives in the travel industry.

CARIBBEAN HOTEL ASSOCIATION (CHA)

18 Marseilles St., Suite 1-A   809-725-9139
Santurce, Puerto Rico 00907

An association existing for the promotion of travel and tourism to the Caribbean.

CARIBBEAN TOURISM ORGANIZATION (CTA)

20 East 46th Street   212-682-0435
New York, NY 10017   Fax   212-697-4258

An organization existing for the purpose of promoting tourism to the Caribbean.

HAWAII VISITORS BUREAU (HVB)

350 5th Avenue, Suite 808   212-947-0717
New York, NY 10118   Fax   212-947-0725

A national membership bureau promoting travel and tourism to the Hawaiian Islands.

INSTITUTE OF CERTIFIED TRAVEL AGENTS (ICTA)

P. O. Box 812059   617-237-0280
Wellesley, MA 02191-0012   Fax   617-237-3860

ICTA is an organization focused on travel agent professionalism. They offer numerous programs of continuing education and certification for the travel community. Two of the programs they offer are the Certified Travel Counselor (CTC) and the Destination Specialist (DS) which are recognized highly in the travel industry.

INTERNATIONAL ASSOCIATION OF CONVENTION AND VISITOR BUREAUS (IACVB)

P. O. Box 6690   217-359-8881
Champaign, IL 61826-6690   Fax   217-359-0965

An association of convention and visitors bureaus in the nation working to promote interest in this segment of the industry.

INTERNATIONAL FEDERATION OF WOMEN'S TRAVEL ORGANIZATIONS (IFWTO)

13901 N. 73rd Street, Suite 210B   602-596-6640
Scottsdale, AZ 85260   Fax   602-596-6638

A non-profit organization with the purpose of promotion and support for women in the travel industry. They have chapters throughout the world that offer chapter meetings and support.

LONG ISLAND TRAVEL AGENTS (LITA)

2961 Merrick Rd.   516-783-6441
Bellmore, NY 11710   Fax   516-783-6785

An association of local retail ARC appointed agencies in a geographic area.

MIDWEST AGENTS SELLING TRAVEL (MAST)

15 Spinning Wheel Rd., Suite 336   708-323-0770
Hinsdale, IL 60521   Fax   708-323-2662

An association of retail ARC and CLIA appointed agencies in a geographic area. This in one of the largest regional agency associations.

NATIONAL AIR CARRIER ASSOCIATION (NACA)

1730 "M" St. NW, Suite 806   202-833-8200
Washington, DC 20036

This is a trade organization for the purpose of representation of small charter service carriers.

NATIONAL AIR TRANSPORT ASSOCIATION (NATA)
4226 King St.   703-845-9000
Alexandria, CA 22302   Fax   703-845-8176

A national trade association representing air charter, air taxi and air ambulance operators.

NATIONAL ASSOCIATION OF BUSINESS TRAVEL AGENTS (NABTA)
3225 Wilshire Blvd., Suite 1601   213-382-3335
Los Angeles, CA 90010-1418

NATIONAL ASSOCIATION OF COMMISSIONED TRAVEL AGENTS (NACTA)
P. O. Box 2398   619-751-1007
Valley Center, CA 92082-2398   Fax   619-751-1309

NACTA is the association for outside sales people, independent contractors, cruise only travel agencies and ARC agencies interested in developing sales forces. NACTA conducts numerous training seminars for non ARC appointed travel entities. NACTA offers local chapter meetings. NACTA is available to members on-line via CompuServe Information Service and the internet. NACTA is primarily an association of leisure agents in the industry and enjoys over members nation wide. NACTA is an excellent place to start your investigation into the travel industry.

NATIONAL ASSOCIATION OF CRUISE ONLY AGENTS (NACOA)
3191 Coral Way, Suite 622   305-446-7732
Miami, FL 33145   Fax   305-446-9732

This is a growing association comprised of cruise only travel agencies and or other agencies with specialized cruise departments. They offer professional support and ongoing educational seminars and forums on land and at sea. They also offer an extensive newsletter to members as well as other group benefits.

NATIONAL BUSINESS TRAVEL ASSOCIATION (NBTA)
1650 King St., Suite 401   703-684-0836
Alexandria, VA 22314

Fax

703-684-0263

NATIONAL TOUR ASSOCIATION (NTA)   800-755-8687
546 East Main Street   Fax   606-226-4444
Lexington, KY 40508

This is a trade organization comprised of tour operators, suppliers and destination marketing associations in the United States and Canada. Such offerings as a consumer guide and Consumer Protection Plan exist for the travel industry.

PACIFIC AREA TRAVEL ASSOCIATION (PATA)
1 Montgomery Street   415-986-4646
Telesis Tower, Suite 1000   Fax   415-986-3458
San Francisco, California 94104

PATA enjoys a membership of approximately 2000 various companies all with a vested interest in tourism within the Pacific Rim and Asia. In addition to the above membership, there are about 65 local chapters throughout the world with an individual membership of over 15,000. PATA's objective is to promote tourism to and within the Pacific Rim countries and Asia. Members enjoy destination seminars, trade shows, conventions and educational materials.

SACRAMENTO AREA TRAVEL AGENTS (SATA)
P. O. Box 15424   916-929-1603
Sacramento, CA 95851-0424

A regional association of retail travel agents.

SOCIETY FOR THE ADVANCEMENT OF TRAVEL FOR THE HANDICAPPED (SATH)
347 Fifth Avenue, Suite 610   212-447-7284
New York, NY 10016   Fax   212-725-8253

This organization makes information available to disabled persons about facilities in foreign countries. The mission of this organization is to assist in the needs of the disabled.

SOCIETY OF INCENTIVE TRAVEL EXECUTIVES (SITE)
21 W. 38th Street, 10th Floor   212-575-0910
New York, New York 10018   Fax   212-575-1838

An international professional organization for individuals in the incentive travel segment of the industry. SITE provides worldwide seminars, networking, and social functions as well as research into the nature and effectiveness of incentive travel.

SOCIETY OF TRAVEL AGENTS IN GOVERNMENT (STAG)

6935 Wisconsin Ave. NW, Suite 200   301-654-8595
Bethesda, Maryland 20815   Fax   301-654-6663

This association exists for continued growth and professionalism in the government travel market. It is an educational forum made up of travel agencies, suppliers, federal and other government travel managers and contractors.

TOURISM INDUSTRY ASSOCIATION OF CANADA (TIAC)
1016-130 Albert Street   613-238-3883
Ottawa, Ontario, K1P 5G4   Fax 613-238-3878
CANADA

The TIAC mission is to promote policies and programs which will enhance the sustained viability and prosperity of the Canadian Tourism Industry.

TRAVEL AGENTS OF THE CAROLINAS (TAC)   919-676-0400
8224 Creedmoor Rd., Suite 101   Fax   919-676-8211
Raleigh, NC 27613

A professional association of localized ARC appointed travel agents including North and South Carolina.

TRAVEL AND TOURISM RESEARCH ASSOCIATION (TTRA)
10200 W. 44TH Ave., Suite 304   303-940-6557
Wheat Ridge, CO 80033   Fax   303-422-8894

This is a national association with a mission to educate others about the travel and tourism industry.

TRAVELERIANS   818-795-8656
c/o Carriage House Travel   Fax   818-795-0113
350 S. Lake St., Suite 210
Pasadena, CA 91101

A regional association of travel professionals in the San Gabriel Valley Area of Southern California offering monthly member meetings. The mission is to provide continued education and support for the regions travel community.

TRAVEL INFORMATION SERVICE (TIS)   215-456-9600
                 For the hearing impaired   215-456-9602

A service which provides information and resources by phone for those with physical disabilities.

UNITED STATES TOUR OPERATORS ASSOCIATION (USTOA)   212-750-7371
211 East 51st Street, Suite 12B   Fax   212-421-1285
New York, NY 10022

A national trade association representing the travel industry. The membership is comprised of large and medium sized tour operators and it offers insurance for travelers against members default and lack of service.

UNITED STATES TRAVEL AND TOURISM ADMINISTRA-TION (USTTA)
14th Street & Constitution Avenue NW, Suite 1860 212-482-4904
New York, NY 10022   Fax   212-484-2887

This administrations purpose is to promote travel and tourism by foreign countries to the United States of America.

WESTERN ASSOCIATION OF RETAIL TRAVEL AGENTS (WATA)   408-777-8170
12280 S. Saratoga Sunnyvale Rd.   Fax   408-777-8173
Suite 111
Saratoga, CA 95070

An association of approximately 155 member retail ARC appointed travel agencies in a geographic area.

UNITED STATES DEPARTMENT OF TRANSPORTATION (DOT)   202-366-4000
400 7th Street SW
Washington, DC 20590

This is the United States government agency that controls transportation. It is available as a body to accept public concerns and complaints regarding transportation and tourism.

Chapter 28
TRADE MAGAZINES, PUBLI-CATIONS AND REFERENCE MATERIALS

TRAVEL PUBLICATIONS

ASTA AGENCY MANAGEMENT   800-828-2712
PACE COMMUNICATIONS
1301 Carolina St.
Greensboro, NC 27401

This is a monthly magazine that is provided to members of ASTA the American Society of Travel Agents. For non-members the cost is approximately $40 a year. It features editorials on current happenings in the industry as well as columns written by ASTA board members.

BUSINESS TRAVEL NEWS   800-447-0138
P. O. Box 1187   Fax   708-647-5972
Skokie, IL 60076

A semi-monthly newspaper of the commercial side of the industry that is provided free to qualified commercial agents, corporate travel arrangers, and business travel suppliers. Subscription is $95.00 annually to all others.

CORPORATE & INCENTIVE TRAVEL   407-989-0600
2600 N. Military Trail   Fax   407-989-9509
Boca Raton, FL 33431

This is a publication geared to the corporate and incentive side of the travel industry. It is available only to high volume large corporate agencies.

CRUISE & VACATION VIEWS   201-605-2442
25 Washington St.   Fax   201-605-2722
Morristown, New Jersey 07960

This is a leisure travel sales and marketing magazine. It is complimentary to qualified travel agents and sales personnel.

CRUISE TRAVEL MAGAZINE   708-491-6440
P. O. Box 342
Mount Morris, IL 61054-0342

A monthly consumer oriented magazine with the total focus being on cruising. Although this is a retail publication, it is an invaluable tool for keeping up to date on the various cruise ships, ports of call, and other cruise related information. The cost is $18.00 a year.

HOTEL AND TRAVEL INDEX   800-360-0015
REED TRAVEL GROUP

This is the "big book" with over 45,000 hotels, motels, resorts, and inns in the world listed with all the fact you need. It features pictures, maps, contacts, address, toll-free numbers, fax numbers, representatives and reservation codes, commission policies, CRS access codes and more. A yearly subscription includes four quarterly issues. It is truly a must if you are selling hotels and resorts. For rates and subscription information contact the above 800#.

THE INDEPENDENT TRAVEL AGENTS DESKTOP GUIDE
TOM OGG & ASSOCIATES - Publishers   619-751-1007
P. O. Box 2398   Fax   619-751-1309
Valley Center, CA 92082-2398

This desktop guide is jam packed with reference information for your home office. In this handy desktop guide you will find the all important two-letter codes for the airlines, the three-letter airport codes around the world as well as supplier contact information. This handy guide is a must as you embark on your travel career. To order this guide see "Tools To Use" in the back of the book and simply complete the order form in that section.

JAX FAX   203-655-8746
Jet Airtransport Exchange, Inc.   Fax   203-655-6257

This is a monthly magazine featuring information on consolidator fares, tours, familiarization trips, and even some cruises. It is organized by destination. It is a wealth of information at an incredibly reasonable cost of only $15 a year.

K. L. SMITH'S CRUISELETTER
http://www.chevychase.com/cruise/

This is a monthly newsletter of approximately ten pages of cruise articles. This publication is geared to the consumer but has some very interesting columns about various ships, protocol, etc. The newsletter is only available via the world wide web. It is free to all.

MEETING NEWS   800-447-0138
P.O. Box 1189   Fax   708-647-5972
Skokie, IL 60076

A magazine of 18 issues a year and two meeting guides. It is published for industry members involved in planning meetings and conventions. It is provided qualified individuals and agencies and is available to others for a subscription rate of $65.00 per year.

NACTA INDEPENDENT TRAVEL AGENT NEWS 619-751-1007
P. O. Box 2398   Fax   619-751-1309
Valley Center, CA 92082-2398

This is "The Newsletter for the Independent Travel Agents of Today". A national newsletter dealing with pertinent issues for the independent contractors and outside sales agents. This magazine sized newsletter is published six times a year. The information in this extensive newsletter will provide you with the tools you need to be a "true independent" making your own commissions and controlling your business destiny. To begin receiving your copy see "Tools To Use" in the back of the book and simply complete the order form in that section.

OFFICIAL AIRLINE GUIDES BUSINESS TRAVEL PLANNER
NORTH AMERICAN, EUROPEAN AND ASIA PACIFIC EDITIONS
REED TRAVEL GROUP   800-360-0015

These are complete guides to destination information for travel agents, frequent business travelers and corporate travel planners. These publications assist in making informed decisions about business destinations and lodging. 32,000 hotels are listed that are suited to business travel. Other items such as metro maps, location details and distances from airports, convention and meeting facilities, local attractions and more are listed. These also feature calendars of events and trade shows in major cities throughout the year. These books are published quarterly. You may purchase one or all editions separately. For rates and subscription information contact the 800 # above.

OFFICIAL CRUISE GUIDE   800-360-0015
REED TRAVEL GROUP

As mentioned in the previous Chapter 13 this is a comprehensive source of detailed cruise ship information for over 375 ships. Included are rates, recreation, accommodations, dining, toll-free numbers, commissions and contact information. It features booking and reservation policies for over 150 cruise lines as well as four color coded deck plans for many of the ships. It offers editorial reviews of ports-of-call and destinations as well as detailed ship profiles with ship size and specifications. Other helpful information are clientele profiles and sailing schedules. It is published annually. For rates and subscription information contact the 800# listed above.

OFFICIAL HOTEL GUIDE   800-360-0015
REED TRAVEL GROUP

This is a very comprehensive hotel reference with unique editorial and exclusive hotel classifications. This publication offers profiles of 30,000 hotel and resorts worldwide. It includes rates, location, amenities, accommodations, entertainment, dining, commissions and other important information. It features a specialty travel section on tennis, golf, skiing, spas and other travel offerings. Advertorials are shown with four-color hotel photos and information. With over 350 maps showing attractions, hotels, and airports resourcing information is made easy. It is published annually in three volumes with a protective case. For information on rates and subscriptions refer to the 800# listed above.

OFFICIAL MEETING FACILITIES GUIDE   800-360-0015
REED TRAVEL GROUP

This is the essential reference tool for travel agents who are meeting planners. The in-depth profiles of over 1,100 hotels, resorts and convention centers make it invaluable. There are 350 Convention and Visitors Bureaus listed as well as over 70 Destination Reports about transportation, entertainment, attractions, shopping and more. It also provides current contact names, addresses, phone and fax numbers for the listings. A one year subscription includes two issues and it is updated semi-annually. For information on rates and subscriptions refer to the 800 # listed above.

STAR SERVICE   800-360-0015
REED TRAVEL GROUP

The Star Service is a critical guide to hotels and cruise ships. This travel reference tool gives true information about 10,000 hotels and over 150 cruise ships around the world. The hotels and ships are visited and reviewed by a Star Service travel correspondent.

The ratings are honest and in-depth information about what your client might experience. Some consider this tool to be the key to making well-informed recommendations about properties and cruise ships. It is a yearly subscription with quarterly updates and includes a binder to contain the information provided. For rates and subscription information refer to the 800 # listed above.

TRADE MAGAZINES

TOUR AND TRAVEL NEWS   800-447-0138
P.O. Box 1190
Skokie, IL 60076

A weekly newspaper covering leisure and corporate industry features. It is provided free to qualified sales personnel in the travel business. Subscriptions available to others at $95 per year in the United States. *Tour & Travel News* has become very active at travel conventions bringing panels and exciting industry speakers to events.

TRAVELAGE WEST   800-446-6551
REED TRAVEL GROUP   ext. 4445
49 Stevenson, Suite 460
San Francisco, CA 94105

A weekly magazine focusing on industry events within the eleven western states and Canada. Free to qualified full-time agency sales personnel when requested in writing on agency letterhead. Subscriptions available to others at $63.00 per year. *TRAVELAGE WEST* is extremely well read in the Western U.S and Canada.

TRAVELAGE MIDAMERICA   800-446-6551
REED TRAVEL GROUP   ext.4445
320 North Michigan, Suite 601
Chicago, IL 60601

A weekly magazine focusing on the midwestern states industry events. Free to qualified full-time agency sales personnel when requested in writing on agency letterhead. Subscriptions available to others at $63.00 per year. *TRAVELAGE MID-AMERICA* is extremely well read in the mid-western states.

TRAVELAGE EAST   800-446-6551
500 Plaza Drive   ext.4445
Secaucus, New Jersey 07096

A weekly magazine focusing on industry events on the east coast.

Free to qualified full-time agency sales personnel when requested in writing on agency letterhead. Subscriptions available to others at $63.00 per year. *TRAVELAGE EAST* is extremely well read in the eastern states.

TRAVEL AGENT   609-786-0127
801 Second Avenue   Fax   212-599-8297
New York, NY 10017

This is a weekly trade magazine offering current editorials and articles on travel trends and happenings. The yearly subscription price is $250.00 for non-industry individuals and complimentary for travel agents when certain criteria is met.

TRAVEL COUNSELOR   800-447-0138
P. O. Box 1191   Fax   708-647-5972
Skokie, IL 60076

This publication is offered quarterly to the graduates of the Institute of Certified Travel Agents ICTA, CTC, and DS programs. The focus is on continuing education and business promotional ideas and suggestions. It is associated with Tour & Travel News.

TRAVEL MANAGEMENT DAILY   800-360-0015
REED TRAVEL GROUP

A daily newsletter of current happenings and events within the industry via fax.. The fast breaking news arrives on your fax machine daily. Subscriptions cost $735 annually and $420 for six months. For raates and subscription information refer to the toll free number shown above.

TRAVEL MANAGEMENT NEWSLETTER   800-360-0015
REED TRAVEL GROUP

A twice weekly newsletter of current happenings within the industry distributed via fax. For rates and subscription information refer to the 800# listed above.

TRAVEL TRADE   212-730-6600
15 W. 44th Street
New York, New York 10036

A weekly publication of current events which costs $10.00 per year. The publisher and editor is a veteran of the industry and offers incredible insight into coming trends and happenings. It is a fun and informative publication and offers an unbeatable value.

TRAVEL WEEKLY　　　　　　　　　800-360-0015
REED TRAVEL GROUP

A twice weekly magazine of industry affairs and events. It offers a wealth of information for the travel agent. As it is circulated twice a week the information is current and up to the minute. It features monthly cruise guides and many other reference and destination guides. For rates and subscription information refer to the 800# listed above.

TRAVEL WORLD NEWS　　　　　　　203-853-4955
1 Morgan Ave.
Norwalk, CT 06851-5017

This is a free subscription distributed monthly to qualified travel industry personnel. For others to subscribe is $25 per year. It features industry news items as well as detailed consolidator fares and familiarization information.

TRAVEL VIDEO SUPPLIERS

VACATIONS ON VIDEO　　　　　　602-483-1551
7642 East Gray Road, Suite 103　　Fax　602-483-0785
Scottsdale, Arizona 85260

Vacations on Video offers hundreds of travel videos. They are the only company to offer all of the CLIA member line cruise videos and have a fabulous selection. Their videos are priced extremely well for travel agents. Write or fax for a catalog.

INTERNATIONAL VIDEO NETWORK　　510-866-1121
2246 Camino Ramon　　　　　　Fax　510-866-9262
San Ramon, California 84583

IVN is the distributor of Fodor's Video Travel Guides and their own travel videos. known as the International Travel Video Collection, IVN offers numerous titles on destinations in the United States and worldwide.

PREVIEW MEDIA　　　　　　　　　415-397-2494
1160 Battery Street. Suite 100
San Francisco, California 94111

Preview Media offers a good number of travel videos on various destinations around the world. Their videos are narrated by news professionals and are of short duration. They are an excellent way to give clients a brief overview of a destination or port.

QUESTAR VIDEO   800-633-5633
P.O. Box 11345
FAX   312-266-9523
Chicago, Illinois 60611

Questar Video offers a limited number of superb videos on international destinations such as the South Pacific, Korea, China, Hawaii and so on. Call or write for information.

Chapter 29
A CHECKLIST FOR GETTING STARTED

To help you get started on your venture and to establish a starting budget following is a breakdown of activities with the appropriate budget allocation to get going. Where you do not know the amount of money that may be required you can simply resource the information from the appropriate source to complete the information.

PLANNING ACTIVITY

Every business should start with a well thought out concept and plan before the first dime is spent. Without this roadmap it is very difficult to engage in a meaningful venture.

Develop a Business Concept _____

Develop a Business Plan _____

Develop a Marketing Plan _____

ORGANIZATIONAL ACTIVITY

Setting up the business: These first steps are necessary to establish yourself in the travel industry.

File a Fictitious Business Name Statement _____

Obtain local business license _____

Open bank account(s) _____

Obtain Seller of Travel bond of restitution fund _____
(Check state requirements)

Register with state as Seller of Travel _____
(Check state requirements)

Design and print stationery

Letter head _____

Envelops _____

Business cards _____

Brochure _____

Other _____

TOTAL ORGANIZATIONAL COSTS _____

START UP ACTIVITY

Furnishing your home office: While you may be tempted to use the kitchen table as your base until you get going, an investment in quality office furniture will yield huge dividends in productivity.

Desk _____

Office Chair _____

Lighting _____

File Cabinet _____

Book Cases _____

Supplies _____

Equipping your home office: You probably already have a personal computer and telephone that would suffice until your business expands to a point where you need to upgrade. You should factor in any cost you are likely to incur the first year.

Personal Computer _____

Printer _____

Software

Office Suite _____

Publishing _____

Facsimile Management _____

On-Line _____

Reservations _____

Facsimile Machine _____

Telephone _____

Joining Industry Associations: You may only want to join one or more of these groups depending on the depth of your involvement.

NACTA _____

ASTA _____

CLIA _____

ARTA _____

NACOA _____

Setting up you reference library: You will need the trade publications to really get going in your business. The rest may not be the most important place to spend money unless you are specializing and need detailed information.

Trade Publications _____

Hotel Books _____

Travel Magazines _____

Travel Videos _____

Other _____

Other _____

TOTAL START UP COSTS _____

SUPPLIER ACTIVITY

Making initial contract and securing working relationship with suppliers is a key chore to establishing your business. One person may simply work with a local agency requiring no investment while others may elect to join IC Networks and consortiums and invest thousands.

Your Host Agency _____

Independent Contractor Network _____

Consortiums _____

Miscellaneous Suppliers _____

ESTABLISHING YOUR MONTHLY OPERATING BUDGET

One of the most important tasks you should undertake before launching your new business is to determine the average monthly cash flow needed to maintain your business. Following are some of the more common monthly expenses you will experience. By understanding the nature of your overhead it will help you adjust your activity for maximum productivity.

Advertising
Yellow Pages _____
Newspaper _____
Newsletters _____
Advertising Specialties _____
Other _____

Automated Reservations System
User's Fees _____
On-Line Services Fees _____

Bank Charges
Checking Account _____
Trust Account _____
Interest on Loans _____

Dues
NACTA _____
CLIA _____

ASTA _____

ARTA _____

NACOA _____

PATA _____

Other _____

Equipment Rental

    Office Equipment _____

    Postage Equipment _____

    Other _____

Insurance

    Business Liability _____

    E & O _____

    Workman's Comp _____

Licenses

    Business License _____

    State Registration _____

Postage and Delivery

    Postage _____

    Bulk Mail _____

    Delivery Charges _____

    Other _____

Printing

    Stationery _____

    Business Cards _____

    Brochure _____

    Other _____

Professional Fees

    Consultant _____

    Attorney _____

    Accountant _____

Subscriptions

    OAG _____

    Hotel & Travel Index _____

    Trade Publications

        TravelAge _____

        Travel Weekly _____

        Travel Trade _____

        Tour & Travel News _____

Travel Agent _____

Other _____

Other _____

Other _____

Telephone & Communications

Business Lines _____

Facsimile Lines _____

Long Distance Usage _____

Local Usage _____

Other _____

Travel

Sales Calls _____

Inspection Tours _____

Ticket Delivery _____

Fam/Cruise/Seminars _____

Utilities

Electricity _____

Gas _____

Other _____

Miscellaneous Expenses _____

_____

TOTAL MONTHLY EXPENSES _____

Chapter 30
WHERE DO I GO FROM HERE?

You should have enough information to make a decision regarding the viability of starting a home based travel business and you should also have enough information to start your agency. File your fictitious business name statement, open your bank account, satisfy whatever state registration requirements your state imposes, and join NACTA. Once you have organized your agency and established your relationship with your suppliers you are on your way to one of the most rewarding business experiences you can imagine.

Enjoy the earnings you can generate while still enjoying your home and family. Let the tax advantages of operating a home based business offer relief from overbearing taxation. Savor the independence of owning and operating your own entrepreneurial enterprise and take advantage of the many opportunities to explore the world.

Whether you operate the smallest part time home agency or the largest is of little consequence as long as you understand your own personal motivation for entering the travel industry and accept your own personal objectives as well. Once underway you may find you need assistance with your business and that is where Tom Ogg and Associates may be able to help you.

WHAT SERVICES DOES TOM OGG AND ASSOCIATES PROVIDE?

Tom Ogg & Associates is an organization formed to help individuals enter and succeed in the travel business. Whether you are buying an agency, starting one, or simply need information about the travel industry, Tom Ogg & Associates is the place to go for help

TRAVEL AGENCY BROKER

Tom Ogg is a licensed Real Estate and Business Broker

specializing in the sale of quality travel agencies and start-up locations. Tom works with sellers in several different ways to market agencies depending on the seller's needs. Tom will work on a traditional listing/commission basis for those agencies desiring full representation and will work on an hourly or flat fee basis for agencies requiring less involvement.

BUYER REPRESENTATION

Tom Ogg represents buyers in the purchase transaction by helping develop a business plan, locate a travel agency, evaluate it, and negotiate the purchase transaction. Tom is most helpful in a transaction where the seller is fully represented and the seller's broker is either a single agent of the seller, or a dual agent.

CONSULTATION AND TRAINING

Tom Ogg and Associates provides consultation to many agencies on an ongoing basis. Consultation and training are available for all agency owners and include access to travel agency operational support available by phone every working day to solve any operating, ticketing, or miscellaneous problem as it occurs. This pay as you use service is mandatory for all new owners who are inexperienced in the daily operation of a travel agency. Established agents use Tom Ogg and Associates electronic filing priority status with the A.R.C. for expediting their miscellaneous A.R.C. applications.

INDEPENDENT CONTRACTOR CONSULTING

Tom Ogg & Associates consults for independent contractors in the travel industry on a number of issues regarding the operation of their business.

TOM OGG AND ASSOCIATES SEMINARS

Tom Ogg and Associates does a number of seminars during the year on various topics. "How to Buy or Sell a Travel Agency", "How To Start a Home Based Travel Agency", "Independent Agents, Issues and Answers", "How to Recruit a Professional Sales Force to Sell Leisure Travel Products", and "How to Start a Cruise Only travel Agency" are topics Tom and Joanie speak on. If you are interested in hearing Tom or Joanie on any of the above subjects simply drop a note to Tom Ogg and Associates for a list of our scheduled speaking agenda. If you have a group and are interested in having Tom speak call, fax, or write for rates and availability.

FAM/CRUISE/SEMINARS

Interested in hearing Tom or Joanie speak while you familiarize yourself with one of the many wonderful cruise ships that sail the waters over the world? Simply give Tom Ogg & Associates a call with your 24 hour facsimile number and we will advise you of upcoming sailings.

WHAT OTHER TRAVEL INDUSTRY BOOKS ARE AVAILABLE FROM TOM OGG AND ASSOCIATES?

"HOW TO BUY OR SELL A TRAVEL AGENCY"

Interested in locating a travel agency to purchase? Find out how to go about the transaction with a minimum of exposure. Find out how to evaluate agencies and how to establish a purchase price, terms, and conditions of purchase. Especially valuable are the chapters entitled *"Buyers Beware"* and *"Sellers Beware"*. *"How to Buy or Sell a Travel Agency"* is twenty seven chapters of hard core information you need to take advantage of the most recent trends in the travel industry. Written by Tom Ogg, this book is a must have at only $29.95 direct from Tom Ogg and Associates, P.O. Box 2398, Valley Center, California 92082.

"HOW TO START A CRUISE ONLY TRAVEL AGENCY"

Love to cruise and want to get into the travel industry? Start your own cruise only travel agency and make excellent money selling cruises...forget airline tickets and put your focus where the money is. Cruising is the largest growth market in the travel industry with opportunity all its own. *"How to Start a Cruise Only Travel Agency"* is the most definitive work on the subject and authors Tom and Joanie Ogg hold nothing back. Everything you need to know to get going is laid out perfectly at only $29.95 direct from Tom Ogg and Associates, P.O. Box 2398, Valley Center, California 92082

TRAVEL TERMS

The nomenclature of the travel industry is unique and difficult to understand for those new to the business, and some of the financial and legal terms used in the buy/sell process are just as unfamiliar. The following are some of the more common terms and phrases one might encounter while negotiating the purchase of an agency:

AFFINITY GROUP: Any club, school, trade association, company, religious organization, etc. whose primary purpose is other than travel and is a formal organization with an established set of bylaws or other recognized organizational format. Affinity groups normally are represented by a group organizer who negotiates on the group's behalf.

AGENCY MANAGER: The person who qualifies an agency for conference appointments and also manages the daily operation of an agency.

AIRLINE CODES: The system of abbreviations for airlines, airports, fares, and such.

AIR-SEA: Any tour/cruise program in which one or more major transportation legs are provided by air and sea, and may also contain other types of transportation and accommodations.

AIRLINES REPORTING CORP. (ARC): The industry body representing domestic airlines which appoints travel agencies to represent the member carriers.

AIR TRANSPORT ASSOCIATION OF AMERICA (ATA): The trade association of U.S. and Canadian scheduled airlines including: international, trunk, local service, intra-Hawaiian, intra-Alaskan, helicopter, and cargo carriers.

THE ASSOCIATION OF INCENTIVE TRAVEL OPERATORS (AITO): A national organization of firms whose major service is providing travel incentive programs to industry in general.

AMERICAN PLAN: A hotel rate that includes three meals per day.

AMERICAN SOCIETY OF TRAVEL AGENTS (USA): The leading trade association of United States travel agents and various allied members of travel agency suppliers.

APPOINTMENT: Official designation to act as a sales and ticketing outlet for various air carriers and cruise lines, or be designated as a wholesale supplier for hotels and condominiums.

ASSOCIATION OF RETAIL TRAVEL AGENTS (ARTA): A trade association of American retail travel agencies.

BOARDING PASS PRINTER: A printer in an airline automated reservation system dedicated to the generation of boarding passes only, or an invoice/itinerary printer with boarding pass capabilities.

BLOCKED SPACE: Airline, hotel, cruise, or other reservations under deposit and blocked for resale.

BULK FARE: Fares available for purchase in specific blocks from carriers at low gross or net fare levels. Purchasers commit with the intent of marking up and resaling for profit.

CERTIFIED TRAVEL COUNSELOR (CTC): Designation made by the Institute of Certified Travel Agents upon the completion of an indepth study of the travel business and is considered, by many, as the professional designation of the industry.

CHARTER: The hiring for exclusive use of an aircraft or vessel.

CITY TICKET OFFICE: A carrier's retail ticket office or counter located outside an airline terminal.

DEBIT MEMO: An invoice generated by a carrier for the purpose of collecting money from the debited agency. Debit memos are used to correct ticketing errors, refunded tickets and commissions, commission recalls, and other situations requiring agencies to reimburse carriers monies due.

ESCORTED TOUR: A prearranged travel program fully escorted by a tour manager, normally the organizing agent.

EXCHANGE ORDER: A document issued by a carrier, or it's agent, requesting the issue of a ticket. Exchange orders are used by agencies to claim commissions upon appointment by the ARC.

FAMILIARIZATION TOUR: A complimentary or reduced rate travel program for travel agents that are designed to acquaint them with specific destinations and motivate new interest from the agents and their clients in the featured product.

F.E.T.: A foreign escorted tour.

F.I.T.: Foreign independent travel or free independent travel. An itinerary designed specifically for the client by booking the various componants of the trip separately.

F.I.T. OPERATOR OR WHOLESALER: A destination specialist operating detailed, individual itineraries for the agency community.

FULLY APPOINTED: Refers to a travel agency fully recognized and authorized by the leading air carrier, cruise, and railroad conferences to issue tickets and collect funds on their behalf.

GIT FARES: Group Inclusive airfares.

GROUP INCLUSIVE TOUR: A prepaid tour of miniumum size, ingredients, and value.

HOTEL AND TRAVEL INDEX: A quarterly publication of hotels, resorts, and condominiums both domestically and internationally.

INCENTIVE TRAVEL: A trip offered as a prize, particularly to stimulate the productivity of employees of industry.

INCLUSIVE TOUR: A tour in which the basic elements of air, transportation, and lodging are offered for one all inclusive price.

IN-PLANT AGENCY: A remote travel agent's sales and ticketing outlet on the premises of a client company, doing business with only that company at that location.

INTERNATIONAL AIR TRANSPORT ASSOCIATION (IATA): An organization of international airlines which operate domestic and international services making the worldwide system of transportation possible.

ITINERARY INVOICE PRINTER: A printer in an airline reservation system dedicated to the generation of itineraries and invoices. Boarding passes may be generated on this printer in some systems as well.

IT NUMBER: The code designator appearing on a prepaid tour indicating the tour has been approved for extended airline commission by ARC or IATAN.

MISCELLANEOUS CHARGE ORDER (MCO): The standard miscellaneous charge order is an ARC accountable document which is issued when standard ticket stock cannot be used. It is a device to handle the reporting of certain air transportation, surface transportation, land arrangements for inclusive tours, car hire, hotel accommodations, and other related miscellaneous transactions.

NATIONAL ASSOCIATION OF COMMISSIONED TRAVEL AGENTS (NACTA): The national assoication of outside sales, independent contractors, cruise only travel agencies, and ARC agencies that use outside sales forces to expand their business.

OFFICIAL AIRLINE GUIDE (OAG): The reference books for both domestic and international flight schedules used manually by an agency.

OFFICIAL HOTEL AND RESORT GUIDE: A comprehensive directory of numerous hotels, resorts and condominiums worldwide.

OFFICIAL MEETING FACILITIES GUIDE: A leading publication cataloging meeting and convention facilities of hotels and resorts throughout the world.

PACIFIC AREA TRAVEL ASSOCIATION (PATA): An organization of nations, suppliers, and retail agencies interested in promoting tourism throughout the Pacific and Indian Ocean areas.

PASSENGER NAME RECORD (PNR): The official name for the record of a passenger reservation in an airline reservation system.

PRE-PAID TICKET ADVICE (PTA): An ARC accountable

document which serves as notification for a carrier in another city to issue prepaid transportation to a passenger.

REVENUE PASSENGER MILE (RPM): One paying passenger carried one mile, a basic statistical unit of the airline industry.

RUN OF THE HOUSE ROOM RATE (ROH): A flat price at which a hotel agrees to offer any of it's rooms regardless of category.

STANDARD TICKET AND AREA BANK SETTLEMENT PLAN: A system established by the ARC under which travel agents report and remit airline ticket sales to banking institutions established as area banks.

TICKET STOCK: Blank tickets to be filled out and validated at the time of passenger ticketing. Ticket stock is individually numbered and accounted for each week to the ARC.

TOUR OPERATOR: A company which creates and markets inclusive tours through travel agencies and to the public.

TOUR ORGANIZER: An individual who organizes a group of passengers to participate in a special prepaid tour or event.

UNITED STATES TOUR OPERATORS ASSOCIATION (USTOA): An organization of tour operators created to elevate minimum operating standards for tour companies.

UNIVERSAL AIR TRAVEL PLAN (UATP): The credit card system originally organized by the U.S. domestic carriers but now includes most international carriers as well.

COMPUTER TERMS

BASIC: A widely used programming language.

BINARY: The "base two" numbering system used by all computers tostore and represent information and instructions.

BIT: Short for binary digit. This is the basic unit information in all computer systems. Each BIT has a value of either one or zero, and all data is made up of a combinations of BITS.

BYTE: A string of BITS usually eight, but more recently, sixteen, that represents one character. A combination of bytes is used by computers to represent words or numbers and the storage capacity of computers is measured in bytes. For instance a computer with 640K RAM, has 640,000 bytes of random access memory.

CENTERAL PROCESSING UNIT (CPU): That part of a computer which performs the data manipulation and controls the sequence of operation of the computer.

COMMERCIAL CRT: A user friendly CRT used by commercial accounts to communicate their needs to a specific queue within the hosting agency's system. The process may involve stand alone hardware provided by the agency or a floppy disk for use with a PC and MODEM.

CP/M: An obsolete operating system sometimes found in back office automation systems.

CURSOR: The blinking light on a CRT screen indicating the position of the next character to be entered.

CRT (CATHODE RAY TUBE): The device sitting in travel agencies that resembles a television set.

DATA BASE: The collection of information accessed by the CRT in an agency, and maintained by the hosting carrier's automated reservaton system.

DISPLAY: The images of a schedule, fare, PNR, or fare rules as shown on the CRT screen at a particular moment.

DIRECT ACCESS: The ability of an airline reservations system to communicate with another system to offer direct access for last seat availability.

FILE: Another name for a PNR or passenger name record, or any other collection of data accessed by a file name or code.

FLOPPY DISK: The flexible plastic disk inserted into the computer housing that contains various programs and backroom software.

HARD COPY: Printed output from the computer of various records and information.

HARD DISK: A rigid version of a floppy disk made of aluminum and used for storing large amounts of data.

HARDWARE: The physical devices that constitute a computer system.

INTERNAL MEMORY: The storage facilities in a computer system where programs and data are held while being worked on.

Kb: A kilobyte, or 1,024 bytes of information.

KEYBOARD: The typewriter type device that allows you to enter information into your computer or CRT.

Mb: A megabyte, or 1,024,000 bytes of information.

MODEM: Acronym of MOdulator DEModulator which is a device that lets you link one computer with another over a telephone line.

MS/DOS: A common operating system being replaced by Windows.

PNR: Stands for Party Now Recorded, or Passenger Name Record, and is used to identify a single passenger reservation.

RAM: Random Access Memory or the kind of computer memory available to the user most often in a small computer.

RECORD LOCATOR: A six character, alpha-numeric code, assigned to each PNR to identify it's address within the computer. A record may be located by this address code, the passenger's name, or departing flight information.

ROM: Read Only Memory, or the type of memory already built into a computer used for permanent storage of program instructions, which cannot be altered or added to by users.

SATELITE TICKET PRINTER (STP): A remotely located ticket printer where tickets can be generated from a centralized source. Normally found in commercial accounts.

SOFTWARE: The general term for all computer programs, as opposed to the actual physical devices, or hardware.

SPLIT SCREEN: The ability of a CRT to split information into several screens, or viewing areas.

TICKET PRINTER: A printer in an automated reservations

system dedicated solely to the generation of airline tickets.

QUEUE: A specific area of the computer where communications occur.

ZOOM: The ability of a CRT to enlarge a specific screen on a split screen display.

FINANCIAL AND LEGAL TERMS

ACCELERATED COST RECOVERY SYSTEMS (ACRES): A method of depreciation allowing accelerated depreciation of a capital asset applicable to almost all property acquired when purchasing an agency.

ACCELERATED DEPRECIATION: A method of depreciation which allows the deduction of the cost of assets more rapidly than straight line depreciation.

ACCELERATION CLAUSE: A clause usually found in a promissory note or installment sale contract providing for full payment of the outstanding balance owed the seller, or his or her assignee, in case of any kind of default by the maker of the note.

ACCURAL METHOD OF ACCOUNTING: An accounting system where income and expenses are adjusted to reflect the true period in which they are incurred.

AMORTIZATION: A deductible expense allowed as a method of recovering an investment in an intangible asset which is similar to the depreciation of a tangible asset.

ARBITRATION CLAUSE: A clause usually appearing in a purchase contract allowing for any dispute to be arbitrated under the rules of the American Arbitration Association and commits both the buyer and seller to accept the arbitrator's decision as binding.

ASSET: Any property that has value.

AUDIT: An examination of financial records.

BASIS: Generally, the cost of an asset adjusted for depreciation.

CAPITAL ASSET: Assets or property held for investment or personal use.

CASH METHOD OF ACCOUNTING: A system of accounting in which income is reported when actually, or constructively received, and expenses are reported when actually paid.

CLOSING: The end of a business sale transaction, as evidenced by the escrow agent's delivery of a bill of sale to the buyer, and the contemporaneous transfer to the seller of the purchase price remaining after payment of all seller's charges assessed.

COMMUNITY PROPERTY: Assets belonging to husband and wife equally.

DECLINING BALANCE DEPRECIATION: A method of accelerated depreciation in which each year's depreciation is a reduction in the asset's basis.

COVENANT NOT TO COMPETE: The provision in an agreement of sale restricting the seller's activities within prescribed limitations to compete with the agency's activities within it's effective marketing area after the sale of the agency is completed.

CRS: Computerized Reservation System.

DEPRECIABLE ASSET: Property used in business with an effective life of one year or more.

DEPRECIATION: A deductible expense calculated many different ways, that reflects a reasonable allowance for the wear and tear of the property of a business with a useful life of one year or more.

DUE ON SALE CLAUSE: A clause in a promissory note or security agreement requiring the payment of the outstanding balance of money due upon the sale or other disposition of the original property sold or any property securing the subject note and security agreement.

FAIR MARKET VALUE: The price a willing buyer would pay, and willing seller would accept, neither being under any compulsion to buy or sell

FISCAL YEAR: Any twelve-month period elected by a business to report their financial activity.

INSTALLMENT SALE METHOD OF ACCOUNTING: A system of reporting the gain from a sale throughout the years, as various payments are received instead of reporting the gain from the original sale in the year it was executed.

JOINT TENANCY: Title held by two or more natural persons in equal shares with the right of survivorship, ususally used as a means of ownership by husband and wife.

LETTER OF INTENT: A document supplied by a buyer to the seller specifying his interest to purchase the agency and guaranteeing all disclosed information will be held in strict confidence from any third parties.

NET OPERATING LOSS: A business loss that has been offset by income, which may be carried back three years, or forward for fifteen years to reduce taxes in one or more of those years.

PROPRIETOR: An individual who is the sole owner of an agency or other business.

REALIZED GAIN OR LOSS: The difference between the amount you realize on the sale of an agency and it's adjusted basis.

RECONGNIZED GAIN OR LOSS: The amount of gain or loss realized that will be included in your taxable income.

SUBCHAPTER S CORPORATION: A corporation that meets the requirements and elects to be taxed under the Subchapter S provisions of the I.R.S. code that allows the operating profits or losses to be passed through to the shareholder's individual tax returns, much like a sole proprietorship or partnership.

SECURED TRANSACTION: Any sale in which an interest in personal property is given to secure payment of a promissory note or performance of some other obligation.

SECURITY INTEREST: An interest in property intended to secure or guarantee payment of a debt or performance of some other obligation.

STRAIGHT LINE DEPRECIATION: A method of depreciation

in which the cost of an asset or adjusted basis is deducted in equal amounts over the asset's useful life.

SUM OF THE YEARS DIGIT DEPRECIATION: A method of accelerated depreciation based on a formula developed from the anticipated useful life of the property.

TAX LOSS CARRY FORWARD: A net operating loss unable to be applied to the last three-year carryback period, which may be applied against future income during the next fifteen years of the business.

TENANTS IN COMMON: Two or more parties, each of whom hold an undivided share of the entire property, which may be disposed of by the decedent's will.

TIME IS OF THE ESSANCE CLAUSE: A clause used to describe a contract provision that requires one party's performance within the time specified in the contract as a prerequisite to the other party's performance.

USEFUL LIFE: The number of years an asset may reasonably be expected to be in use at a travel agency.

Chapter 32
WHERE CAN I GET A PROFESSIONAL TRAVEL EDUCATION

Primum Travel Company offers the country's most popular travel agent training program, working in partnership with local colleges and universities. For the past ten years, Primum's travel agent training program has operated successfully in over one hundred Continuing Education Departments nationwide. The Program is a proven, successful method for motivated people to begin a career in the travel industry and offers real value to the students within a one semester time frame. This certificate program teaches the basic skills needed to operate a computer reservation system, whether with the airlines, travel agencies, cruise lines, hotels or as home based agents, in a concise sixty-hour format.

The program consists of three courses:

Travel Career Training is an introductory course covering the fundamentals of the travel industry. Students learn the basic skills and gain knowledge unique to the travel business. Topics covered include: (1) Travel Agency Operations-Opening an Agency, Agency Operations, Employment Opportunities, Discount Benefits and Industry Associations (2) Introduction to Domestic Air Travel-Obtaining lowest fares, scheduling and Itinerary Planning, Airfare Construction, Reservations, Ticketing, Industry Codes, Use of Travel Planners and Resource Materials (3) Introduction to International Travel, Passports, Visas, Customs Regulations, Airline Operations and Terminology, Basic World Geography (4) Introduction to Ground Transportation, Car Rentals, Rates and Codes, Rail Travel, Eurail and Britrail (5) Introduction to Hotel Accommodations, Hotel Reservations and Payments, Hotel References and Resources Accommodations (6) Introduction to Tours-Tour Operators and Tour Programs, Reading and Understanding Tour Brochures, Steps in Selling Tour packages, Selecting and Booking Tours, Payments and Tour Documents, Tour Planning and Group Tours (7) Introduction to Cruise Travel-Types of Cruises, Cruise Details, Ship Services and Tipping, Nautical Terms, Documentation and Safety, Reading and Understanding Cruise Brochures, Selecting the Right Cruise, Reservations, Payments and Documentation, Cruise Lines, Ships, and Associations, (8) Overview of Travel Agency Automation, Airline Computer Reservation Systems (9) Travel Industry Sales Techniques-Listening Skills and Telephone Courtesy, Effective Handling of Complaints and Customer Service, Writing Resumes, Job Interviews, Job Search and Preparation

This class will meet two evenings per week for four weeks, a workbook is provided.

Reservation Computer Training is Hands-On Computer Training on one of the various Reservation Computer Systems. As a prerequisite, students must have completed the Travel Career Training course and have a basic understanding of: Airline/Car/Hotel reservation procedures, Airport/City Codes, Day to Day Operations of the Travel Agency. This comprehensive course will include: (1) Introduction to the computer and software used in the travel industry (2) Basic Computer Formats for Domestic and International Ticketing (3) Building a Passenger Name Record (4) How to Book, Cancel and Rebook a Reservation (5) Understanding Flight Information (6) Decoding City/Airport Codes (7) City Pair Availability Displays, Selling from CPA Displays (8) Understanding Action/Status Codes (9) Itinerary Pricing (10) How to Quote and Shop for Air Fares (11) Rental Car Reservations (12) Hotel Reservations (13) Printing Customer Invoices and Itineraries (14) Issuing Airline Tickets (15) Seat Assignments (16) Sending Queue Messages

This class meets two evenings a week for six weeks, a workbook is provided.

Travel Destination Geography is optional but highly recommended. Students research, identify and learn to describe important destinations for business and leisure travel. This information is a valuable tool for planning and constructing itineraries. The various cultures, climates and attractions for destinations worldwide will be covered. The following topics will be discussed: (1) Introductory topics-Latitude and Longitude, Use of the Atlas-Thematic and Locational Maps (2) Continental North America-California, Florida, Northeast USA, Southeast Canada, Southwest Canada (3) Noncontiguous United States-Hawaii, Alaska (4) Mexico, Central America-Coastal and Colonial Mexico, Costa Rica (5) South America-Galapagos (6) Caribbean-Jamaica, Island Groups (7) Southern Europe-Italy, Spain (8) Northwest Continental Europe- British Isles, United Kingdom, France, Netherlands, Switzerland (9) Scandinavia, Eastern Europe-Bergen, Stockholm, Budapest, Moscow, St. Petersburg (10) Africa, Middle East-Israel, Egypt, Kenya, South Africa (11) South

Asia, Southeast Asia-Bali, Thailand (12) East Asia-China (13) South Pacific-Australia (14) Geography and the Travel Industry-Integrating Geography with your Career

This class meets one evening per week for seven weeks, a textbook is provided.

These three courses are offered at a more than reasonable cost to the students, especially when compared to the $2,800 average cost of attending a proprietary school. All courses are instructed by qualified, local personnel, actively involved in the travel industry. All course materials and workbooks are included in the cost of the course.

A list of the colleges and universities currently offering the Travel Agent Training Program follows and detailed information is available by calling 1-800-299-3726 or via the Internet on Primum's Homepage at the following WEB address: http://www.primum.com.

Primum Travel Company is proud to announce their Travel Career Training Program is being offered in partnership with these fine educational institutions for 1997:

Alabama
Troy State University
334-241-9769

University of South Alabama
334-431-6411

Arizona
Chandler-Gilbert Community College
602-732-7114

Glendale Community College
602-435-3805

Mesa Community College
602-461-7414

Northern Arizona University
520-523-8063

Yuba College
916-741-6825

Arkansas
University of Arkansas at Little Rock
501-375-3690

California
Bakersfield College
805-395-4177

California State University - Fresno
209-278-0333

California State University - Hayward
510-885-3605

California State University Hayward   Concord Campus
510-885-3605

Cerritos Community College
310-860-2451

Chaffey College
909-477-2954

De Anza College
408-864-8275

Golden Gate University
415-442-6508

Irvine Valley College
714-559-3333

Pasadena City College
818-585-7608

Riverside Community College
909-222-8090

Ventura College
805-654-6459

West Valley Community College
408-741-2096

Colorado
Aims Community College
970-330-8008

Front Range Community College
303-466-8811

Connecticut
University of Connecticut - Storrs
860-486-3231

University of Connecticut - West Hartford
860-486-3231

Florida
Broward Community College
305-351-9584

Edison Community College -
Fort Myers
813-489-9235

Edison Community College - Naples
813-732-3707

Embry-Riddle Aeronautical University
904-226-6188

Florida State University
904-644-7554

Jacksonville University
904-745-7050

Palm Beach Community College
Boca Raton
407-367-4517

Palm Beach Community College
Palm Beach Gardens
407-625-2535

St. Petersburg Junior College
813-341-4455

University of Miami
305-284-4777

Georgia
Coastal Georgia Center
912-651-2550

Georgia State University
404-651-3450

Macon College
912-471-2770

University of Georgia
706-542-7537

Where Can I Get a Professional Travel Education?

**How To Start a
Home Based
Travel Agency**

Illinois
South Suburban College
708-596-2000

University of Illinois at Chicago
312-413-5055

Indiana
Indiana University South Bend
219-237-4167

Indiana-Purdue University-Fort Wayne
219-481-6624

Kansas
Wichita State University
316-689-3731

Kentucky
University of Louisville
502-852-6614

Western Kentucky University
502-745-1912

Louisiana
Louisiana State University
504-388-6621

University of New Orleans
504-568-8593

University of Southwestern   Louisiana
318-482-6344

Maine
University of Maine at Augusta   207-621-3174

University of Maine at Augusta -   Bath/Brunswick
207-621-3174

University of Maine at Augusta -   Lewiston
207-621-3174

University of Maine at Augusta -   Portland
207-621-3174

Maryland
Frederick Community College
301-846-2400

Michigan
Kalamazoo Valley Community College
616-373-7800

Mott Community College
810-762-0587

Saginaw Valley State University
517-891-4002

Wayne State University
 Farmington Hills
313-577-6693

Wayne State University
 Sterling Heights
313-577-6693

Minnesota
Minneapolis Community & Technical College
612-341-7697

St. Paul Technical College
612-221-1370

Mississippi
University of Mississippi - Jackson
601-232-7282

University of Mississippi - Biloxi
601-232-7282

Missouri
University of Missouri at Kansas City
816-235-2736

Nevada
Community College of Southern Nevada
702-651-4287

New Mexico
University of New Mexico
505-277-1166

New Jersey
Burlington County College
609-494-9311

Fairleigh Dickinson University
201-692-6500

Where Can I Get a Professional Travel Education?

Gloucester County College
609-468-5000

Passaic County Community College
201-684-6202

Sussex County College
201-300-2141

New York
Hofstra University
516-463-5999

Hudson Valley Community College
518-270-7338

North Carolina
University of North Carolina - Wilmington
910-395-3000

Winston Salem State University
910-750-2630

Ohio
University of Cincinnati
513-556-5994

Columbus State Community College
614-227-2579

Cuyahoga Community College - Eastern Campus
216-987-2234

Cuyahoga Community College - Western Campus
216-987-2234

University College
419-321-5129

Oklahoma
Oklahoma State University
405-945-3373

Oregon
Lane Community College
503-726-2252
Portland Community College
503-244-1818

Pennsylvania
Community College of Philadelphia
215-751-8024

Community College of Philadelphia - Northeast
215-751-8024

South Carolina
Converse College
803-573-6948

University of South Carolina
803-777-9466

Tennessee
University of Memphis
901-678-2877

Texas
Eastfield College
214-860-7623

Galveston College
409-763-6551, ext 115

McLennan Community College
817-750-3528

Midland College
915-685-47223

Northlake College
214-659-5106

Southwest Texas State University
512-245-2507

Tarrant County Junior College
817-531-4592

Texarkana College
903-838-4541

Texas Tech University
806-742-2352

Tyler Junior College
903-510-2900

University of Houston Cinco Ranch
713-395-2800

University of North Texas
817-565-2656

Where Can I Get a Professional Travel Education?

University of Texas at Austin
512- 475-6684

University of Texas Pan American
210-381-2120

University of Texas at San Antonio
210-691-4670

West Texas A&M University
806-656-2000

Utah
Utah State University
801-269-9422

Virginia
J. Sargeant Reynolds Community College
804-371-3413

Northern Virginia Community College
Alexandria Campus
703-845-6229

Old Dominion University
804-683-4603

Washington
Everett Community College
206-388-9214

Renton Technical College
206-235-2285

Tacoma Community College
206-566-5019

Chapter 33
FOR MORE INFORMATION

By now you should have enough information to decide if you are interested in pursuing your own home based travel agency and how you intend to go about it. As you can see there is a myriad of decisions to make and people to see, I am sure you can also see the opportunity that awaits those brave enough to venture into the travel industry.

There are numerous sources of further information about the travel industry. Trade Associations, books, video tapes, business opportunity offerings, seminars and so on. Your best bet is to jump right into the mainstream of the Independent Travel Agent community and get as much exposure as necessary to ensure your success.

You should always be cautious when approached by organizations offering home based travel businesses that require an investment of hundreds or thousands of dollars. While there a quite a few reputable organizations that offer excellent opportunities that require an investment there are also some disreputable scoundrels as well. Be sure you understand the nature of the offering and the reputation of the company making the offer.

Here are some ideas on how to proceed with your home based travel agency.

Join NACTA!

The National Association of Commissioned Travel Agents is the association of home based travel agents (See Chapter 26) and is well worth the investment. NACTA will provide you with information to speed you along the way to setting your business up with a minimum of investment and a maximum of benefit for each dollar invested. NACTA's newsletters will guide you through the myriad of decisions a home based travel agency faces. You can communicate with NACTA on CompuServe or America On-Line or by simply picking up the telephone to ask questions.

There is no question that NACTA membership should be one of the first things you do when starting up.

Attend a "HOW TO START A HOME BASED TRAVEL AGENCY" seminar or seminar/cruise!

How To Start a Home Based Travel Agency

If you liked this book you will love one of Tom's *"HOW TO START A HOME BASED TRAVEL AGENCY"* seminars. These seminars are offered throughout the United States in major cities and pick up where this book leaves off. It is the next natural step to get all of your questions answered with up to the minute information. The seminars take place on Saturdays and last a minimum of six hours. They are in-depth work shops and enrollment is limited to a maximum of twenty people. These seminars are available for the nominal fee of $79.00 ($49.00 for NACTA members) and includes the seminar, seminar materials, and lunch.

The "*HOW TO START A HOME BASED TRAVEL AGENCY*" cruise/seminars are similar to the hotel based seminars but are 6 hours for 3-4 day cruises and 10 hours for seven day cruises. In addition to the seminar there is lots of time for one on one discussions and consultation with Tom, of course, it is all included in the cruise price. Best of all, the cruises are usually available at special travel agent's familiarization rates that make it almost impossible to stay home. Examples of cruise seminar rates are on Carnival's Holiday, departed January 29th, 1996 from Los Angels for a four day cruise at $189 per person, double occupancy (including the seminar).....7 day Caribbean cruises (East, West and Southern) around $450 per person (Including seminars) and so on. If you can take the time these cruise/seminars are the very best way to get tons of information at an affordable price plus enjoy a nice cruise experience.

Information Order Form

Use the following order form to order additional books and to be listed on the seminar mailing/fax broadcast list.

ORDER FORM

Please put me on your mailing list/fax list for seminars in my area: ————————
Please put me on your mailing list/fax list for your cruise seminars: ————————

I am interested in cruises to the following destinations (circle applicable cruises)
W. Coast, Mexico   Eastern Caribbean Western Caribbean Southern Caribbean
Alaska Panama Canal Mediterranean South Pacific Indian Ocean South America

I have enclosed a NACTA membership application. $95.00 _____

Please send me the following books from Tom Ogg & Associates:

"HOW TO START A CRUISE ONLY TRAVEL AGENCY" $29.95 _____
*(33 chapters of hardcore information about the biggest opportunity the travel
industry has ever seen. Every detail you need to get going immediately!)*

'HOW TO BUY OR SELL A TRAVEL AGENCY" $29.95 _____
*(Everything you ever need to know about buying or selling a travel agency
...and then some in 29 chapters)*

"NACTA's INDEPENDENT TRAVEL AGENT HANDBOOK" $49.95 _____
*(Everything you need to know to maximize your profits as an outside sales
agent, independent contractor, or cruise and your only travel agent. Included
with every NACTA membership but also available to non-members.)*

                                              Total $ _____
                                      CA Sales Tax $ _____
                        (CA Residents add 7% tax on books only)
                                          Postage $ _____
                  (Add $3 for 1 book, $5 for 2 or more books)
                                              Total $ _____

Please charge my credit card # _____   **Exp Date** _____
Check Enclosed _____

Signature_____   **Date** _____

Mail to: Name _____
              Address _____
              City _____   State _____ Zip _____
              Phone #_____   24 Hr. Fax #_____

Make check payable and mail or fax to:

Tom Ogg & Associates
P.O. Box 2398
Valley Center, CA 92082-2398
619-751-1007   Fax 619-751-1309